SEVENTY TIMES SEVEN

ALSO BY ALEX MAR

Witches of America

SEVENTY TIMES SEVEN

A True Story of
MURDER AND MERCY

Alex Mar

Penguin Press
New York
2023

PENGUIN PRESS
An imprint of Penguin Random House LLC
penguinrandomhouse.com

Image credits appear on page 355.

LIBRARY OF CONGRESS CATALOGING-IN-PUBLICATION DATA
Names: Mar, Alex, author.
Title: Seventy times seven : a true
story of murder and mercy / Alex Mar.
Description: New York : Penguin Press, 2023. |
Includes bibliographical references and index.
Identifiers: LCCN 2022029831 | ISBN 9780525522157 (hardcover) |
ISBN 9780525522164 (ebook)
Subjects: LCSH: Cooper, Paula, 1970–2015. |
Murder—Indiana—Gary—Case studies. |
Female juvenile delinquents–Indiana—Gary—Case studies. |
African American juvenile delinquents–Indiana—Gary—Case studies. |
Capital punishment—Indiana—Gary—Case studies. |
Forgiveness—Indiana—Gary—Case studies.
Classification: LCC HV6534.G37 M357 2023 |
DDC 362.88/2930977299—dc23/eng/20221230
LC record available at https://lccn.loc.gov/2022029831

Printed in the United States of America
1st Printing

Designed by Amanda Dewey

For Todd
And then you arrived.

Then Peter came to Jesus and asked, "Lord, how many times shall I forgive my brother or sister who sins against me? Up to seven times?"

Jesus answered, "I tell you, not seven times, but seventy times seven."

—*The Gospel of Matthew*

Contents

SEVENTY TIMES SEVEN

PROLOGUE

On a spring afternoon in 1985, in Gary, Indiana, four teenage girls enter the home of an elderly woman under false pretenses, and when they leave she is dead. One of them, a fifteen-year-old, will soon be sentenced to death for murder. There is no question of her guilt; this is not a story of wrongful conviction.

The crime was violent enough to *shock the conscience*—a legal phrase the prosecutor invokes—and so no voices of protest will rise up in that city, or in broader Lake County or farther south in the capital, at the impending execution of a tenth grader. Not until a man very close to the victim, her grandson, publicly forgives the girl—against the wishes of his family—and campaigns to spare her life. Not until the crime is featured on the front pages of newspapers and television programs five thousand miles away, across the ocean, where petitions are signed by millions, does the American media begin to question the outcome of this case. A tragedy in a midwestern steel town will continue to play out, have its second act, as far away as the Vatican. From criminal court in northern Indiana, the reverberations of the case will eventually be felt in the highest court of the United States.

Over the past five years, I have read thousands of pages of documents, personal letters, and newspaper features, and scanned through thousands of photographs and dozens of hours of footage. I have conducted interviews with some eighty individuals, culminating in hundreds of hours of conversation. Throughout, I was asking myself about the nature of belief, of conviction, the source of our guiding principles. I have asked myself what our common definition of *justice* might be, if there is even a shared understanding of the word.

Unlike some of the people whose lives and choices I will describe here, I am not a practicing Christian. But I have returned again and again to a moment from the Gospel of Matthew that has special meaning for someone at the center of this story: the moment when the disciple Peter asks Jesus how many times he should forgive those who harm him. The answer is *seventy times seven*—an enormous number, as if Jesus were suggesting his followers be prepared to forgive an infinite number of times. It is hard to imagine someone who could carry this out; it is hard to know if such a request is even fair. Anger is a very human, instinctual response. The act of forgiveness, I think, is more alien, and requires something tougher: a belief that none of us is solely defined by the worst thing we have ever done. That each of us remains human, sometimes in spite of our actions. And that sometimes, our actions are a response to forces larger than ourselves.

This is a story that asks what any community is willing to accept as just consequences—as justice—for harm done. It is a difficult question, one that each person in this book has been forced to confront. Because whatever the answer, its impact will be more sprawling than predicted, hard to contain. Whether or not we choose to acknowledge it, in ways very great or very small, the fates of neighbors are linked.

I

THE CARE
OF CHILDREN

One house of the many that make up a city: a pale-yellow house, an hour after sunup in Gary, Indiana. A woman lives here, on Wisconsin Street, with her two daughters. Rhonda is twelve, her sister Paula is nine. It is 1979.

Their mother—her name is Gloria—hustles them outside into the morning light, and then into the dark of the garage and the back seat of her red Chevy Vega. The girls are very young, and they are powerfully tired. They understand what their mother intends to do—she has kept them up all night softly talking then shouting then whimpering to them about where they'll be traveling together, about what must happen next—and they are no longer resistant.

With her daughters inside, Gloria tugs at the garage door until it slides down to meet the concrete. She slips into the driver's side, rolls down the windows, turns the key in the ignition: the engine gives off a deep, thrumming sound. Then she waits for them to close their eyes and fall into that steady rhythm; she can see their faces in the rearview mirror, small and brown and perfect. All three are still, their limbs grown heavy as if underwater.

The engine continues running; the minutes accumulate; the air thickens.

Outside the garage, the neighborhood is awakening. Inside the garage, the girls are passing into an unnatural sleep.

What Rhonda remembers next: she and Paula laying side by side on their bottom bunk, not knowing how they got there. They have not exited the world. Gloria is leaning over them, her daughters: they will be all right, she says. Just before leaving.

Rhonda does not know how much time has passed before she is able to move her body. She rises slowly. A letter is taped to the door, from their mother: She is finishing what she set out to do. Rhonda rushes to the kitchen and calls her aunt, who tells her to run, get their neighbor. Through the window, she thinks she sees exhaust seeping out from under the garage door, into the bright daylight.

Mr. Hollis drags Gloria out of the garage and lays her on her back on the lawn. He drops to his knees and with elbows locked, hand over hand, pushes hard on her chest. Again and again. The neighbor across the street, a nurse, rushes over and takes her turn trying to pump breath back into Gloria's body.

The ambulance arrives, and the fire department, and a medic becomes the third person in line to tend to Gloria. By now, Paula is standing outside, watching. Rhonda sees her younger sister grow hysterical at the sight of this stranger bearing down on their mother's chest, and Gloria not responding, not responding.

Something Rhonda will not forget: no one examines them, the girls. The firemen, the medics—no one so much as takes their pulse. When Gloria is swept off to the hospital, the sisters go stay with their aunt. When after a week their mother checks herself out early, no one asks any questions; when she comes to retrieve her daughters, no one stops her.

For years, Rhonda has said that she does not know what transformed her sister. But now she tells me, as if untangling the question aloud, that this was it. This must have been the start of a change in Paula. "Because you have to understand: We were all supposed to have been dead. That's what we were expecting, that's what we were hoping." But they were still alive. And what now—another day in the yellow house?

The house stands in Marshalltown, a subdivision of the Pulaski neighborhood, integrated by Black working-class families in the 1950s. Theirs is one of a collection of streets lined with neat, ranch-style homes, single-family, with small front yards.

About a mile west of here is Midtown, or the Central District, once the sole, clearly delineated quarter of Gary's entire Black community. And a mile into Midtown is Broadway, which runs north-south the entire length of the city. That four-lane street leads you north into downtown, where the architecture collapses time: an ornate brick department store, now boarded up; a children's clothing store, now boarded up; the former headquarters of a major regional bank, its Greco-Roman façade left to grow tarnished. People still shop here, but more and more, steel accordion gates have been pulled shut across entranceways and display windows and left that way. More and more, businesses have closed up or moved south, into the malls of the white suburbs.

Broadway's final destination in the north, at the edge of downtown, is the Gary Works, along the southern shoreline of Lake Michigan. The United States Steel Corporation dominates the waterfront, the plant's rows of smokestacks darkening the air overhead; at night the compound glows red. At this moment, thousands rotate shifts here day and night, unaware that, within the next three years, more than two thirds of them will lose their jobs. About 150,000 people live in this town, most of them linked to the mill. It is the reason the city exists.

Just three generations ago, this area was all sand and swampland, a great expanse of nothing thirty miles from Chicago. It was the start of the 1900s, and the state of Indiana, shaped like a boot pointed West, was very rural and very white, its nearly one hundred counties distinguished by the sheer number of railway lines crisscrossing through it. Lake County, some six hundred square miles at its northwest corner, pressed against the shoreline. The county's most desolate stretch, along the water, was used as a private hunting and fishing club by Chicago's wealthier men, and as a hideaway by that city's fugitives. Winding rivers and tributaries, dense marshland, the rough terrain of the dunes—territory to *pass through*. It was here that U.S. Steel decided to buy nine thousand acres. They leveled the dunes, filled a half mile stretch of the lake, packed the marshes, rerouted part of the Grand Calumet River, dug out a mile-long ship canal, and began construction of the mill itself, with its massive blast furnaces and coke ovens. Within a handful of years, the Gary Works was completed, along with the beginnings of a company town.

In the building of every city, decisions are made as to who gets what. These decisions are built into the layout of the streets, the digging of trenches, the laying down of water pipes and sewer drains, the doling out of permits and licenses, the paving of roads and the rolling out of sidewalks, the planning and funding of schools and parks. There are many accidents along the way, the unintended aftershocks of these choices, but a city's framework, the bones of it, is laid down with intent. Some groups of residents are protected and served, while others are left isolated and exposed. This is the tension underlying all American cities, and in Gary this tension was extreme from the start.

O f the two sisters in the yellow house, Paula is a much gentler girl, *a wuss, a baby, the biggest chicken*—that's how her sister thinks of her—and Rhonda is *the boss*. They live around the corner from Bethune Elementary, where they're both enrolled, a quick run from door to door. Which is helpful, because Paula gets into fights after school. That is, she starts something she can't finish, and then she races back home with two or three angry girls in pursuit, and she runs them toward her big sister, and Rhonda has to do the fighting. Every time. Paula gets into it with someone, and Rhonda has to come swinging, and some girl ends up yanking at her long hair and making her look a mess. Paula, always a joker, stands in their doorway laughing. This works out fine for her—until one day their grandmother comes to stay with them, and now Rhonda has a witness. Their grandma sees this drama unfold out the front door three days in a row, and on the fourth she pulls Rhonda aside and pushes Paula out the door. "Get your butt out there and fight! Rhonda's not going to help you today. Rhonda been saving you *all week!*"

Paula can't fight, but she can dance. Whenever it's just the two of them in the house, they play music all the time. Rhonda has a Jackson 5 record from the back of a cereal box, and they play it over and over. Paula tries to teach her sister new moves, but it's a crack-up. "No, Rhonda, the beat is over here. It's over *here*. Come over here, Rhonda, and get on the beat!"

They like the neighborhood: so many kids around, riding their bikes after school or playing on the block. But the sisters are kept apart from the others. No one is allowed over to the house, and they are not allowed to visit other kids' homes; they can only sit inside. And so they make up games that can be played with friends from their doorway.

Most days and nights, Rhonda is expected to babysit Paula while their mother works long hours as a lab technician at Methodist Hospital and their father is nowhere to be found. She gets Paula up and dressed for school; she makes biscuits for breakfast; she sets a time for homework and cooks dinner. She is made to play the role of the *other* mother, and she makes sure Paula knows her rank, even if it means tearing through the house fighting. But sometimes they stop playing mother-daughter and have girl time, fix each other's hair, sit in front of the TV together and binge on cake and cookies. Sometimes Rhonda lets Paula turn the dial to *The Three Stooges* because it's her favorite. She *loves* watching those grown men squeeze into phone booths, smack each other in the forehead, fall down a set of stairs, get a pie in the face. Rhonda thinks of it as ignorant stuff, but it lights her sister up.

Bethune Elementary School portraits of Paula (left) and Rhonda (right)

The girls were both born in Chicago. That's where their mother and her family are from, and where she met Ron Williams, the man she started dating right after high school. About a year later, she became pregnant, and the two got engaged. But then something went wrong. The idea was to have a wedding quickly—but when they got down to making the arrangements, they began to argue, and the arguments unfolded at a pitch that did not make sense. Ron started to worry that Gloria might be unstable, and he decided to wait. They broke up; they got back together; they did it all over again. By the time she gave birth to Rhonda, Gloria seemed so erratic to Ron, so forgetful and volatile, that he wanted to sue for full custody. But when he told his own mother, she could not condone him taking a woman's child away. And so he let it go.

Within a few months, Gloria did marry—a man named Herman Cooper. She convinced him to raise Rhonda as his own; if Ron wanted to visit with the girl, they would simply tell people he was her uncle. Soon they had Paula, and she and Rhonda might as well believe they were full sisters.

When the girls were eight and five, the family packed up and moved to Gary. They rented a small three-bedroom house in Marshalltown. Herman did odd jobs as a mechanic, and Gloria found work at the hospital. Over the years, Herman became quick to anger at the smallest things—if the girls were slow to take out the garbage or wash the dishes. If they were in any way out of step with his moods, he was within his rights to hit them hard. That was fair punishment in their home.

The yellow house is directly across from a small storefront church, New Testament Baptist. After they settled in, Gloria ordered the girls to start heading there for Sunday school, though neither she nor their father had any plans to join. Rhonda and Paula were too young to choose their own church or faith or to make any personal decisions about God, but they did as they were told, and it got them out of the house. On the day of the girls' baptism, Gloria decided not to attend. One of the church mothers stood in for her.

Herman disappears for weeks at a time; he comes and goes when he feels like it. When he is home, he repeatedly beats the girls—with an electrical cord or a belt or his fists. He calls to them in their bedroom and orders them to come out with all their clothes off—that way, he says, they'll really feel it when he whips them. Gloria is drinking heavily. On the occasions when she locks him out, Herman breaks in. Late at night, Paula and Rhonda listen to their shouting through the wall. When neither of their parents is home, the girls put the chaos out of their minds and live what Rhonda will later call their "imaginary type of life."

Gloria and Herman make a habit of separating then getting back together. It is during one of their breakups that Gloria, in the early morning, leads the girls out to the garage, ushers them into the car, and runs the engine. And it is months later that Rhonda learns Herman is not her father, that her father is "Uncle" Ron, a nice man who's come by a few times. The abuse has been focused on her, and now Rhonda thinks she understands: Herman treats her this way because she is not actually his child; he does not feel obliged to be careful with her. She packs a few things and leaves. She is thirteen years old.

Gloria reports her missing, and Rhonda is picked up by the police and returned to the house. This happens again and again. By leaving home, she becomes, in legal terms, a *status offender:* a category that's broadly defined—truancy, "immoral conduct," "incorrigibility"—a label a juvenile court judge can use, more or less, as they'd like. Eventually a judge sends her to the juvenile detention center—what has become a catchall remedy for children who act out. She spends months in the institution, a massive sterile building, packed in with kids who have done far worse. And then she is sent back to her mother.

Eventually, as Rhonda plans yet another exit, Paula begs to come along. *Begs* her. And so this time, in the middle of the night, they set out together.

Rhonda feels terrible about it: there's a big difference between being on her own and bringing a ten-year-old with her. Paula needs to be taken care of, and soon it's starting to rain. Rhonda spots an abandoned house (there are more and more in Gary), and they find a way inside and fall asleep. The next day, they make it to the home of a friend, who says their parents are looking for them. Rhonda refuses to return; she wants to file a report with the police. A pair of officers arrive, sit with the girls, take down what they have to say. Then they load them into the patrol car and drive them back to Gloria's. The court mandates that the entire Cooper family take part in family therapy—but the parents refuse. So the girls attend sessions alone. And Gloria and Herman are never ordered before the judge.

More escape attempts follow, and the girls are placed, together, in a string of homes. There is the Thelma Marshall Children's Home, three and a half blocks from the Jackson 5 family house (the boys' father had worked at the mill too), there are emergency shelters and foster homes. Every placement is temporary. This is the design of the system, based on the belief that a child's parents are their best caretakers, and reliant upon government employees who are often overwhelmed. When Rhonda's father Ron asks their caseworker how he can adopt the sisters himself, she tells him that the Cooper parents are "crazy," and that she does not want any complications to interfere with her own retirement, six months away.

Finally, when Rhonda is fourteen, she moves in with her father, and Gloria does not try to stop her. Rhonda leaves the yellow house, without her younger sister. She will not return.

Paula begins skipping classes and fighting girls at school—at one school after another, transferring two or three times a year. And with Rhonda gone, Herman turns his attention to his daughter.

She learns to run away on her own. And on one of those nights, after a beating from her father, Paula runs all the way to the police station and begs to be given somewhere to live other than home.

Paula is thirteen. She will be passed from stranger to stranger for the next two years—foster homes, shelters, juvenile detention. But these stays are punctuated by time with her parents, a few weeks or months at a stretch, miserable.

One morning at home, soon after turning fourteen, Paula does not get out of bed. Does not talk to anyone. Does not open her eyes. She seems completely catatonic, and nothing Gloria says or does can stir her. Eventually, her mother cannot ignore how bad the situation looks and decides to take her for an evaluation. Paula is placed in a mental health center in East Chicago for observation.

After four days, she will be released. She will be released, again, into the care of her parents.

Two

SOUTH OF THE
LITTLE CALUMET

A white house with slender columns in the Glen Park neighborhood, south of the Little Calumet River. This piece of Gary is just three miles from the Marshalltown development, but for much of its history, that distance was pronounced: until the late 1960s, Glen Park was within the city's borders but kept apart, strictly white.

It is the spring of 1985, and a lot has changed. Glen Park, like much of the city, has become integrated; and, like much of the city, the neighborhood is less well tended, its residents more likely to be in search of a job after the massive layoffs at the mill.

Ruth Pelke will turn seventy-nine in a few days, and she has lived in the white house on Adams Street since the early 1940s. But most of the friends she and her husband made have already chosen to relocate farther south, into the suburbs. It seems to her that the families to move in since have each been a little poorer than the ones before. Now when a front gate, a drain pipe, or even a window breaks, many neighbors leave it that way. Police cars regularly patrol the area. Ruth has a sign on her front door that reads: *The owner of this property is armed. There is nothing inside worth risking your life for.* In spite of the warning, her home has been robbed four times in the last two years. One of her stepdaughters suggested they move in together; a stepson offered to help make some repairs and sell. But even after Ruth's husband died—one year and nine months ago—she's remained committed to living out her days in the home they shared. She has no interest in leaving.

Ruth spent nearly the first half of her life on a farm in Erie Township on the outskirts of Peru, a town about two hours southeast of Gary. She was Ruth Zimmerman then, and from a very early age she did her part, milking and feeding the cows before sunup, driving the wagon. The rhythm of that life was so distant from her future in Gary: the cool, silent mornings with only the sound of the livestock; the long, slow walks through the cornfields. The community was small, and out in its farther-flung countryside she could stand in one spot and look around in every direction and count only about half a dozen houses dotting the fields; they were so spread out, so dependent upon one another. When a neighbor's wife was ready to give birth, Ruth's parents would send her over to help out with the family's chores.

The Zimmermans were part of a Church of the Brethren community, followers of a German branch of Protestant Christianity, and they attended services and prayer meetings at Center Chapel four or five times a week. It was a one-room church then, very small, and they would keep the windows open during service so the spillover crowd would be able to hear the sermon from where they huddled outside. Each member was baptized—in a tub inside the church or in the swimming hole near Squirrel Creek—not as a young child but only when they were old enough to understand the beliefs of the congregation, as the Brethren require. How can you accept something you do not understand? Ruth sang in the church choir, hymns like "In the Garden," and she taught Sunday school. She had an easy way with the children, keeping them in line without ever raising her voice; she'd lost her younger brother Russell, when she was five and he was just a toddler, and she remained drawn to the younger kids.

Ruth's social life revolved entirely around whatever was going on at the church. She was just a child during the First World War, and she watched the older boys in the town leave in droves. But, with the start of World War II, she was already thirty-three and not afraid of hard labor, and she took a job at a tire factory in Wabash. The long days of work, and the nights and weekends at Center Chapel, kept her occupied. This was partly the reason that Ruth turned thirty-five before she began dating someone with serious intentions.

By then, Ruth's second cousin Dorothy, up in Gary, had been married for some time to a man named Oscar Pelke. Ruth would see the Pelkes when they took trips south to visit, and she always enjoyed the kids. She'd let their son Bob, already a teenager, drive the hay wagon; she didn't even give him a hard time when once, taking a turn too quickly, he tipped the whole thing over. Dorothy and Oscar named their daughter Ruth too—a name that means "compassion"—and when Ruthie was as young as four, Ruth would send her out to the pasture to bring in the cows and then let the girl watch her milk them. Ruthie would trail after Ruth all across the property, right at her heels, totally in love with her.

Dorothy died of leukemia in 1941. A year later, Oscar and Ruth began seeing each other; another year went by, and he asked her to marry him. First, she insisted, he had to ask the children, never mind that they were hardly children anymore. Everyone was excited about it. Ruth would become the only grandmother their kids would know. She eventually had nine grandchildren and fifteen great-grandchildren, and the entire circus called her Nana. Holidays were always at Nana and Granddad's house; she crocheted them gifts, which took much longer than shopping. When the family went fishing, she and Oscar would invite everyone over for a fish fry, and they'd make a spread in the basement, like in a church rec room, to hold all two dozen of them.

As they grew older, she and Oscar were openly affectionate, kissing and holding each other in front of friends and family. It had been like that between them since the beginning: in a photograph of Ruth and Oscar standing on Adams Street, taken early in their marriage, there's a serious, easy closeness between the couple, he in a broad tie, hair combed back, and she in a pillbox hat and pearls. They are pressed close together, his arm hooked into hers, and though they are both staring straight into the camera, they each have a recognizable look in their eyes: the look of someone very aware of the person beside them.

There is the story of the layoffs at the mills, the downswing of yet another steel town. And then there's the story that many white residents of Lake County tell about the decline of Gary, whites whose families used to have a foothold in the city, and that can be reduced to: *It was left to Black people*, or *A Black man got elected mayor*. But Gary's is the story of a city whose resources were bled from it by many of its white officials and white citizens.

As in many American cities, tiers of segregation were built into this place, fair conditions and fair treatment defined differently for each sector of the population. When the corporation erected Gary, they constructed a showcase of a mill, among the most advanced of its time, and a *piece* of a city—just enough housing and services to cover the needs of their executives and foremen and supervisors. But the majority at the Gary Works—and, soon, throughout the town—was comprised of unskilled workers who streamed in from across Eastern Europe, Greece, Turkey, Italy, and Russia. These immigrants were pushed south of the small grid of the established city, where there were no building regulations and few paved streets. Developers descended and sold them poorly constructed houses and shacks, crowded together, without running water, for grossly inflated prices. Within about ten years, by 1920, more than half of Gary's residents were foreign-born or first-generation American—"white ethnics"—and their piece of the city was not built to last.

During the 1910s, once the influx of immigrant workers was cut off during World War I, Black workers and families from the American South streamed into industrial cities in the North, better able to compete for jobs in the factories and mills. They steadily grew to become the dominant presence in Gary's Southside, and as they moved in, upwardly mobile white immigrant families moved out—into new neighborhoods to the east, west, and farther south. Early on, many immigrants and Black newcomers had considered each other neighbors and fellow settlers; they worked alongside one another; they sometimes shared church buildings and meeting halls. An Eastern European might learn English from his Black neighbor; some Black workers picked up Serbian or Croatian. But white, American-born locals, though the minority in Gary, maintained their advantage through a very American strategy: they pitted vulnerable groups, who had needs and grievances in common, against each other—through hiring practices, a segregated school system, whites-only businesses, whites-only public parks. Many immigrants undoubtedly experienced a sort of relief at discovering a community that was lower in rank and even more marginalized than their own.

The city, whose population had grown to about seventy thousand by the early 1920s, was becoming deeply segregated along racial lines: Black residents could only live in inferior housing in the Midtown area, attend inferior schools, and be hired for dangerous jobs (where they were first in line to be fired). The Ku Klux Klan, then at the peak of their influence in Indiana, campaigned loudly against Blacks, immigrants, and Catholics; the white supremacist group ruled Gary's Republican Party, producing a string of mayors and city councilmen. The city's Black residents may have come looking for a respite from the racism and Jim Crow laws of the South, but their hopes were misplaced. By the 1940s, the degree of segregation equaled that of many Deep South communities. It was not until after World War II that Black residents slowly began moving beyond the boundaries of Midtown.

Meanwhile, many white families continued relocating farther away from the mill and into neighborhoods like Glen Park, at the city's southernmost edge. The Little Calumet River—and by the mid-1950s, Interstate 94, to the river's north—demarcated the border between comfortable white Gary and everyone else. It is a boundary that one Indiana federal judge would later refer to as "the Berlin Wall."

Over time, the Black residents of Gary came to make up nearly half the population. And so what happened in 1967, against great resistance, could have been seen as part of the city's natural evolution: the election of a Black mayor, one of the very first in the country's history.

That mayoral race would be a defining moment in the story of the city, an episode retold for generations. For the first time, a Black resident announced his candidacy for the Democratic primary. The twelfth child of a factory worker in Michigan City, Richard Hatcher had earned a law degree while working a night job, and went on to become a Lake County deputy prosecutor and a legal adviser to the Gary chapter of the NAACP (the National Association for the Advancement of Colored People). As a city councilman in the mid-1960s, he helped pass an omnibus civil rights bill and fought hard to end housing segregation through the enforcement of open occupancy laws. Hatcher's campaign announcement came only three years after Alabama governor George Wallace—"Segregation now, segregation tomorrow, segregation forever!"—swept Lake County's white vote in the Democratic presidential primary, and the party had not run a Black candidate for any office more influential than city coroner.

Hatcher ran on a broad anticorruption platform—local lore had it that Robert Kennedy, as U.S. attorney general, referred to Lake County as the most corrupt county in the country—but he was most identified with his commitment to Gary's Black community. For decades, the local Democrats had relied on the conservative white steelworkers' votes, and Hatcher would have to win without them. When he beat the incumbent in the party's primary, in a heavily Democratic city, it was considered as good as winning the race.

Party leadership, shocked, did not throw him their full support. Instead, his platform, with its focus on public housing, was found suspect. Some white officials insisted that the needs of Gary's Black population could be met quickly by throwing up projects in Midtown; Hatcher said the city had a duty to provide public housing *throughout* its neighborhoods, including the white enclaves of Glen Park and Miller. He called on "the moral conscience of the city." The white Democratic machine was concerned that they would not hold sway over a Hatcher administration. The chairman of the county party withheld campaign funds; he demanded that Hatcher publicly denounce the Black Power movement and agree to allow the party certain key appointments to his cabinet.

Rather than give in, Hatcher appealed to outside donors through a full-page ad in *The New York Times*: "We're at War, You Know. With Ourselves," the ad opened, and featured a photo of a white policeman clubbing a Black man. It called for "Peace and unity for all men—black and white (and every shade in between)." Hatcher deployed armies of student volunteers to register voters in Gary's Black-majority neighborhoods. He received public support from Indiana senator Birch Bayh, now senator Robert Kennedy, President Lyndon Johnson (who invited him to the White House), and Vice President Hubert Humphrey (who embraced him on camera). The Lake County Democratic Party, in the meantime, had thrown its support behind the Republican candidate. The last time Gary had a Republican mayor was in the 1920s, during the heyday of the Klan.

When Hatcher won the race, he and Carl Stokes of Cleveland, Illinois, became the first two Black mayors of major cities in American history.

There is a version of the story of Gary that might have come to pass then—the story of a city, half Black and half white, that became, if not fully integrated, the home of two equally thriving communities. Midtown was growing—Black-owned businesses, clothing stores, record shops, breakfast spots and nightclubs, packed Black churches—and the civil rights movement had injected a new energy into the area. Young Black talent from the region and around Chicago came to work for the Hatcher administration. The *Post-Tribune* had been a successful white-run newspaper since the city's founding, but Black Gary had the recently founded weeklies *Info* and *The Gary Crusader*—the self-described *Militant Voice of the People*, with its motto *Blacks Must Control Their Own Community*. The *Crusader*, in particular, was full of mentions of local students who had made the state college's dean's list, or earned an Eagle Scout award or an Army Reserve award, or been named a teen pageant finalist; of Gary residents who'd been elected to the board of the Lake County Young Democrats; announcements of a new children's summer theater program or a teen pianist's recital. The community was telling itself the story of what it could become, was on the verge of becoming.

But over the next several years, white flight from the city accelerated. The image of a Black mayor—and one committed to civil rights and open housing—helped lead a city that was half Black to become, by the end of the 1970s, more than 70 percent Black. White families relocated to suburbs farther south, such as Merrillville and Portage, where developers spent their money on new shopping centers that catered to white Lake County. The big banks followed, as well as nearly all white-owned businesses. The gutted population meant a gutted tax base and the beginning of a decades-long decay of the city's infrastructure. Abandoned buildings became part of the downtown landscape. People needed work, and crime was rising.

Half the city's residents had abandoned it because they refused to recognize themselves in its other half.

Four blocks away from Ruth's house is Lew Wallace High School, a large redbrick schoolhouse where her stepson Bob studied long ago. It is lunch break on a Tuesday morning, and Paula Cooper, fifteen now, walks out with Karen and April. In the pocket of her white denim jacket, she has a prescription and a note from her mother: permission to leave early today to refill her birth control pills. The three tenth graders decide to head over to Candyland Arcade around the corner.

Paula has been at Lew Wallace for just a few weeks—it's her fourth high school—and Karen is her best friend here. At sixteen, Karen's a large girl, often out of breath; everyone calls her Pooky, maybe because of her sweet face (in spite of the scar through her eyebrow). She has a child, who's three, and he mostly stays at home with her godmother. April's about to have the same problem—though she can still hide it at seven months.

The girls walk a few long blocks through Glen Park, down 45th to Broadway. At the arcade, they play games, talk to boys, buy candy. Not much is happening; everyone is growing bored.

They decide to skip school for the rest of the afternoon. April invites along a younger girl the others don't really know—Denise, who's fourteen, a freshman—and together they walk the three blocks to the house where April stays with her siblings, to sit on her porch and drink Wild Irish Rose. Earlier in the week, the girls had robbed a neighbor—broke a window near the back door, slipped in, and came away with ninety dollars—but they've spent most of that money. After buying candy, they're down to a few quarters between them.

Paula watches April look up and down the block, sizing up the houses she can see from the porch: a lazy kind of recon. April mentions an old woman who lives in the house just behind hers. "Remember that lady we saw standing out back?" Paula and Karen remember her. "Well, we could go over to her house," she says. "Because she has a lot of money and jewelry and different things."

The place the girls are talking about across the alley, the bright white house with the columns out front, is the home of Ruth Pelke. What they know about Mrs. Pelke is what April tells them: she is a Bible teacher, she is elderly, and she lives alone. The key to getting into her house, April says, is to ask about Bible study.

Outside of her church, Ruth used to volunteer with Child Evangelism Fellowship, driving into downtown Gary once a week to teach children eight and under in an after-school program. Ruth also organized local 5-Day Clubs for CEF, usually during the summer, in which she talked to slightly older kids about her faith, and when kids didn't have parents to take them to church, she'd bring them along to Glen Park Baptist herself. This is what she'd done for April a few years back—though, out on her porch this afternoon, April has told Paula and Karen and Denise none of this. They do not understand how well she knows the lady across the alleyway.

April had been among Mrs. Pelke's last students, two years ago—shortly before Ruth's husband died and she retired from teaching and began keeping more to herself. She had even driven April and her brother to church for their first time—to the Pelkes' newer church, Christ Temple, since their longtime congregation had moved farther south. After April's mother died, Mrs. Pelke reached out to her again: she invited April over for meals and packed her lunches for school. This is how, today, April knows that Mrs. Pelke will be alone; this is why, today, April assumes that the woman must have money in the house—because of the many little things she has done for her. If a person gives freely, they must have more than others.

One Mother's Day several years earlier, Ruth's pastor had asked the mothers in the congregation to stand up to be recognized. Because

Ruth had no children of her own, she remained seated in her pew. Her grandson Bill noticed this, and it bothered him: she had never allowed them to celebrate her on Mother's Day. And so a few days later, when Ruth turned seventy, her family threw her a combined birthday and "Nana's Day" party. They dressed her in a store-bought crown and a homemade queen's robe trimmed with faux fur.

In four days, Ruth will have her birthday, and her great-grandson will turn fifteen. There's also her great-granddaughter's high school graduation coming up fast; maybe, for the celebration, she'll bring over the macaroni salad everyone likes, the kind with watermelon pickles.

Since settling in Gary more than forty years ago, Ruth has taught hundreds of children stories from the Bible. In a string of neighborhood living rooms, she's gathered kids together, lining them up on the sofa or seating them cross-legged on the carpet, and served them Kool-Aid and cookies. She's mounted a flannel board on an easel and walked cutouts across that field of blue—of Joseph and his coat of many colors; of Jonah and the whale, its mouth wide open; of Daniel and the lions.

Though her own people, on the farm near Peru, were Church of the Brethren, once Ruth married into the Pelke clan, she became part of a family that was resolutely Baptist. The Pelkes were part of a Baptist community in Gary that, like her own, revolved entirely around church life: if the doors were open, and you weren't at work or at school, you were at church. You showed up for service, for Bible study, for after-work prayer meetings and volunteer projects. Glen Park Baptist had been just a few blocks from Ruth and Oscar's house, and there they could worship alongside most of the kids and grandkids. She taught their early Sunday school class before attending morning service; on Wednesdays, she went to prayer meetings and Pioneer Girls meetings, followed by choir practice. She made quilts for visiting missionaries with the women's circle and hosted the visitors in her home. She knitted booties for the new babies in the congregation; she drove her friends to church; she tithed any extra money she and Oscar had—even when the dryer broke and then the TV set too.

In the two years following Oscar's death, holidays are hosted by other family members. The house is quiet. But Ruth can draw on the independent spirit of her earlier life. She gardens and mows her own lawn with a push mower, goes out for her own groceries—and she can't imagine moving. She isn't foolish or superstitious, but maybe some piece of Oscar's presence lingers.

I t's after three p.m. and hot when the girls leave April's porch to visit the Bible teacher. April stays behind: she is a too-familiar face. Paula and the others cross the alley behind the white house on Adams Street.

They walk across the stretch of flat, no-fuss lawn and up the front steps. They pass between a pair of neatly tended ferns with drippy tendrils, under the archway, two columns on either side, and crowd onto the porch.

Karen rings the bell.

The three stand and wait, quietly. Paula listens: the sound of slow steps across the floorboards; she can see movement behind the glass panel. Mrs. Pelke opens the door.

From behind Karen, Paula looks at the lady for the first time. Mrs. Pelke may have grown up on farm and factory work, but she is an elegant woman, with a slim white neck. Her hair is set in bright white curls, and her eyeglasses curve upward at either end; the look in her eyes is gentle and steady. She's only slightly shorter than Paula, but she looks so much smaller. She is someone's good grandmother, somebody's soft mother.

"My auntie would like to know about Bible classes," Karen says. "When you all hold them."

"Well, now's not a good time," the lady says. "But if you and your auntie come over on a Saturday, I can give you both some information." And Mrs. Pelke closes the door.

Slowly, the girls turn around and file back down the walkway as they came.

W ell, you could scare the lady with *this*"—that's what April says to Paula back at her house. They are standing in the kitchen, and she's pulled a knife out of a drawer. The blade is wide and twelve inches long. A butcher knife.

This time, April says, they should go to the lady's house and tell her they need all the information about the classes written down—dates, address, phone number. Paula removes her white denim jacket and wraps the knife inside.

And so they cross the alley and round the corner and, once again, they round the corner and file up that walkway on Adams Street.

Once again, Karen rings the bell.

Once again, as if the possible paths their lives might take were being rearranged, Mrs. Pelke comes to the door. Paula stands behind the others, gripping her jacket to her chest.

Mrs. Pelke opens the screen door. And one, two, three: the girls each step across the threshold.

They enter the living room, with its large fireplace. An ivy-like pattern covers the walls; the davenport is printed with leaves. Here and there are hung small pictures of modest landscapes, a barn covered in snow. Paula carefully sets her jacket down on the sofa.

They trail the old woman into the dining room, where there is a large table, a pump organ, and a writing desk. Above the desk is a black-and-white photograph of Oscar as a boy, standing beside a horse—not that the girls would know who he is, why his picture matters in this house. Mrs. Pelke pauses at the desk and pulls a pen and pad out of the drawer: she will write a note for the girls, all they need to know. The lady leans over—and Paula comes up from behind and knocks her down.

Mrs. Pelke lands seated on the carpet, legs splayed in front of her, the tips of her thick-soled shoes pointed toward the ceiling. Just within reach, on the table, is a glass paperweight: Paula picks it up and brings it down hard on the lady's head.

For a moment, nothing moves. And then it springs forth from the woman's head: a red rush of blood. The blood spills out, true red against white hair.

Mrs. Pelke does not stir. Paula looks down at the lady. She has never before laid someone low like this, not an adult. Now Mrs. Pelke is no longer who she was when she answered the door, that well-kept church-woman with the bright curls.

Paula will remember what comes next like this: that suddenly, there on the tabletop, is the knife. *Right there*, within reach. And she reaches for it.

Her movements are exaggerated now, double time. She slashes at the lady—little sideways cuts, at her arms, her legs. She is shouting: "*Where's the money, bitch?*" She shouts it again, then again, slashing at the woman's dress, growing more determined, cutting through skin. Mrs. Pelke, overwhelmed, tips over, falling flat on her back.

Paula climbs on top of her. From this vantage point, peering down at the lady's face, straddling her thighs, she sees Mrs. Pelke's earrings, like silver buttons, and the blood trapped under the rim of her glasses, and those dark freckles that old people get on their skin. She can hear sounds coming from the lady's mouth, a stream of words. Paula can just make them out: "*If you do this, you'll be sorry.*"

A key deep inside Paula turns and catches, and she is set in motion. She stabs the woman in her chest; she pulls out the knife; she stabs her again. Her hand comes down more than thirty times before she stops, leaving the blade in Mrs. Pelke's stomach.

Paula is finally used up. She looks at Denise—she's been standing there the whole time, her back against the wall. "Come here," Paula says, "and hold the knife."

Denise shakes, every part of her: she can't—she's a baby. Karen will do it. Paula gets up to let her take her place.

But Karen pauses. "I can't look at the lady." She leaves the dining room, then returns with a bath towel. Karen drops it, that piece of white terry cloth, over Mrs. Pelke's face. Now she can sit across the legs of the dying woman.

Paula searches the house. In one of the bedrooms, she finds a key ring on top of the bureau. She rushes past Denise (tearing through the closet) and Karen (with the lady on the floor) and out to the sedan where it's parked in the garage. She tries it in the lock: Not. It.

Just then, she sees April cross the alley, and the two enter the house together. They join Denise in the rummaging. They drag bags and hangers and blankets out of the bedroom closet, pull out dresser drawers and sofa cushions, until they find it: the key to the Plymouth. That, and ten dollars.

During the time the search takes, Karen remains crouched over Mrs. Pelke, holding on to the knife. And after the first fifteen minutes have passed, Karen decides to test something: she wants to see if the blade will go in deeper. So she shoves it in. She pushes it down, through the woman's chest, until the tip comes out the other side—out through her back, through the carpet, and into the wooden floorboard below. And then she rocks the handle from side to side, feeling how the point is now fixed in place.

Ruth is pinned like a specimen to her own dining-room floor, and she can see nothing. She will die soon, and the young girls are still circling, stalking, moving through the house, overturning the photos of the grandkids and touching and tossing aside Oscar's things. These are children, like the hundreds of others who've passed through Ruth's house. That was why she'd let them in.

Three

THE MAKING
OF A PROSECUTOR

Seven years earlier, in 1978, Jack Crawford had decided to run for Lake County prosecutor. A campaign ad shows him at twenty-nine, outdoors on a sunny day in a rugby shirt, giving the camera a full-toothed grin. The ad communicates that he's young! and fresh!, belying the tough-on-crime campaign he's about to run. *The so-called political experts say Jack Crawford can't win the race for Lake County Prosecutor. Jack Crawford doesn't depend on the experts. He depends on You!*

Jack had been in his first semester at the University of Notre Dame, in a suburb about an hour east of Gary, when Richard Hatcher was first rumored to be running for mayor. It was all the adults around him seemed to be talking about, and Jack, who was Irish American, was struck by the amount of sheer white animus directed toward the man: talk of how he would ruin the city, how he was a secret communist or a Black Panther or both. During his childhood, Jack's idea of what it meant to be Black had something to do with the view he and his grandfather saw out the window of the elevated train as it passed through Wrigleyville in Chicago on the way to watch a Cubs game: small tenement apartments packed with families, the kids wearing shabby clothes. He heard his father tell a few jokes about Black people that he looked back on with discomfort.

Jack had grown up in Hammond, a town fifteen minutes from Gary that would later inspire the Rockwellesque setting of the movie *A Christmas Story*. It was a small city that, like parts of Gary then, was split along several white-ethnic fault lines—Greeks, Serbs, Croatians, Yugoslavians, Poles—each with its own churches and taverns. Most had emigrated for the abundance of jobs in the mills; for many young men, the paycheck would be solid and the unions would provide security. Jack considered his upbringing middle-class, leaning toward lower-middle-class: His mother was a schoolteacher; his father was a barber and a worker at Standard Oil; the family was union all the way. He was raised to believe the union had given his family its start, and that meant you voted straight Democrat, without question. Industry had long ago turned Lake County blue in a doggedly red state.

They were Catholic in very Protestant Northwest Indiana, and Jack had attended one of the two area Catholic schools, Bishop Noll Institute, where teachers wore clerical black. In yearbook photos, in his navy blazer, he looked young and clean and eager to please. Many of his classmates at Bishop Noll were of Irish descent, and many of those were first- or second-generation American; Jack was raised on stories of how hard the Irish experience had been, coming to the States. It was through that lens, as the civil rights movement was becoming visible to mainstream America (Jack was a sophomore when the March on Washington took place), that he decided he related to the Black experience. In high school, Jack would sometimes drive into Midtown—he wasn't afraid the way some of his friends were. He'd shop for records, check out some cool clothes, go to Miller Beach, where he could see the Gary Works stacks in the distance, and the dark smoke that shrouded them. The guys he brought along would ask, "Okay, what did you want to come here for?" He was curious.

At Notre Dame in the late 1960s, politics were at the center of campus life, and Jack wanted to be a part of it. John F. Kennedy, the country's first Irish Catholic president, was shot when Jack was in high school, and now Kennedy's younger brother Robert was his personal hero. He saw him as less cerebral and detached than his brother, more of a "doer," a tough prosecutor who helped mount an aggressive investigation of Jimmy Hoffa and an attack on organized crime as attorney general. In the spring of 1968, Bobby Kennedy, now grown into an idealist and an advocate for civil rights, entered the presidential race late, and he needed to win the Democratic primary in Indiana. On his first day in the state, he would find himself in Indianapolis, informing a shocked crowd of the assassination of Martin Luther King Jr.—but earlier, in the afternoon, he'd made an appearance at Notre Dame. As a volunteer, Jack helped coordinate the candidate's visit, escorting him down the packed streets toward the campus. In the auditorium, full far beyond capacity, young men listened to Kennedy talk about their "personal responsibility" to invest in the country's political process, to find solutions to poverty and hunger and inequality. When asked about the Vietnam draft, in motion for four years already, Kennedy said he did not believe in college deferments. Jack would remember him saying something like, *The only reason you're here is you're children of privilege. The unfairness of that should strike you in your heart. That means you don't have to die, and someone who did not have your privileges has to go to Vietnam. If the children of wealthy, privileged, white Americans were forced to go off to the jungles of Vietnam to fight, this war would be over tomorrow.*

Two months later, Kennedy, like his brother, was assassinated. And the following year, the draft became a lottery. For the lottery's launch, "youth advisory council" delegates were sent to D.C. from around the country to pick numbers onstage on live TV; Father Hesburgh, the long-time president of Notre Dame, chose Jack to go, as student-body president. When his turn came, he reached inside a glass jar full of blue capsules, each containing a birth date and its assigned draft status. He did this five times, and then the next delegate took their turn. This was how, in a single night, about 850,000 men learned their likelihood of being killed in the war. At Notre Dame, students began burning their draft cards during Mass on campus. Jack applied to law school to pursue a career in public office, but also in the hope of extending his deferment.

After graduate school at Indiana University at Bloomington, Jack was hired by Chicago firm Kirkland & Ellis. In the meantime, he'd married Ann, a woman he'd met in college. She was two years younger, also Irish Catholic, and a staunch liberal from Long Island, New York. She could relate to Jack's fascination with the Kennedy mystique, and she understood that he had a larger plan. And so, when he left his lucrative job to become a poorly paid assistant city attorney back in Hammond, she supported this first small step in what she assumed would be a long career.

Jack planned to make his start with or without the support of the Democratic machine. He bided his time until he saw an opening: Hammond city court judge. As someone without political allies, experience, or endorsements, few thought Jack could win. But he and Ann went door to door throughout the city, thousands of doors. He won in a landslide. It was a modest position—he was, essentially, in "traffic court"—but he had become one of the youngest judges in Indiana. And he was certainly much younger than the other officials in the court building. While they waited for the elevator, Jack made a habit of running up the stairs.

After about two years on the bench, Jack began considering a big leap: Lake County prosecutor. Jack, with little experience in criminal law or as a trial lawyer, coveted the office. Across the country, prosecutors (or district attorneys) have almost total discretion in deciding whether or not someone should be indicted, whether or not a case should go to trial, and how high the stakes will be for the defendant: real influence.

The party machine was not pleased: you were not supposed to run against the incumbent; there was a pecking order. The county Democratic chairman came to Jack and asked him to wait another nine, ten years. But Jack's successes would always be driven by appetite; his drive grew in proportion to the size of the obstacles in front of him. If his campaign for prosecutor was pissing a lot of people off, he was prepared to hustle hard enough to make up the difference. He and Ann went door to door again—a *lot* more doors. He packed in appearances, giving talks to PTA groups and women's clubs, at local bingo games and house parties of fifteen people. A natural politician, he remembered *everyone's* name. Jack would put in a full day of shaking hands and at the last minute, at ten-thirty p.m., ask his volunteer driver to turn into the parking lot at Bethlehem Steel because he knew the men would be changing shifts.

Jack's key campaign issue was plea bargaining: he accused the incumbent of bargaining 90 percent of his cases—a percentage Jack admitted was an "educated guess" (the incumbent, Ray Sufana, suggested it was closer to 55 percent for felony cases). Lake County had about a thousand criminal cases filed each year, and it was impossible for all of them to go to trial and not have the courts collapse. But Jack's instinct told him that comeuppance would sell well. On the day before the May election, he ran a last-minute ad: a photo of Jack and his pretty wife strolling together, looking middle-class relatable and carefree, with the message "Don't Plea Bargain Your Safety Away!"

Jack had developed a new level of savvy since his Hammond campaign. Running for city judge, he performed very poorly with the Black community, losing their vote 10 to 1, and his immediate reaction had been: *I'm not racist—what is this about?* On a countywide level now, he could not win without Black support, so he became more deliberate in his strategy. He approached the more influential ministers in the Black community. Among the most prominent was the Reverend A. R. Burns, pastor of Mount Zion Missionary Baptist Church in Hammond for over thirty years and a father of twelve. When Jack learned that Reverend Burns had a daughter, Mary, who was a receptionist for the police department, he hired her to work in his office as an investment in his own future. Jack found her charming and attractive, and she helped him make the rounds at the major Black churches.

He became a regular at Black services, whether with Ann or with Mary, and was often asked, as an elected official, to come up front to say a few words. Jack learned to make his case as a candidate up there by the pulpit, an approach he couldn't have taken at the white churches he knew. Mary was used to politicians (who were predominantly white) coming into the Black community for a drop-in, announcing with fanfare that they'd be bringing "turkey and ham and bingo and prizes!" to their campaign event—and assuming that was enough to bring people out and secure their votes. As if Black residents in the county never thought about the issues, never cared about whether someone was going to follow through on their promises. Jack, however, struck Mary as a fair person, and someone who spoke to Black and white voters in the same way; she didn't mind introducing him at a house party in Hammond, or suggesting an appearance at some prominent couple's fiftieth-anniversary celebration. He would make late-night stops at a Black club like the Blue Room, without an entourage or security, and bring Ann along on his arm. This was not something white officials were doing.

Behind the scenes, Jack also formed an allegiance with Mayor Hatcher, who had heard about this candidate's style. During a private lunch in the mayor's office, Hatcher said, "You and your wife, I know that you go to Black clubs at night to campaign. You go by yourself, I've been told. That means something to me, that you feel comfortable coming into the community and participating. You strike me as a young man who knows what time it is." Hatcher told his precinct captains—his lieutenants throughout the city—that they were going for Crawford.

Jack won. And in Sufana's final week, a long line stretched from his office down the hall—a line of people trying to make deals before the new no-deals prosecutor took office. Some in the building referred to it as a "going-out-of-business sale."

————————— ✳ —————————

When Jack took office in January 1979, he inherited eight hundred open cases, in addition to the thousand he could expect to be filed that year. But he was determined to make a reputation for himself as a hard-line prosecutor, and that meant avoiding plea bargaining wherever he could. In a move that would become commonplace on a national level, Jack soon set up a Career Criminal Unit that made more aggressive use of the state's habitual offender law: Three strikes automatically earned a person thirty additional years on their sentence, regardless of the level of seriousness of that third charge. If someone was brought in who had two prior felony convictions and was up for a third, Jack's staff always took the option of adding the habitual as a consecutive sentence, known around the office (and in the prison system) as "the bitch." What would have been a ten-year under Sufana became a forty-year; twenty years became fifty. Jack was "three strikes" all the way.

Tom Vanes, a veteran of the previous administration, was made head of the Career Criminal Unit—but Jack otherwise got rid of nearly the entire staff. He was able to hire a lot of talented young attorneys, a diverse group, because they knew they'd have a chance to try cases rather than regularly plead them out. And despite the county being much smaller than New York or Chicago, it had more than its share of crime; as Vanes put it, Lake County just had "one or two fewer zeros in the amounts of money stolen." For some of the same reasons that made recruiting easy, Jack's job was made riskier. He was a visible, aggressive prosecutor whose name was known throughout the region. When he went out in public, he often brought an armed investigator with him.

When it came time for the next Democratic primary, no one ran against Jack Crawford because they knew they'd lose. He was a man of grand ambitions. As one public defender put it: "You could just tell he was doing *The Jeffersons*. He was *movin' on up*." Such comments were not always intended to flatter. A female assistant to one of the judges said Jack "came in like on stardust, so full of himself," flirty, like he thought he was "hot shit."

For someone who denied that he had his sights on the White House, Jack seemed very conscious of his trajectory. In 1983, a year into his second term as prosecutor, he decided to run in the Democratic con-gressional primary in

Indiana's 1st District—a mainly Democratic district that included Lake and Porter counties. Once again, Jack was counting on the support of voters, rather than party insiders who felt he was rushing, pushing too hard. It was with this run for Congress that his upward mobility hit a wall.

He was confident he would win. But, through a combination of bad timing, some poor strategic choices, and significantly less time spent shaking hands than in his earlier campaigns, Jack not only lost but came in third. The winner, Pete Visclosky, was low on charisma but solid; in contrast to Jack's reputation as a "political animal," he came off as no-frills and sincere. On election night, as it became increasingly apparent that Jack was going to lose, he was a no-show at his campaign office, where his volunteers were gathered waiting to hear from him. The fol-lowing day, gutted, Jack took off from work and went to see the Cubs play. One local news outlet found a way to make a story out of it, along the lines of *Jack Crawford drowns his sorrows with another loser, the Chicago Cubs.*

The question became: What next? He would likely hold on to the Prosecutor's Office for another term or two—that was the platform he had at his disposal. His future might depend on how much of a statement he could make in Lake County.

And now it is 1985. Gary continues to take turns with Detroit as the FBI's "murder capital" of the country. Two high-profile assassinations in the city in recent years remain unsolved: that of Hank "Babe" Lopez, the former president of the steel workers' union at Inland Steel; and that of Jay Given, a powerful East Chicago attorney. The Prosecutor's Office is regularly charged with handling home invasions, rapes, "dismemberment slayings," and gang wars, and it seems that a weekend cannot go by without a homicide. At the same time, mill jobs across Lake County have dramatically declined throughout Jack's tenure, mainly because of the importing of steel, and many people are desperate.

In response, the prosecutor continues to shore up his aggressive reputation. And a key weapon in his arsenal is the death penalty.

In the 1970s, the United States had a five-year nationwide moratorium on capital punishment. It began in 1972 with a landmark case won by the NAACP's Legal and Educational Defense Fund (or LDF) as led by the attorney Anthony Amsterdam. In *Furman v. Georgia*, Amsterdam argued that the death penalty was unconstitutional under the Eighth Amendment barring "cruel and unusual punishment"—and the Supreme Court agreed. In their decision, the Court focused on the penalty's arbitrariness as carried out by the states: Justice Potter Stewart wrote, *These death sentences are cruel and unusual in the same way that being struck by lightning is cruel and unusual.* But over the following years, several death-penalty states wrote new statutes giving greater guidance to juries in capital cases. These new laws created a two-phase trial procedure: the jury would first decide whether the defendant was guilty, and then it would consider, after a presentation of "aggravating" and "mitigating" circumstances, whether they should be sentenced to death. And so in 1976, in *Gregg v. Georgia*, the Court ruled that these new statutes prevented capital punishment from stepping beyond the bounds of the

Eighth Amendment. The door was opened to hundreds more death sentences—a revival. In January 1977, executions resumed.

About a year later, under Jack's predecessor, Tom Vanes caught the first death-penalty case in the state after the moratorium—and won. Soon Jack Crawford was elected, and prepared to make full use of the country's most severe sentence. He quickly handed Tom his second and third capital cases, and it rolled on from there. Most of Tom's colleagues, many still in their twenties, were eager for this kind of high-profile work. Tom thought the office had that air of competition most people associate with sports.

When weighing whether or not to pursue death, after six years in office, Jack feels he has a fairly straightforward approach. The first two questions he asks himself are obvious ones: Is the evidence strong?, and What is the defendant's record or background? But then he gets a little more abstract, more interpretive: Do the facts of this murder *shock the conscience?* Does society have to make a statement? This last question is one that Jack spends particular time considering. Lake County recently had a rash of murders committed by young people: Does the prosecutor, representing the community, have to draw a line and say *Even though you are not an adult, we're going to hold you responsible as an adult under the law and extract the maximum penalty?* His answer is yes nearly every time. Always in the background is his mandate: no pleas, if he can avoid them. A hard line.

Jack was taught that to be Catholic was to be adamantly, uncompromisingly pro-life. But as prosecutor, he sees that plenty of Catholics—plenty of devout Christians of *any* denomination—are willing to accept the death penalty, even call for it, for crimes they decide are heinous enough. He and Ann attend Mass each week, and neither of them sees this as a contradiction. Specific cases can always be the exception to a moral rule: no matter how fixed a rule is *in theory*, there is always the question of *in practice*. He has come to believe that a person's religion has little to do with their feelings about the death penalty. People often invoke their faith when talking about justice—but what they are drawing on, their instinctive need for retribution, is more primal.

Jack continues going to Mass on Sundays, but he feels his Catholicism falling away. Attending church has become one more obligation; his faith makes less and less sense to him. The cases that come to him nearly every day, the crime-scene photos: they have begun to wear on him. There are the gang killings; there are the toddlers whose parents dipped their feet into scalding hot bathwater as punishment, their baby skin swollen with such long, angry blisters they can't walk. There are theological explanations for why God would allow this kind of suffering, and Jack has heard them. But if He is truly all-powerful and all-seeing, then couldn't He, wouldn't He, prevent these things from happening? Soon, Jack will stop going to church altogether.

Four

MALICE SUPPLIES
THE AGE

In the early afternoon on the day after her death, a Wednesday, Ruth Pelke's stepson Bob stops by her house for a visit. He and his wife had gone over for dinner the night before last, but Bob is worried: when he called Ruth that morning, as he does nearly every day, no one answered.

He steps up onto the front porch and rings the bell. Nothing. He bends over and calls through the mail slot, as he sometimes does: no answer. Peering through the opening, he can see a slice of the dining room: the carpet is strewn with stuff. And Ruth Pelke is a meticulous Christian woman.

Nervous now, Bob walks around back and picks up the extra key, tucked under a wooden board above the basement entrance. He returns to the porch, pulls open the storm door, and lets himself in.

In the living room, he finds sofa cushions thrown all across the floor, and through the doorway, he can see chaos in the dining room.

There he finds Ruth lying on the dark carpet. A towel over her face. Her head pressed against the leg of a dinner chair. The hem of her dress hiked up to expose much of her thighs.

Her arms are stiff and bent at the elbows, hands high on her chest, as if to defend herself. The backs of her hands are coated in blood. Her eyeglasses lie on the rug, against her bloodied elbow.

On the far side of the room, fresh white stationery is scattered across the green carpet like snow. And stamps and pens and pencils, coupons and plastic bags, letters Ruth had saved, all shaken out of desk drawers.

Bob drops to his knees and pulls the towel off her face. He calls to her. He touches her, and her body is cold, and he knows that she is gone.

He rushes to the phone: torn out of the wall, it sits on the dining-room table; the cord hangs like a limp tail off the edge of the lace table-cloth.

He runs out into the street in search of help. He runs up the neighbor's walkway and bangs on their door: no answer. He tries another house: no answer. He tries a few more, but no one responds, and all the while his stepmother lies on her dining-room floor, and he is the only person who knows it.

Finally, Bob sees a car turn south onto Adams and pull up a few doors down. A couple steps out. He rushes to them: *Please call the police my mother's been killed!* Bob has never used that word for Ruth before, *mother,* but that's how it comes out of him today. He gives them the address and rushes back to wait for the police.

About ten minutes later, detectives begin streaming in, and the white house becomes a public place. Bob stands outside, aimless, as cars continue to pull up—until someone tells him there is nothing more for him to do, that they are sealing Ruth's home. Someone uses the phrase *home invasion.*

Children in the neighborhood are returning from school, and the news ripples through them. They stand in clusters on the sidewalk near Mrs. Pelke's house and across the street, young boys and girls and some teenagers; a few are crying.

Soon the media appear: a camera crew is on hand to film the removal of the elderly woman. Two men in ties carry the loaded gurney over the front steps and roll it, slowly, down the walkway.

That evening, the Pelke clan gathers at Bob's house. About a dozen family members stand around large plates of food, stare at the table, exchange looks, share theories. A robbery—it must be. Drug-related—these things so often are.

That night, on television, Ruth's death makes the local news. Bob is shown standing off to the side, talking to the police. He has never appeared in public this way. He does not speak on air. He does not want to talk about it.

The next day, Ruth's murder is on the front pages of Lake County's major papers: BIBLE TEACHER, 77, MURDERED IN HER HOME is the lead story of the Gary *Post-Tribune*; "SOMEONE SPECIAL" KILLED reads *The Times* of Northwest Indiana. The killing is covered as a robbery—but a detail that will not be remarked upon, in all the press that follows, is this: when Ruth was left alone on her floor to die, she was still wearing her diamond ring; whoever entered the house had not taken it off her finger. If they had struggled to remove it, there's no evidence they tried very hard. But thieves would have known what to do with jewelry, would have known where to pawn it, would not have killed the old woman and then stopped short of yanking a diamond off her finger. That, after all, would have been what they were there for: a clear purpose.

That same morning, two students are arrested at Lew Wallace High School. By evening, two others will be delivered to the station. Girls, all of them—fourteen, fifteen, sixteen years old.

K aren and Denise sit at Detective Kennedy's desk at the Gary Police Department while he waits for their parents to arrive.

Kennedy has been with the department for three years, and for the past year and a half he's worked at Lew Wallace as a security officer. He is used to seeing these girls in the halls, used to them calling out to him—*Hi there, Kennedy*, that kind of thing. He knows Denise as a "little skinny girl" who's only pushed back once, said a few curse words when he caught her outside of class after the bell. But that morning, assigned to the Ruth Pelke murder, he went to the school specifically in search of her and three other students. A classmate had reported that the girls had given her a ride in Mrs. Pelke's car, and Paula Cooper had left a white jacket at the scene with a birth-control prescription in its pocket made out to her name. Gloria had just filed yet another missing person report about her daughter.

When Denise's father and stepmother get there, Detective Papadakis leads them to an interrogation room in the back. They are told that their daughter is bound for the jail in Crown Point. Only now do they learn that Denise has been skipping school all year.

Kennedy did not find Paula and April at school: unbeknownst to the authorities, they have spent the past two days living in the baby-blue Plymouth, getting as far as Chicago before running out of gas. That afternoon, April calls her older sister Gurseel for a ride back from Illinois. What else could they do? They are young, and as they moved farther away from home, their imaginations came to a halt. Gurseel drives them to the Gary police station that night: she has talked April and Paula into turning themselves in. By the time they arrive, more parents are streaming in. When each girl, in her own room, is ready to make a statement, a detective rolls in a typewriter.

From Karen's statement:

Q: Did you stab the lady after you took hold of the knife?
A: No. I just pushed it in a little bit.
Q: Why did you push the knife?
A: To see how far it would go in.
Q: . . . Was the lady still alive while you held the knife?
A: While I was holding it she was still breathing. I held it for about ten or fifteen minutes, then she died.
Q: How did you [know] the lady was dead?
A: After I did not see her stomach move anymore . . .

Herman and Gloria Cooper show up around ten p.m. They sit in an interrogation room with Paula and Detective Kennedy, refusing to say much of anything. Eventually, the Coopers go downstairs, and Kennedy leaves Paula on her own.

Around this time, nearly midnight, her sister arrives. Rhonda learned the news when she called her mother, just as Gloria was leaving for the station.

At fourteen, Rhonda found relief when she moved into her father Ron's house in Chicago Heights, and she now lives part-time with a girlfriend in Gary. When she turned eighteen last year, she started partying a lot, going out to clubs—so when she heard about Paula, she had to drink a lot of coffee to clear her head. This could not be happening. The police must have made a mistake—it would not be the first time. Rhonda took a shower, put on clean clothes, and got a ride to the station.

In an interrogation room, she and Gloria are given some time to sit with Paula on their own. When Detective Kennedy returns—Paula recognizes him from school—Rhonda encourages her sister to tell him what happened, only the parts she wants him to know. The rest, she says, Paula can tell a lawyer when they get one. And this is when Paula says she does not want them to look at her when she speaks. So they all glance away, and she begins to talk.

Paula tells them everything.

By late that night, Karen, Denise, Paula, and April have given statements, each flanked by some combination of parents, stepparents, older siblings, and unofficial guardians, and entirely without lawyers.

And now it is Friday, and the girls are in custody in Crown Point, just a few minutes' drive from Bob Pelke's house, expected to be charged later in the day. The police have not released their names to the media.

The day before, Jack Crawford's deputy prosecutor Jim McNew had rushed into his office with a detective: "Jack, you've got to pay attention to this one." He laid it out: *Bible studies teacher . . . home invasion . . . torture . . . robbery . . . four girls from Lew Wallace High School.*

"You're shitting me."

The detective said there was no doubt they had the right people: one of the girls had left a doctor's prescription at the scene; they had confessions; they had witnesses. Jack was struck by the fact that it had happened in Glen Park, which had long been one of Gary's last white holdouts. People were going to care about this case—*people* meaning people of influence, and the media. He believes he has an instinct for cases that have "legs." There is a saying in Lake County legal circles: "The most dangerous place to be is between Jack Crawford and a camera."

"This moves up to number 1," he told McNew—and then he added, "D-F-U." Don't fuck up.

A robbery-murder qualifies for the death penalty, and so Jack ran through his list of questions. The girls had no prior records, but the evidence in this case seemed solid. The facts of the murder definitely *shocked the human conscience*: such a violent crime, such young defendants. The prosecutor would be expected to come out strong. Making this a capital case, against four juvenile girls, would seize the public's attention.

Thus far, not halfway through the year, Ruth Pelke's was the twenty-fourth murder, and one of two killings in Gary in three days. That May alone, the *Post-Tribune* had covered the Lake County stories of: two seventeen-year-olds in Gary arrested for the rape and stabbing of a sixty-two-year-old kindergarten teacher; a man in St. John who'd gone on a shooting spree outside a Kmart, killing three people; a Valparaiso woman, her son, and her mother charged in the poisoning death and the crossbow killing of two family members. None of these crimes, however, will hold the public imagination, throughout the county, like the Pelke murder. Almost precisely one year after his congressional run ended in failure, this could become the biggest case of Jack's career.

———— ⚓ ————

Beginning in the late 1960s, a phrase came to dominate politics: "law and order." It was a weapon of both Alabama governor George Wallace, the populist and segregationist, and Richard Nixon during the 1968 presidential campaign, and those words were wielded by Ronald Reagan throughout his administration. The term was tied to the idea that many of the country's problems stemmed from "soft" enforcement of the laws, at every level of the system. Democrats and Republicans alike began vying to be seen as "tough on crime" by voters, and that attitude trickled down to prosecutors around the country. Jack Crawford had created a Career Criminal Unit because large amounts of federal grant money were available for that specific purpose, and "three strikes" laws would become normalized throughout the country in the mid-1990s. Popular support for capital punishment was rising, and had reached a new high of over 70 percent; the number of prisoners on death rows around the country was climbing.

Jack has always been attuned to the way justice is shaped by public opinion, and he reads the room. Over the course of what will be a decade as Lake County prosecutor (he's now at year seven), he will push for the death sentence twenty-two times and will win seventeen: one of the highest death-penalty conviction rates of a county prosecutor in Indiana history. He earns a new nickname: "Smilin' Jack," used by those who don't appreciate his political ambitions, has been supplanted by "Maximum Jack," a name he can live with. By the time the Pelke murder is brought to his attention, Jack is in the press insisting on a death-penalty prosecution for Alton Coleman and Debra Brown: a pair of serial killers of young girls, one of whom has already been sentenced to death in the state of Ohio.

But there is a difference between pursuing death for killers of girls and pursuing the deaths of defendants who are girls themselves. Added to

Paula Cooper

this is the sensitivity Jack feels regarding his standing with Black voters: he can imagine the political blowback of pursuing capital punishment for these four defendants. And so he consults with some of the county's Black ministers whom he'd made a point of meeting during his run for prosecutor, to gauge the mood of the community.

There is no resistance. No one Jack speaks with has an objection. The act was too violent, and the victim a devout Christian woman, a Bible teacher—that fact alone seems to transcend race, to evoke the need for an Old Testament form of justice.

He calls a press conference. That Friday afternoon, Jack Crawford sits behind his large wooden desk, a set of scales—his personal "scales of justice"—at hand to his left, a small bust of JFK to his right. He is flanked on either side by Gary's police chief and chief of detectives.

In front of about twenty of his favorite reporters and TV journalists, the prosecutor leans into a pair of microphones perched on his desktop. He confirms that the suspects in custody are teenagers. The knife used to stab Mrs. Pelke has been recovered, and so has her car. He has petitioned to have all four tried in adult court—and now he reveals their names and ages: Karen Corder, 16; Paula Cooper, 15; April Beverly, 15; and Denise Thomas, 14. (Their home addresses will be published in at least one local paper the next day.) But his most important announcement, made with special emphasis, is that the state has already filed a death penalty count against Karen Corder, as the oldest, potentially setting a historic precedent: this, the prosecutor says, could be the first death sentence for a female juvenile in Indiana. If he's able to try the other girls in adult court, he promises, he will pursue the death sentence for one or two of them as well.

While Karen is held at the Lake County Jail, on the fifth floor of the criminal courts building, the other girls are kept in the juvenile detention center, waiting to see if they will also be tried as adults. When each of them is marched into court for her detention hearing, heads turn. Many comment that Denise, in particular, looks young for her years, more like a ten-year-old. The *Post-Tribune* describes her as "so petite that handcuffs barely stay on her wrists."

The Lake County Juvenile Detention Center represents a distinction between the culpability of a juvenile and an adult—a distinction that was not made formal in the United States until 1899, when the first juvenile court was created in Chicago. The idea, the imperative, was to hold children apart from adults—to protect them, in recognition that they are especially vulnerable. It was a shift away from the earlier notion, inherited from English common law, that *malitia supplet aetatem,* or "malice supplies the age": If a child of seven or above understood the difference between what was considered right or wrong, that was enough for them to be held accountable. More than a century after the country's founding, with the Industrial Revolution—and with it, the exploitation of children as cheap labor—there finally arose a movement to treat children as a separate class. A parallel juvenile court system would serve as, in reformer Jane Addams's words, a "kind and just parent."

That is not how the system played out in 1985 in Lake County, Indiana. Because, in reality, the detention center has become a cross between an emergency shelter and a jail, mixing together kids being held for a whole spectrum of reasons—from children who've run away from home to those who've committed robbery or rape or another violent crime. There is not much in the way of rehabilitation.

Paula is the only one of the three already familiar with this place—a detention officer, Karen Brilmyer, recognizes her from when she'd stayed there as a runaway at thirteen. Back then, she thinks, the girl was different, someone you could talk to, a kid who expressed a range of emotions. Ms. Brilmyer hadn't known Paula's reasons for running away, but she remembers the girl cried when she talked about leaving home. Now Paula strikes her as distant, cocky. Other than her arrest in the Pelke murder, the officer knows nothing about the last two years of Paula's life, whether she was placed in foster care or sent back to her parents. That's not part of her job, and she does not look into it.

Paula lasts a week and a half at the detention center. One evening during "quiet hour" in the dayroom—the girls are supposedly writing letters—another officer, Bridgette Garringer, asks Paula and her friends to break into smaller groups. When she continues being loud, Ms. Garringer asks her to return to her room for "isolation time." Paula starts arguing—then hits the woman across the nose. The two struggle, until a pair of male officers tackles the girl to the ground and handcuffs her. When they drag her back to her room, she tells them she'll find a way to get even with Ms. Garringer. The next morning, she announces that if she is not moved across the street to the jail, she will kill the woman. And so Paula is transferred to a cell near Karen's.

In the last week of June, six weeks after the murder, Magistrate Bonaventura waives April, Paula, and Denise into adult court, one after the other. That Friday, Jack Crawford files death-penalty charges against Paula and April. The nature of their crime has aged them up in the eyes of the system.

The first juvenile executed in the American colonies was a sixteen-year-old boy, hanged in Plymouth, Massachusetts, in 1642. By 1985, nearly three hundred and fifty legal executions in the United States have been for crimes committed under the age of eighteen—a number that will not be made public record for a few more years. A fifth of those took place during a very different time—before 1900—but nearly two hundred have been carried out in the twentieth century. Although no such executions have occurred since 1964, thirty individuals condemned for crimes committed as juveniles are on death row at the time of Ruth Pelke's murder, and that number will continue to rise. The vast majority— 79 percent—of children executed since 1945 have been Black; looking only at the Southern states, that percentage is as high as 86.

The fact that the juvenile death penalty is permitted in twenty-seven states in 1985 stands in tension with the practice of keeping children separate. Of classifying them as different from adults, "special." It also defies the minimum age for capital punishment advocated by the United Nations and adopted by three fourths of the world's countries: eighteen years old. The Reagan administration's "tough on crime" approach to criminal justice questions the value of rehabilitation, even for the young. And if a society is saying that a teenager cannot be rehabilitated over the many years left in their life, to the degree that their execution is the only option, then it is unclear who the system considers salvageable.

Though Jack Crawford now felt confident that the county's Black community would not oppose the death penalty for the girls in the Pelke murder, he wanted to proceed with caution. The optics had to make sense. There was only one Black judge in Lake County Criminal Court, and the prosecutor wanted *him* to hear the case.

By law, a judge is assigned through a randomized process—but Jack decides to break the rules. He tells Jim McNew, the prosecutor he's put on the case, that he wants James Kimbrough on this. And one morning, McNew comes into his office and says he's gotten it done. This is how Judge Kimbrough—the county's first Black public defender, first Black chief public defender, first Black criminal court commissioner, and now the single Black criminal-court judge in its history—takes on the murder of Ruth Pelke.

This is not a case he wants. If the legal community thinks of Jack Crawford as a hard-liner, the word often used to describe Judge Kimbrough is *fair.* He is seen as more liberal than his fellow judges in criminal court, but he has a reputation, across political lines, of being straight-ahead and deeply informed, a careful thinker, someone whose rulings are always well considered.

He also has a history of being conservative with punishment; he's a believer in shorter sentences and more likely than his three colleagues to place someone on probation as an alternative to prison. Just after he was appointed to the bench, in late 1973, Kimbrough called for a new trial for a man who'd served over sixteen years for a rape and murder committed as a teenager, arguing that he'd been too young to waive his rights and that his mental-health issues had not been made clear. A few months later, a man appeared in Kimbrough's court who'd confessed to beating an older woman to death with a bowling ball, and the judge allowed him to walk free: he was considered sane at the time of his trial but declared insane at the time of the murder. When, after 1977, defendants in his court were up against a death-penalty charge, Kimbrough did not bite—as in the trial of a two-time car thief who had committed his first homicide, someone Crawford's office saw as a strong candidate for death.

Then, in the fall of 1978, the judge heard the case of Larry Hicks, a twenty-one-year-old accused of fatally stabbing two men in Gary. It was a capital case, and following the letter of the law, Judge Kimbrough handed down the death penalty—his first and only time to date. But in a hearing a year and a half later, he declared the need for a retrial, agreeing with his new attorney that Hicks's competence to stand trial had never been determined. (Jack, new in office and clearly peeved, told the press this was "highly unusual.") In a second trial, the jury acquitted him based on new information about his alibi. Kimbrough attended the freedom party the defense team threw for their client, along with most of the jurors, at a nearby Holiday Inn.

Jim Kimbrough was raised in segregated Selma, Alabama, where his parents had marched in Selma behind Martin Luther King Jr. and John Lewis. Kimbrough and his family felt the limitations of the law painfully—how few protections the system offered them, the stark imbalance of it. Just a few weeks after Kimbrough's graduation from law school at DePaul in Chicago, George Wallace, the governor of his home state, made national headlines for standing in the doorway of an auditorium at the University of Alabama to block the entry of two Black students. (Kennedy had to issue an executive order federalizing the state National Guard in order to force Wallace aside.) In 1963, Kimbrough and Fred Work, his friend from their time at historically Black Fisk University, moved north together, to Gary, and opened their own firm. In just a few years, they built up a serious client list and a reputation as two of the best criminal defense attorneys in the county. Fred was the charismatic figure—tall, lean, and strikingly handsome, a dramatic speaker; Jim was the cool one—short and a little round, low-key. At one point, they hit a streak of about twenty not-guilty verdicts in a row. By late 1967, Richard Hatcher, with his strong background in civil rights, had been elected mayor—but Kimbrough and Work were not supporters. They were willing to work with the county's white Democratic power structure.

About six years later, a legislative decree expanded the number of judges in Lake County Criminal Court from one to four, and Kimbrough was promoted from court commissioner to a judgeship. Among the county's Black lawyers, this was cause for celebration, the result of years of lobbying to increase the Black presence on the bench.

Now that Kimbrough is a judge, attorneys on both sides do not worry when they end up in his courtroom: they may be in Lake County, but he goes by the book. Consistent, predictable. If an offer is on the table (though there are few deals under Crawford), the attorney has a good sense of whether Kimbrough might offer something lower. The judge also has a talent for wearing his work lightly. His fellow criminal court

Indiana Senator Birch Bayh and
Judge James Kimbrough

judge Richard Maroc, a newer appointment by just a few years, can't shake the feeling that the job is *easier* for Jim. Every morning, Richard gets uptight about what's on the docket for the day, getting his reports done, reviewing files—and each day, at quarter to noon, Jim comes by his office with a newspaper tucked under his arm, maybe a toothpick in his mouth, and he laughs and says, "Oh, you're up to it again! I'll be over at Broadmoor for lunch. If you need anything, call me." No case seems to bother him.

His personal assistant, Patti Wolter, cannot imagine any of the judge's staff having a bad thing to say about him; she thinks of him as their hero. In 1978, a few months before Jack Crawford took office, Patti had recently been divorced; she had a seven-year-old son, and she had been working a string of jobs in pediatricians' offices. An attorney friend told her about an opening in criminal court for an assistant to the judge, which would mean a pay raise and much better benefits. But Patti had almost no relevant experience, only a few college courses in criminology; she didn't even know where in Crown Point the Government Center was. When she was called in for an interview, she lied about her weak secretarial skills and her scant familiarity with legal proceedings. "Are you telling the truth?" the judge asked. "Pretty much," she said. Patti was a Gary native, her father a Teamster, and her grandfather a Norwegian immigrant who had shown up to find work with U.S. Steel. By the time she was starting grade school, crime in the city was rising, and her father saved to move them out to a small house in Valparaiso. The entire family was ecstatic when Patti became the first among them to go to college,, but now she really needed some good luck. One kind act. "Why are you here?" the judge asked. And Patti admitted she was a single mother and in dire need of health insurance. A pause. He had one more question: "What do you like to drink?" "Tequila?" She was hired.

During a major trial, if Judge Kimbrough thinks he might need more help or the jury is still there, the staff is expected to stay—even if it's midnight or one a.m. But if they have finished their work, if Patti is done typing up the docket sheets on her Selectric and has taken them to the clerk's office, they're supposed to go home. Many days, the motley legal crew drinks together—their local place is the German Inn, a Tudor-style building a few blocks away. Whenever they've been out for a couple of hours already, the judge likes to enable that last, *last* round by announcing to the group, "Okay, one more and we'll *all* go home!" His staff jokes that this will be the title of his memoir.

But Kimbrough has also made the German Inn his think tank. He takes young attorneys there after work to talk about the law or review what happened in court that day—and he will not hesitate to tell them, after a trial is over, what he'd have done differently in their position. After any major case has wrapped, he invites the lawyers and jury members out, dinner on him. With one rule: everyone is allowed to ask questions of the jurors—like *Why did you hold out for so long?* or *What finally changed your mind?* They don't have to answer, but many of them do. Everyone taking part in the process is made to feel connected, all players in an urgent mess of an experiment.

By the summer, the supervisor of the female residents in juvenile detention, Greta Smith, has noticed a pattern with Denise: as the youngest of the residents, she is too eager to become friends with the older kids, the sixteen- and seventeen-year-olds; when girls her age or younger come in, she's just not interested. She is drawn, inexorably, to what Ms. Smith thinks of as the "hardcore kids," the ones who have "war stories a mile long to tell," kids she sees again and again. Maybe Denise wants to avoid trouble from these tougher girls, form an allegiance—but they use her. She has received a lot of isolation time, and it is always for a plot hatched by some other kid.

April's recent evaluation at the center was marked "poor." The staff accused her of manipulating another girl into being fresh with them—so April stopped speaking. In their presence, she now tilts her chin down and does not make eye contact unless she has to. She's also been refusing to eat, claiming that she "only eats at McDonald's." But she is pregnant—seven months, now eight—and the staff has been trying to explain how unhealthy this is for her unborn child. In late July, April has a cesarean because of complications with her pregnancy.

The very next day, across the street in the county jail, Paula and Karen are put on suicide watch. Lately, whenever a corrections officer, Frances Irons, makes the rounds to collect the inmates' medical cards, she sees that the two girls have written on theirs variations on *Give me the electric chair* and *Give me that shock. I want to die.* And on this particular day, one of their cards announces that they are going to kill themselves. So Ms. Irons follows protocol and takes away their possessions and clothes, strips their cells of mattress and sheets.

Maybe Paula and Karen had not expected this, because in response the two start yelling and banging on the bars. Irons takes them to medical, where an officer gives Karen an oral sedative. Paula, aggressively resistant, refuses her pill, and so the officer tries to give her a shot. But while Ms. Irons holds the girl down for the injection, Paula hits her in the shoulder. As they struggle, the officer tells her, "Oh, you tough, huh? You stabbed an old lady." And Paula says, "Yeah, I stabbed an old lady. And I'd stab the bitch again. I'd stab *your* fucking grandmother."

This is possibly a moment of adolescent bravado, of Paula doubling down on her new reputation in the way that teenagers often do. But Ms. Irons will not forget it.

April's family hires an established local law firm, but the other parents cannot or will not pay for counsel. And so Paula, Karen, and Denise are appointed public defenders. Capital cases require a much greater number of prep hours than average, but in 1985 these attorneys will be paid the same rate as for every other case on their very full slates. The Pelke cases will be a strain.

The first of the girls to be tried, in early fall, is Denise. This is exactly what her defender wants. Rich Wolter's client is the youngest of the group, and she still looks it—but Rich knows that she may hit a growth spurt at any moment. If Denise gets a little taller, and her breasts and hips come in, they may lose the jury. If found guilty, a decade could be added to her sentence.

But for now, she's small and skinny. Rich and his wife, Patti (of Judge Kimbrough's staff) go shopping for clothes for her court appearances. For her first hearing, Patti buys her a white blouse with a bow, to make her look "like a choir girl," and their friend Jim McNew has a fit: "You dressed her! You can't tell me you didn't!" Patti says, "I don't have to tell you anything." People want a girl to look a certain way, and maybe the right blouse and skirt will help prevent this one from growing up in prison.

In Kimbrough's court, Rich argues that Denise was not knowingly involved in the crime, that she was not an "aider and abettor" (Indiana's term for an accessory). There are two days of testimony—from crime-lab technicians and police officers and Lew Wallace students. Rich feels good about the jury, about their attitude toward his client. But after a detective offers a ride home to three stranded jurors, the judge declares a mistrial. They will have to start the process over again. And Denise is growing.

When the retrial begins on November 5, Rich takes the same approach. But now there is the fact of Denise's body. In the months since her last appearance in court, Denise hit her growth spurt. Rich looks over at her, seated beside him at the defense table, and he has a bad feeling. She has gone from looking "like a pencil" to looking like a woman, the way some girls in school leave for summer break and come back in the fall a different person.

Denise takes the stand and is so soft-spoken that the judge and both attorneys take turns asking her to speak up. She may be maturing, but she remains petite enough that she needs a booster seat to be visible to the jury when she slumps her shoulders. She cries as she takes them through the events of that May afternoon.

A heavy emphasis is placed on the question of Denise's intentions when she went along with Paula and Karen that day. Rich asks why, after Paula said she planned to rob and beat this woman, did Denise follow her?

"Because I wanted to see what she was going to do," Denise says. "I didn't believe that she was going to do what she said." She says this like a kid divorced from the consequences of her actions.

The initial jury vote is 6–6, and, as Rich would later say, "We just didn't have the strong ones." When the jury re-enters the courtroom, they have found his client guilty.

At Denise Thomas's sentencing, Judge Kimbrough confesses that he has been unable to sleep for a week. Early this year, he presided over a string of cases involving crimes committed in Gary by young men, with nine or ten of those defendants under the age of twenty-one; immediately after this streak came the Pelke murder. The judge does not know what to make of this trend, but it troubles him. He says he's been asked many times over the past few months for the age at which juveniles should be charged as adults, and he does not know the answer. He recently read in the paper that Lake County is now considering murder charges against a thirteen-year-old—"And the question goes on to 'Will there be a twelve-year-old next year? Or at what point will we stop?'"

That downward trajectory clearly disturbs him. "Whose fault is that? I'm not sure. It may very well be the fault of the community at large . . . But I don't know enough about that to make that judgment."

In pleading for the minimum for Denise—fifteen years—Rich Wolter had emphasized what the length of the judge's sentence would mean to someone as young as her, someone with no prior record:

> The only thing that would cause this child to commit another crime is if she gets so pounded out of shape as a person, from seemingly endless years of incarceration, that she's unable to function. But that is not the case today. . . .
>
> She was at that age when people are all grown up in the morning, they are children again at night. They flip-flop back and forth a great deal, and oftentimes as parents we wonder if they are gonna make it. That was the person who was there in May. It's a different person here now. And what I'm asking the court is to give her the minimum sentence. It will certainly crush her as much as twenty years, twenty-five, thirty years would; but it at least leaves her some hope.

The judge has spent many heavy-laden, drawn-out hours considering the fitting punishment for Denise. He admits that, in drafting his sentence to be read aloud today, he realized he would not be speaking directly *to* the defendant: she is simply too young to process his statement.

> Her maturity and development is going to happen later. Unfortunately, that's going to be in a penal institution. . . . All of the good things that can happen to human beings are going to happen while she is in prison. And that pains me; it hurts me. I cannot help but cry for Denise and others.

But his job is also to answer a call for retribution, for some level of satisfaction, on behalf of the community. And so the judge steels himself, and he leans on the system, which gives him the lens through which to look at the girl. "Because I may have some sympathy for her," he says, "there is always the refuge of the law when there are difficult decisions to be made, because law offers us some direction. And we can be consistent, if we follow the law, and not be swayed by the passions of the moment."

Judge Kimbrough then sentences Denise Thomas to thirty-five years in prison. By Indiana law, if she handles her time well, she may be released while she's in her thirties. If she acts out, she will not rejoin the world until she is fifty years old.

Five

THE QUESTION
OF CONSCIENCE

Two weeks before Denise's second trial began, William Vandiver, a Hammond man who had killed and dismembered his father-in-law, was executed. Jack Crawford had promised the public the ultimate punishment in this case, and the state meted it out. But the procedure did not go as planned.

In a way, Vandiver had made it easier for the courts and the Department of Correction: he had volunteered for his execution. He'd shown up for a hearing and explained his reasoning: compared to growing old on death row, death by electrocution would be no more dramatic than "getting a tooth pulled." He asked for an October date, and he got one. In his last week, he was allowed to see many of his family members, and in the hours before his electrocution, in the death house in Michigan City, he and his wife had a last meal of pizza and soda. He took a shower, had his head shaved, spoke to a priest.

Although the prosecutor is always welcome to do so, Jack had never witnessed an execution. In Vandiver's case, the state prison decided to make that invitation explicit—but Jack passed on the offer. Once a verdict is handed down, he believes, machinations are set in motion that go beyond his office, a process that is neither his responsibility nor his concern. He imagines some may consider it standard for a prosecutor to attend an execution he'd sought—and Jack *had* sought Vandiver's death, and many others. But the idea of watching a man go to the electric chair reminds him of history books about the days in England "when they had public executions in the town square, and it was a huge jamboree." To Jack, it seems "pretty low" to watch a man be put to death. He would later acknowledge that it was "kind of somewhat hypocritical" to decline the invitation. "But I just didn't want to go. And talking to people that were there, it didn't work too well on this guy."

The chair on Indiana's death row is known as Old Betsy, built from wood salvaged from the state's gallows. The last execution in Indiana, in 1981, had gone as expected, and the Department of Correction had recently run a test on the equipment. But on Vandiver's date, just past midnight, after the first jolt of electricity—2,300 volts sent through his body for ten seconds, intended to kill—he hung on, breathing audibly. Five hundred volts followed for twenty seconds, and Vandiver was still breathing. They administered another charge, and his heart continued beating; two more followed. It took seventeen minutes for Vandiver to die, his fists clenched throughout. Smoke was seen rising from his head, and a terrible burning smell flooded the witness room.

The botched electrocution made every major national newspaper and front pages across Indiana. Meanwhile, Paula Cooper and Karen Corder sit in the Lake County Jail, awaiting their capital trials. *Give me that shock*: it has been months since the girls wrote those words. Neither of them wants to die.

The growing fascination with the case is marked by the arrival in Lake County of a production team from *60 Minutes*.

Host Harry Reasoner, white-haired and in a conservative brown suit, is filmed in Glen Park standing inside Ruth Pelke's house. With the camera crew clustered together on the front porch, Reasoner opens the door to them, as if replaying Ruth's actions from that May afternoon. They film him inside her dining room, now empty, gesturing to where a desk used to stand: the spot at which she was knocked to the floor. At the Lake County Government Center, Reasoner interviews Karen and Paula, one by one, in the jail's visitation room, and Jack Crawford in his office in the court building. Jack is very aware of the attention this will bring: the CBS newsmagazine is the fourth most-watched television show in the country.

The house on Adams Street is empty for the crew because it had been cleared out not long ago. When the girls were first interrogated at the Gary police station, Bob Pelke had returned to the place. With everything photographed and cataloged, he was permitted to step inside; his niece joined him there. However necessary, they would restore order to Ruth and Oscar's home.

Bob's only son Bill, Ruth's grandson, came to check on them while he was between shifts at the steel mill. It had been some time since he'd set foot in that house; he had found it harder to visit after his grandfather's death. Nana would cry without warning, and she would ask him, again and again, to try on Granddad's clothes, to take his suits and jackets (each time, he had declined). And now Bill found his family cleaning blood off the walls and scrubbing the floor. Bill did not help—he felt unable to. He was thirty-seven years old and had been wounded in Vietnam, but he could not wipe his grandmother's blood off the floorboards.

Bill stepped into the kitchen. Maybe out of habit, he pulled open the refrigerator door and looked inside: a corsage. Four days ago had been Mother's Day, and he'd asked his parents to give the corsage to Ruth when they visited her for dinner. They had not forgotten.

Bill did not go back to the house for a long while—there was no cause to visit. Bob, after a hospital stay for stress, joined his two sisters in packing up personal things. There was talk about who was promised what; some of the Pelkes took home sentimental items. The photograph of Oscar as a young boy, standing beside a horse.

In a few months' time, the family held an auction at the property. Many of Ruth's and Oscar's possessions, each in turn, were carried out into the yard for bidding. Because it all happened so quickly, no one had time to worry over the auction, and a case of Ruth's jewelry went for almost nothing. Both sides of the family had good jobs, and it did not matter to them whether they got five dollars for this or twenty dollars for that. The desire was to finish things.

Everything would sell. Including, eventually, the house on Adams Street.

Shortly after Jack took office, Jim Kimbrough had learned that Senator Birch Bayh was nominating him for a new federal judgeship in the Northern District of Indiana. This meant that he was poised to possibly become the first Black federal judge in the history of the state. While the news was still merely a rumor, Kimbrough told a reporter, "If that is true, it is beyond my wildest dreams." Bayh's nomination was then forwarded to President Carter.

The FBI spent about three months conducting a background check on the judge for the Department of Justice, interviewing hundreds of people who knew him. But the vetting process dragged on. One reporter suggested the delay was possibly racist—but the theory most repeated was that past financial liens on Kimbrough's property, for overdue taxes and debts, were causing a problem. Still others, in private, wondered if the lag was due to the judge's "overindulgence"—his drinking. During this period, Rich Wolter and Kimbrough went out after court and someone approached the judge: "Aw, Jim, why are you putting yourself through this? Just call them up and tell them you're going to withdraw your name." And Kimbrough said he wouldn't do that. He later told Rich why: If he at least saw the process through, he thought, maybe it would go more smoothly for the next Black nominee.

Several weeks passed: November 1980. Reagan was elected president, and the window for a Democratic nominee closed.

More than four years later, now fifty, the judge catches the Pelke murder—a highly visible case. He understands that his professional career is now destined to end in criminal court; his legacy will be whatever good he can accomplish in Lake County. And he does not like the position this case put him in: a truly terrible crime, in a death-penalty state, and the perpetrators are children.

Nearly a year after the crime, in the spring of 1986, the girls' attorneys learn that the *60 Minutes* segment will air at the end of the month, and they're nervous. Karen's trial is set to begin the morning after. The exposure could go either way, and their juries will not be sequestered. The crime was so violent, and the girls have inspired little to no public sympathy. No civil rights groups have spoken out on their behalf—not the NAACP or the ACLU, no local religious leaders. There has been no talk of plea deals from Crawford's office, no surprise. April is the exception: she hadn't entered the Pelke house until after the stabbing took place, and she's had a deal on the table for months now, with a private law firm behind her. Karen's public defenders, David Olson and David Braatz, ahead of the segment airing, decides to change the girl's plea to guilty. Perhaps the violence of the crime will have less of an impact on the judge than it would on a jury. Best to leave matters in Kimbrough's hands.

Since the death penalty was reinstated, it had been very rare for a Lake County defendant to plead guilty to a capital charge without a deal in place. And so, before appearing in court to do so, Karen's attorneys repeatedly reach out to her father, Walter. Since the man does not have a phone, David shows up at his house and, when no one answers, tapes a letter to the door. He returns the next day: again no answer, but the letter is gone. He leaves another, just in case; he sends a copy of the same letter by certified mail. He never hears from Walter Corder.

60 Minutes airs the segment as planned, on the night of Sunday, March 30—two months before Karen's sentencing hearing and one month before Paula's trial is set to start. There are sound bites throughout from Jack Crawford, seated at his desk. His confidence is striking; he speaks quickly and clearly, rarely pausing, in the style of someone with a well-rehearsed message. He speaks of decades-long imprisonment as insufficient punishment, a "slap on the wrist" when compared with execution. He focuses on the victim and does not waver. At one point, Jack declares, "Well, rehabilitation has never been the sole purpose of sentencing. There is an aspect of justice"—and by *justice* he means *retribution*—"that must be injected into any criminal case. *So what* if these young people, fifteen or twenty years later, could be contributing citizens? That doesn't compensate for the victim in this case and for what happened to her."

While the greater Chicago television market has given plenty of exposure to Jack Crawford, this is the first time the public has seen footage of Karen Corder or Paula Cooper. We meet Karen as she is being escorted down the hallway of the court building, wrists cuffed in front of her, in a dark blue jail uniform, her hair pulled back in short braids. She is overweight, with very round cheeks and gentle eyes. She takes a seat in the slate gray visitation room.

The producers have agreed to avoid direct questions about the case, and so Reasoner keeps it broad. "You're still a kid, really. In spite of the fact that you're a mother, you're still a kid. What do you think about giving kids the death penalty?" "Um, I don't know what to say about that." Her slow, uncertain, quiet speech gives the impression of an overgrown child.

In contrast, when viewers first see Paula walking down that same hallway, her attorney following behind her, she is smirking. It's a lingering, extended shot: Paula in her V-neck uniform, short hair pulled back tight with a white headband, her skin clear and radiant. In spite of the circumstances, her face is undeniably beautiful. Her lawyer whispers something in her ear, and her face drops for a moment—but the smirk quickly reappears. It is not a look that inspires sympathy.

Leaning on the arm of her chair, she speaks softly about how her father had "problems" with her mother, how "he took the problems out on me and my sister. And he constantly beat on us all the time." She would go to her room and cry, she says—and she begins to tear up in front of the camera. Paula, through tears, goes on to describe an episode in which she claims her father told her "You just don't deserve to live. I should kill you. I should just go out in that car right now, get that gun, and blow your brains out." Many viewers are watching to see if this young woman is dissembling, playing the victim, and it is hard to be swayed one way or the other by a few minutes of camera footage.

Until a shift occurs. As her tears continue to come, silently, a deeper misery shows through. And as she answers more questions about her family life, her tone becomes disappointed, pitiful.

"What did you think about all this?" Reasoner asks. "You were what—thirteen, fourteen? Did you think this was the way people lived?"

"Nope." The word has weight to it.

"Did you know your family was different?"

Paula nods.

"Did you see any way out of it, for you?"

She shakes her head slightly. Paula's completely silent now, for fifteen long seconds, tears rolling down her cheeks.

"Just take it easy," Reasoner says. "You want to take a break?"

After a long silence, Paula answers. "Nah, I knew I—I knew we was different 'cause—" She exhales. "I just wanted to be like everybody else, you know?" Exhales. "I just wanted a good family."

Eventually Reasoner asks Paula if the possibility of facing the death penalty scares her. She nods, crying.

"I don't want to get the death penalty," she says, "because I want to live my life."

"Do you think you've still got a chance?"

In what looks like an involuntary response, Paula's head shakes; her mouth quivers. She says, in a voice higher pitched than before: "I don't know."

News of the Pelke case eventually reaches a woman in Washington, D.C., named Cathy. She is startled and upset to see that Jack, her old boyfriend from Bishop Noll high school, is the person who decided to pursue the death penalty for those two teenage girls.

And so Cathy looks up the number for the Lake County Prosecutor's Office and gives Jack a call. He's clearly surprised to hear from her. They haven't spoken in several years, but Jack liked Cathy a great deal and still thinks of her as "a super lady." They'd stopped seeing each other sometime in college, he thinks, because of politics: Cathy was far more liberal than him, wearing a peace symbol before that became fashionable, marching in demonstrations at Georgetown. Hardest for Jack to wrap his head around was the fact that she was a Eugene McCarthy supporter. When Kennedy was shot, it was a rift between them.

But these were not their only differences, from Cathy's perspective. She had grown up in a family with more financial worries than Jack's, and worked her way through college. And while Jack remembered there being only two or three Black students at Bishop Noll, Cathy knew better: she'd been the only white girl on the bus every day with the kids commuting from Gary. She grew up thinking about the differences in the experiences of these particular friends—the time one kid's brother was shot in Midtown; how her friend, the only Black cheerleader, wasn't invited to any of the parties Cathy went to. Cathy also wonders what Jack retained from their Catholic education. She, too, had stopped going to Mass, but she held on to some of the most fundamental lessons: killing of any kind is wrong; mercy is paramount—*turn to them the other cheek*, and all of that.

"What are you *doing*," she says, "asking for the death sentence for those girls?"

"What do you mean?" Jack is unsettled by the question. "Everybody's in support of it."

"It's not right. I don't care what they did, you shouldn't go to that extreme."

And then she tells him, "I'm disappointed in you."

This crushes Jack. "Cathy, what do you mean?" About sixteen years have passed since college, but he realizes he still wants her to think well of him.

Maybe he hadn't explained his position, publicly, as well as he should have, Jack thinks—and so he tries again now, over the phone. But Cathy interrupts him.

"I know you're on and on about how this was a terrible crime, and it was. But asking for the death sentence for a fifteen-year-old girl, it's not right. It's not right. It surprised me about you."

Beyond the girls' defense attorneys—and it's their job to disagree with him—Jack has not personally heard from anyone who opposes the death penalty in this case. And so, strangely, this call from an ex-girlfriend carries special weight. Jack respects her so much that he wonders, for a moment, if he's made a mistake. He will remember this conversation for decades to come.

A few weeks later—just one week before her trial is set to start—Paula's attorney, Kevin Relphorde, changes her plea to guilty, just as Karen's had.

Like Paula, Kevin grew up mostly in Gary, though in a tight-knit, steady family, more upwardly mobile. His father, who'd been one of the Tuskegee Airmen in World War II, had worked as a chemical engineer, and Kevin had become the first Black quarterback at his Catholic high school. After a football career proved unrealistic, he went East to pursue his backup, law school, and returned home to practice. It was 1980, and he found the city totally transformed: during his childhood there had been plenty of fights and the occasional stabbing, but now it seemed to Kevin that people were getting shot and killed in full-fledged gang wars. Five years in, he finds himself with his first death-penalty case, and the defendant is a kid. Despite Paula's confession, he can't process that this girl committed this crime. When he speaks to her, even though he's a young-looking thirty-two, she always responds with "Yes, sir" or "No, sir"; she has never once raised her voice to him.

His inexperience aside, Kevin feels there is nothing they could go to trial on. Paula, after all, gave a detailed confession before she ever met with him; the prosecution has good witnesses and strong evidence. But they have a judge who is uncomfortable with the death penalty, whose alma mater Kevin attended, whose former firm Kevin interned at and now works for, who made him a public defender. Kevin decides they should throw themselves on the mercy of the court. He does not believe that Indiana, no matter how "backward," will actually put a teenage girl to death.

And so Paula changes her plea. She takes the stand and confesses. She recounts, in detail, what happened nearly one year ago, on the afternoon of May 14. It is a terrible story.

On the last Thursday of May, a series of witnesses and experts are paraded before Judge Kimbrough in the hope of influencing his sentencing of Karen Corder.

Perhaps the most important person called, in determining whether or not Karen has the potential for rehabilitation, is Dr. Frank Brogno, a psychologist hired by the defense. He makes note of the fact that Karen (like Paula) changed schools eight or nine times, and when her mother died she was passed among a series of aunts and a babysitter. During this period, she became pregnant at twelve, through sex with a seventeen-year-old, and she compulsively hid the pregnancy—to the point that she gave birth on her own, in the bathroom at an aunt's house. The doctor believes that Karen represses her emotions to an unhealthy degree, and that she is easily dominated—but he sees her as far more capable of rehabilitation than someone with an "antisocial" or "sociopathic" personality type. He says that when he asked her to discuss her feelings about the crime, she was silent and then began to sob; she listed the many people she realized she'd hurt badly. He found her expression of remorse "quite moving—because I felt some real, pure feelings coming out of her."

McNew raises the question of "conscience." He asks Dr. Brogno, "I think on your direct examination that you stated—and again, correct me if I'm wrong—that one of the ways you could determine or tell whether the defendant was not a sociopath was because she had a conscience?"

"Yes."

"Could you tell me," he asks, "where her conscience was when she held the knife in the woman, who was alive by the defendant's own accounts, anywhere from ten to fifteen minutes? Where was her conscience then?"

"I don't know."

Unrelenting, the prosecutor asks this same question, in slightly different forms, three more times. How could the doctor claim that the girl's moral compass is intact, that she is not twisted or irreparably damaged, knowing that she held a butcher knife inside this woman's body, moving it from side to side? Knowing that she did *that*, rather than try to help Mrs. Pelke or go get help? It is a very effective line of argument.

After hours of testimony from experts and witnesses, Karen stands in court to plead for her life. In a voice full of emotion, she apologizes for what she did to Ruth Pelke and her family; she prays for their forgiveness. She says that one of the only reasons she wants to live is for her son, who is four years old—and to prove that she is "not as bad a person" as she is believed to be.

The next morning, Karen becomes the second of the girls to hear her sentence. In a quiet courtroom, the judge asks aloud why the United States is the only country "that executes children." He follows up with another question: "Never in history has a female of any age been executed in Indiana. So the question is, Do we begin with Karen Corder?" His answer: "After substantial thought, reflection, and soul-searching, I believe the answer to that question is no." He has stopped short of the death sentence, he says, because Karen was "in some limited fashion" acting under Paula Cooper's influence. But because of Karen's lack of humanity in her treatment of Ruth Pelke, he hands her the maximum prison sentence: sixty years.

David Olson is elated. Sixty years is far more severe a prison sentence than he would have predicted—but Karen escaped the electric chair, and that, he believes, is a solid win.

On her way out of the courtroom, Karen does not speak to the press. But Bob Pelke does. He says, "The Lord has seen fit to spare her"—as if the workings of the law and the judge himself, his sleepless nights spent deliberating, have been an arbitrary piece of the process. As if sixty years were scant punishment.

After the sentencing, the Prosecutor's Office releases a statement: "We are disappointed, but accept the court's decision. We will continue to vigorously pursue the death penalty against Paula Cooper."

Six

THE LAW
COVERS ALL

Paula's turn comes in July, and Courtroom 3 has rarely been this crowded. Reporters from Indiana papers and international news agencies alike pack the benches for one reason: chances are high that a teenage girl will be sentenced to death today. The calculus is simple: The girl who did *not* stab Mrs. Pelke thirty-three times was given sixty years, and only one penalty is more severe than that.

At the plaintiff's table sit both Jim McNew and, as evidence of the gravity and visibility of the occasion, Jack Crawford. Behind them is the Pelke family.

Across the aisle, Kevin Relphorde awaits the arrival of his client. There, on the defense side, are Paula's grandfather Abraham, Rhonda, Rhonda's father Ron Williams, and her boyfriend Mike LaBroi.

Rhonda had met Mike over a year ago, a few weeks before Paula turned herself in. One night that spring, Rhonda had slipped on her stilettos and headed over to Mister Lucky's, a club on the corner of Grant and 11th, the first place the Jackson 5 ever played, and she and Mike started talking. He was in his late twenties, a jazz and blues guitarist, but kind and not flashy; he'd gotten into music at a young age because of the Jackson kids, who lived around the corner from him (Tito had taught him guitar). Rhonda had gotten into the club that night with a fake ID, and she told Mike she was thirty. He definitely did not believe her—but he thought, *If she got in here, and she's drinking, she must be old enough?* It was all right if she was a little bit of trouble. They started spending time together.

They had only been together for a couple of weeks when her sister Paula was arrested, and Mike thought *Whoa*. Rhonda was completely out of it, overwhelmed with grief; he didn't know if he could handle the situation. His mother asked him, "Hey, you sure you're with the right person?" Plenty of his friends had the same question. But Rhonda told him, "I got to be here for my sister, I'm going to do this for my sister"— and that was all he had to hear. He saw that loyalty and felt good about staying. Rhonda knew Mike had "his own crazy mind."

It was then that their mother left town. Soon after that, Paula's father could no longer be found. Rhonda, at nineteen, became the only person Paula could rely on. For years, she'd been raising Paula, in Gloria and Herman's shadow, but since she was a teenager herself, she had no idea what to do. Before Gloria left, the one message she imparted to her older daughter was: *Say nothing about this to anyone*. Rhonda had other plans: She was going to testify on her sister's behalf, and so was her father Ron. She had to get herself together, become someone people might listen to.

Mike's father happens to be an officer with the Gary police, and he's been good friends with Jim Kimbrough since the judge's days as an attorney. Mike himself was raised to believe in law and order, and that includes the death penalty when the crime fits; Rhonda feels the same way. But he'd met Paula not long before her arrest and could not believe the way she was portrayed in the papers, so much coverage, the statements of those other girls making her out to be a terror and some kind of criminal "ringleader." He thought, *She did a monstrous thing, but she is not a monster.* Three weeks later, a group of Black kids went into a house a block from his grandmother's place and killed a Black couple: the coverage of *that* crime amounted to a short newspaper item and nothing on TV. That was the first time Mike thought, *This is not fair. I'm a college graduate—how have I never noticed this before?* It occurred to him that the special frenzy around this case might have a lot to do with the color of the victim.

Never again did Rhonda see or hear from the people she had considered her friends. The church across the street from Gloria's house, where she and Paula had been baptized: no one from the congregation reached out. Mike had found that "church people figure you're getting what you deserve," but even he was surprised that not a single congregant asked after Rhonda. When she saw someone she knew on the street, they would scatter "like roaches or ants or something, just trying to get the heck away. There were no phone calls, there was no stopping by, there was no peach cobblers, there was no barbecue, there was no hugs. Everybody just disappeared." Rhonda knew, even then, that she did not deserve this treatment—but part of her also knew she'd signed up for this isolation. She refused to reject her sister.

Sometime before Paula's sentencing, Rhonda got a call from their mother: *I'm in Atlanta! I found a guy here, a cab driver. He's rich, rich, rich.* Rhonda told Gloria, "Your daughter is on goddamned death row. Are you kidding me? For real? A rich man? You should be here with me!" And she hung up. And so Gloria is not in the courtroom today, and neither is Herman Cooper—gone to Tennessee. No one knows when either plans to return.

Bill Pelke, Ruth's grandson, finds himself seated with the defense; of his family, he and his girlfriend Judy were the last to show up. He was a conspicuous figure as he rushed through the throng of television crews in the hallway and down the courtroom aisle: sturdy and tall, with an almost bohemian-thick head of hair and dark beard. Bill grabbed the first seats he saw, on the left hand side, not realizing he'd chosen the wrong team.

Bill had not come to any of the previous hearings, but he took time off work to be here today. Bob told the family that, based on the wording of Karen Corder's sentence, the judge would likely give the Cooper girl death. If that happens, Bill wants to be in the room for it. He tells himself that he does not wish anyone *dead*, but he wants the state to hand down the maximum penalty for the taking of his grandmother's life. His father, too, sees it as their responsibility to Ruth to push for death—that it's a way of honoring her. The state has made the Pelkes feel that anything less would be a defeat, a grave disappointment.

At ten a.m., Paula is led into the courtroom by a female officer. All eyes are on her, hands cuffed in front, short hair atop her forehead in a puff of dark curls. As she enters, Paula is smiling, laughing actually, as if in response to something the officer has said. As she takes her place beside her attorney, Bill is watching, disgusted. He thinks, *You won't be smiling when this day is over.*

When Judge Kimbrough enters, everyone rises.

O ver the course of the hearing, McNew will question Beverly Byndum, a Lew Wallace student the girls had given a ride home, along with her sister, in what turned out to be Ruth Pelke's Plymouth; she'll recount how her sister stepped on a bloody knife on the floor of the car. He'll question Officer Wleklinski, head of the crime lab, who collected evidence at the house on Adams Street and the McDonald's in Hammond, where they'd tossed the weapon. He will speak to Bridgette Garringer, who Paula struck in the face at the juvenile detention center: "She said that she would get me later, even if she needed to use a knife." The testimony of Officer Frances Irons will be particularly damaging to Paula: how the girl told her, "I'd stab *your* fucking grandmother."

But McNew begins by calling Bob Pelke. This is Bob's third time testifying in court on behalf of his stepmother, and the third time he is asked in public to look closely and identify a photograph, State's Exhibit #1: a picture of Ruth's body as he found it, a towel over her face. When the prosecutor asks how the murder impacted him, Bob says that he was hospitalized for stress. At an earlier hearing, when he'd had less practice speaking in public, he'd struggled to answer the same question. "Sleep, I don't. I keep the scene of when I found her—keeps recurring. I don't think I've had a full night's sleep in months." For members of his family, he'd said, "Different things happen and they break out crying."

The witnesses today are not speaking before a jury. And so when McNew asks Bob what he believes is the appropriate sentence for Paula Cooper, it's as a suggestion to the judge. Bob spent a good while composing a letter on this topic to the Probation Department, and he unfolds it now and reads it aloud: a clear declaration of his belief that only death would be sufficient. He states that he is "both a Christian and a patriotic American citizen" who fought in World War II; he believes in the judgment of the government of the United States and its ability to mete out justice. "He—God—created governments to protect the people. And I expect our governments and judicial systems to do what they are pledged to do. . . . No one, and I repeat no one, has the right to touch me or any of my family without paying the penalty."

He now turns to the subject of Paula Cooper—*Paula* he calls her, with an unexpected familiarity. Bob speaks of her lack of mercy, says she "reveled in her doings and enjoyed it." He cites Genesis 9:6—*Whoever sheds human blood, by humans shall their blood be shed; for in the image of God has God made mankind*—as biblical support for the death sentence. He closes with a diatribe against the state of the county, and a call for retribution:

It is not easy to write these things, but we must be objective, and crime is crime. I am getting older. I am retired and sitting bait for some ruthless individual to do me in, I do fear, with all the criminals breeding like rats and no one with guts to deter it. Do what has to be done, annihilate the criminals, so that decent people can enjoy the life that God has given them.

Anything less than death for Paula would be "immoral, unbiblical, unproductive, a travesty of justice and a disregard to the rights of victims"—a sore disappointment to "all true Americans."

He signs off aloud: "Respectfully, Robert C. Pelke."

When Kevin Relphorde takes his turn with the victim's stepson, he asks, "Mrs. Pelke was a Christian woman, correct?"

"That's right."

"You are a Christian also?"

"Yes, I am."

"Mrs. Pelke was a woman that didn't see color?"

"No."

"Viewed everyone basically as one, is that correct?"

"Yes."

"I think you have characterized her on occasion as being a forgiving person."

"Yes."

"You wouldn't deny that now, would you? At least in some instances, she was a forgiving person and gave persons a second chance?"

"Well, I don't know about the second chance. In other words, she would forgive them, but don't give—in other words, just watch yourself so it don't happen again."

Kevin returns to the question of Paula's sentence.

"Mr. Pelke, you indicated in your letter that you just read that any sentence less than the maximum would be 'unbiblical' and 'unproductive.' Is that correct?"

"Correct."

Kevin now asks if what Mr. Pelke means by "maximum" is the death penalty, and he confirms this.

"You are asking Judge Kimbrough to kill Paula?"

"No, no."

McNew interrupts: "Your Honor, the state is going to object to the phrasing of that question. This witness—"

Judge Kimbrough sustains the objection. "I am not sure that the court 'kills' anybody."

"Well, I am sorry, Your Honor."

Kevin has managed to land this moment. He will not do much better today.

The defense begins calling its witnesses, and Rhonda is first to take the stand.

Paula's best hope is that Kevin will provide enough evidence of mitigating circumstances—reasons the court might be able to find her less culpable—to outweigh the push for the death sentence. There is her age and the fact that she has no prior record—though she did attack staffers in both the juvenile detention center and the jail. The victim was particularly vulnerable and the violence of the crime excessive and cruel, and it remains unclear whether Paula's remorse is "genuine." Her sentence may come down to the story of her abuse, the chaos in her house.

Rhonda speaks of how she and her sister were mistreated by Herman Cooper. When asked to describe the beatings, she replies: "With extension cords, with all our clothes off." This happened, she says, "a lot."

Kevin asks, "Would you describe those years growing up as happy times?"

"No."

"Okay."

"I mean with *her*, it was," she says of Paula, "because we did a lot of talking."

Kevin asks about Rhonda's discovery that Ron was her biological father, and how she moved into his house. He asks about the morning in the garage, after their mother convinced the girls to end their lives with her—she speaks plainly about all of it. For Bob Pelke, this is the first he has heard of their stories, of the defining experience they have in common with him: that of running to the neighbors for help, panicked over their mother. Who would have shared this with him? Until fourteen months ago, the lives of the girls across the aisle seemed set apart from his own by a hard line, and the state is not interested in what spans one side and the other.

In his cross-examination, McNew reframes the abuse Rhonda described as a form of tough love. He says that her caseworker saw Rhonda as a teenager who wanted to live by her own rules, repeatedly rebelling against "strict" parents.

"But that is just her opinion," Rhonda says.

The caseworker claimed Rhonda never went to class, McNew states, even when her parents took her to school.

"They never took me to school," she says.

McNew establishes that Rhonda left to live with her father when she was about the age at which Paula committed this crime. "You had essentially the same type of background as your sister, correct?"

"Yes, correct."

He points to Paula, at the defense table. "She went out and murdered a seventy-eight-year-old woman. You haven't done that, have you?"

"No."

"Have you thought about doing it?"

"No."

McNew walks around the room and looks knowingly at the crowd. He does this throughout the hearing. Bill Pelke thinks the man struts like a banty rooster.

On the stand, Ron Williams speaks about his former fiancée, Gloria Cooper. The two remained in touch throughout his daughter's childhood, and he claims that Gloria went through periods of regularly taking Valium and drinking about a fifth of hard liquor a day. It was for this reason, beyond her mother's long work hours, that Rhonda had been the one to clean up the house, make meals, keep Paula presentable, call someone to bring the three of them home whenever Gloria was unable to drive.

Ron says that when Rhonda moved in with him at fourteen years old, he realized the damage done by her mother and Herman. "Rhonda couldn't deal with people, period." She and Paula would push people away. At night, he'd often hear Rhonda having nightmares, and he'd go into her room and hold her for a moment in her sleep.

He tells of a time when, after dropping Rhonda off for a visit with her mother and sister, Ron returned to pick her up and heard Paula crying out of sight. He asked what was wrong, and Gloria said, "I'm going to kill that bitch." He returned to his car and sat for a moment, uncertain what to do. And then Paula, who was eleven, came running out to him. He gave her a hug—and he asked if she thought her mother might really try to kill her. When Paula said yes, he went ahead and took her home with him. Gloria threatened to call the police: It was a crime to transport a minor over state lines. And Ron and Paula talked it through: Gloria would never let him keep her legally, so how would Paula enroll in school? And what could he do if her mother did go ahead and call the authorities? "It's best for me to go home," she said. "Because I don't want to get you into no trouble." The girl returned, once more, to the yellow house.

Ron Williams is dismissed—but he asks Judge Kimbrough if he may add something more.

"What is it you wish to say?"

"Well, I came here to testify for Paula's character, or whatever it is, okay. I didn't come here to justify—what Paula did was wrong. Mrs. Pelke and her family is hurt real bad, okay. I understand that. But the child was hurt too, you know. She never had the opportunity that any normal child had. She used to ask me on occasion, she said, you know,

'I just want to be like the other little kids. I just want to be like the other little kids.' This is what the child asked . . .

"I think maybe she needs to be punished. But didn't the system some kind of way let this child down?"

He tells the court that he contacted Paula's caseworker to explain the situation of the two sisters. "She said, 'I'm getting ready to retire. I don't want to get involved.' She told me that. I said, 'What about the child, miss?' . . . She said, 'I gotta put them in a home.' I said, 'What about *my* home?'" He was told they could not be moved to Illinois.

"So what is your recommendation, sir?" the judge asks.

"For Paula?"

"Yes."

Kevin asks the man if he understands the question.

"Yes, I do. I understand what he is asking me. And I am very prejudiced on your answer, sir. I would like to take the child in my arms right now and take her home. I know that is impossible, okay. But that is the closest I can tell you."

Paula's public defender does not do well in his closing argument. He raises solid, basic questions: Over the years, there have been "more gruesome" cases in Lake County that were not capital cases; why is the prosecutor pursuing death here? And why should Paula be singled out for death for a crime that might never have occurred without the participation of the other three girls? But he gives a loose, vague critique of capital punishment, and, with some presumption, he speaks of Ruth Pelke and what she would want if she were in this courtroom today. "I think she would be the first to say 'an eye for an eye' is not the way it is done."

He sounds utterly out of his depths when he says of Paula's character, "I think we have seen . . . a number of bad points, for lack of a better word, bad points that Paula may have. But that is not the only side." He presents no statistics about the death penalty for juveniles—there was more information about child psychology and capital punishment in the *60 Minutes* segment than in his argument before the court.

The defense had called the psychologist Frank Brogno to testify on Paula's behalf, as the doctor had for Karen, and he'd described her overall as "a very grownup young adolescent, one who physically looks mature—but then, when you talk to her, you also hear the little girl, the yearning little girl that seems to be quite dependent and weak and childlike." In his cross, McNew had challenged this portrayal of Paula as "childlike"—or any use of the word *child* in reference to the four girls.

"You will give me they are at least young adults, won't you?"

"No," the doctor had replied. "I think they are *children*."

In his final argument now, McNew, in stark contrast to the defense, opens clear, strong, and without apology, resolutely in the tone of Lake County's aggressive prosecutor. He acknowledges that some believe there is never a justification for capital punishment, regardless of the level of suffering a person has caused or the danger they pose. "This, Your Honor, is not the view of the people of this state or of the majority of the people in this country," he says. Citing "compassionate regard for human life," some in society "appear to exhibit more compassion to the killers than the killers showed to their victims."

McNew goes so far as to reject deterrence and rehabilitation as legitimate aims of sentencing; he argues that "punishment designed to rehabilitate . . . distracts from the crime that has been committed." Today's sentencing, he says, should be a call for retribution, for extreme penance. "Cold-blooded murderers," he says, "should be put to death to atone for crimes they have committed." The people have a fair claim to righteous anger. He cites the large percentage of Americans who favor the death penalty, saying that they "are angry—angry at the sight, sound, and smell of crime and criminals. It would appear to these people that the efforts of criminologists, some judges, law reformers, and the liberal press has been to deprive them of that anger by making them ashamed of it." The people of Indiana, he says, "shall not be bullied into believing that retribution is evil."

And now finally Paula—who has been spoken of today as, alternately, an immature child and a well-developed sociopath—has her chance to speak. She rises to make her statement.

If she has been coached by her counsel, there is scant evidence of it. She is self-pitying and confrontational; she speaks in the passive voice, saying this act of terrible violence "just happened"; she blames others. She begins by demanding credit where she believes credit is due:

> First of all, I want to say when I first got arrested, I never sat up and lied about what I did. I never denied it . . . and what did I get? The other three girls didn't tell all the whole story of what they was involved in—but I didn't want to lie. I didn't want to lie to the court. I didn't want a trial because I didn't want to sit up on the stand and tell a bunch of lies.

Having pled guilty, she frames herself as the victim. "Now, my family life, it hasn't really been good. . . . You all heard the story on what my sister said. You know. Nobody understands how I feel." She says she had no plan to kill Ruth Pelke on May 14; she did not know the lady; she did not make the girls join in.

> But everybody put the blame on me . . . Well, where was all these people at, right here, when I needed somebody? Where was they at? They turned their backs on me and took me through all this. All I can say is: Now look where I'm at now, facing a possible death sentence.

She gestures to Jim McNew.

He wants to take my life. Is that nice? Is that just? . . . Where is his conscience at? He wants to know where is mine. . . . Where is his?

She gestures to the Pelkes—and challenges them.

Now, I would like to talk to you people. I am sure you are the Pelke family . . .

What's going to happen if they take my life? Is that going to bring your mother back, your sister, your aunt? No, that is not going to bring her back. How would you all feel when I am in my grave? What's going to happen to the family? The sorrow in the past still going to be there.

Her apology is a garbled one.

But I didn't do it on purpose. And I can't just sit here and say I'm sorry, because sorry don't do it. Sorry isn't good enough for me. And sorry isn't good enough for you.

Now, if that isn't remorse, Mr. McNew, if I'm not showing you enough, I'm sorry . . .

You never took time out to understand. The first thing, when I got locked up, you said death. That is what you said. You said death. But that is okay? That is okay, for you to take my life? But what about me taking *her* life?

Paula looks at the judge, but he does not meet her eyes.

I would like to say, Judge Kimbrough, today is a hard day for me. I really been upset. . . . I know justice must be done. And whatever the—whatever the consequences, or whatever your decision is, I will accept it, even if it is death. I cannot change things right now. And I am very sorry for what I did. . . .

I hope that one day I can get out and start my life over. I hope that one day I can get my life together. Maybe I can finish school. I haven't even finished school. Will I have a chance? Will I get a chance?

And in closing, she ends much like she began, listing the things she did *not* do:

I didn't tell Karen Corder what to do. I didn't tell April Beverly what to do. I didn't supply a weapon. And I didn't go—I didn't go in the house and get the knife out the drawer. And I didn't kill the lady by myself. And I am sorry for what I did. And I know my involvement in this case is very deep. But all I can ask you is not to take my life. That is all I can ask you. That is all I can ask is to say, *Spare my life.*

At this point, there is a disturbance in the courtroom: In the gallery, in the row just ahead of Bill Pelke, an older man is calling out, "My grandbaby! My grandbaby!" Paula's grandfather.

He is escorted out by the bailiff. As they pass, Bill sees that the old man is crying.

The courtroom is silent as people wait on the judge. He is ready to pronounce his sentence.

Judge Kimbrough begins with the calculus of the death penalty in the state of Indiana, that which has made this crime a capital offense: The defendant committed murder during a robbery, the victim was elderly, the violence was excessive, and she seems to have been the "dominant personality" in the crime. On the other side of the scale: Paula Cooper has no prior record, and she was fifteen when she committed this act. "As to the other mitigating circumstances," he says, "I believe that there are none." It was suggested by Dr. Brogno that Paula may have "antisocial personality traits," but the judge does not believe that significant enough to influence her sentence.

The judge now makes clear his feelings about capital punishment: When he finished law school in 1959, he was adamantly opposed to it. And at the time, about half the population agreed with him.

But, he concedes, that was nearly thirty years ago. For the majority in this country now, the meting out of justice may call for death. The key question here, he says, is whether or not this penalty is appropriate for a minor, for someone who Kimbrough agrees is "a child." He believes *this* is the controversy that has drawn attention to his court. If she were twenty-six years old instead, he says, there would be few people in the audience and an easy decision in his hands, according to the law.

The judge shares that he ran for state representative in 1966: If he had won, he would have been a part of shaping and refining death-penalty law in Indiana after *Furman*—but he lost. "We all in this courtroom would have been better off if they had set out some specific provisions for minors. But they did not. The law is pervasive. It covers all." And the law, in this instance, has thrown him into "turmoil" for many months.

I don't believe that I am ever going to be quite the same after these four cases. They have had a very profound effect on me. They have made me come to grips with the question of whether or not a judge can hold personal beliefs which are inconsistent at all with the laws we are sworn to uphold. And for those of you who have no appreciation of it, it is not a simple question. It is not a simple question for me.

He addresses Bob Pelke, firmly:

I do not believe that the failure to impose the death penalty today would be unbiblical. . . . I don't profess to be an expert in religion, but I know the Bible has passages which are merciful and do not demand and mandate an eye for an eye. It is not a travesty of justice if, in any case, a court does not impose the death penalty, because the statute provides for alternatives. It is a viable alternative; it is reasonable; it is there in the law.

Having disentangled the law from Christianity for the moment, Kimbrough says, "There are many laws that I don't believe in, that I think are poorly drawn and ought to be reworked. This is one. . . . Maybe in twenty years, after we have had our fill of executions, we will swing back the other way and think they are unconstitutional. Maybe."

And now he turns to Paula. "Stand up, Paula."

She rises.

All of the evidence in this case, including your statement, indicate that you stabbed Ruth Pelke thirty-three times.

I am concerned about your background. I am concerned that you were born into a household where your father abused you, and your mother either participated or allowed it to happen. And those seem to be explanations or some indication of why you may be the type of personality that you are.

Jack Crawford leans over to McNew and says, "We're finished. He's not gonna give it."

And then Jack believes he sees Kimbrough's shoulders slump. And the judge says, "They are not excuses, however."

Jack turns to McNew: "Watch out—"

"You committed the act," Kimbrough continues, "and you must pay the penalty. The law requires me to find that the mitigating circumstances outweigh the aggravating circumstances in this case. They do not, they do not . . .

"The law requires me—and I do now impose the death penalty."

"Oh my fucking God," Jack says. He won.

The rows of journalists *jump* over one another to rush from the courtroom, down the hall to one of the few pay phones. They shove in their quarters and call their editors. All along the corridor, you can hear variations on "Death for Cooper."

Paula, still standing, looks at her attorney, then turns back to the judge—but he is already gone. "What did he *say?*" she asks Kevin. When he tells her, she begins to cry openly. Tears darken the front of her uniform.

As the guards lead Paula out, she does not speak. She will be moved to Indianapolis, to a unit of the Indiana Women's Prison that's been designated as women's death row.

Kevin is in a state of shock. The judge has always been against capital punishment—he restated his position even today, on the record and in front of so much press. That very morning, Kevin had told his client, "Don't worry, it's never going to happen. It's never going to happen." A long prison sentence, surely, but not death.

More people stream out into the hall, where reporters have begun gathering quotes. Jack and the Pelkes stand in a cluster. Heads turn when someone shouts in their direction: *"Are you satisfied now?"*

This is the voice of Rhonda Cooper, sobbing.

Neither Jack nor the Pelkes respond.

Jack turns, instead, to the media. "I congratulate the judge on a very difficult but ultimately courageous decision. He followed the law. It was painful for him, and there are no winners in this situation. But the law provides that, for certain kinds of crimes, people even as young as fifteen must pay the ultimate price." It's a political statement, he thinks, but it's what the moment calls for.

Bob Pelke tells reporters, "As far as I'm concerned, justice has been done."

By the end of the day, Jack has followed up with a press release in which he claims that his office made history. "Paula Cooper is the youngest person ever to receive the death sentence in modern American legal history and is the first female juvenile ever to receive that penalty." The message: The prosecutor has set a new precedent in fighting crime.

At the Crawford house, his wife Ann fields calls throughout the day: friends congratulating her and Jack with variations on *Yes! Justice has been served!* Somewhere in the mix, her sister phones, and Ann announces, "We got the death penalty for Paula Cooper!" The line falls quiet, and then her sister's voice: "Who *are* you?"

Looking back years later, Ann will find her own enthusiasm confusing. But at the time, she'd taken it for granted, as part of her role. If her husband championed a cause, she did too.

One week later, April Beverly is sentenced in a brisk proceeding in a nearly empty courtroom.

There has been little interest in her case since the death sentence was taken off the table. Back in January, April's attorneys started negotiating a plea agreement for a lesser charge, and today Judge Kimbrough sentences her to twenty-five years. With good behavior, she can expect to spend about thirteen years in prison.

By the time he has pronounced the last of the four girls' sentences, the judge, in the eyes of his colleagues, is a visibly changed man, as he himself had predicted. Rich Wolter, the judge's mentee, believes a sadness has settled in. Kimbrough seems less able to leave the weight of his responsibilities at the office. Rich believes that the judge's takeaway from the Cooper sentencing is *I wanted to make a difference, and here I am, a part of the problem.* The Pelke case, Rich thinks, was almost a perfect storm of everything the man did not want to be.

Rich and Patti occasionally make the two-and-a-half-hour trip to Indianapolis, to the Indiana Women's Prison, to visit Denise Thomas. They send her letters; they accept a lot of collect calls; now and then they deposit spending money in her prison account. The Wolters travel to the Women's Prison on her birthday, a day on which inmates are allowed to invite guests for an outdoor picnic. This closeness is unusual for Rich, but his client is so young, and she's gotten used to their presence.

Back in May, when the guards led Karen Corder away, her attorney David Olson was struck yet again by how young she was, her softness. But ultimately, he thought, *If she can survive Gary, she can survive the Women's Prison.* And that was where he left it. In the first letter he receives from Karen, she asks him to buy her a TV. That's the sort of reason why he'll hear from her in years to come. Mostly, he will not write back.

The morning after Paula's sentencing, Kevin Relphorde gets out of bed. In court, it's as if nothing happened; there are new cases. Colleagues tell him, "I would have handled it the same way" and "I wouldn't have done anything differently," whether or not they mean it. He does not sleep and he loses his appetite.

He talks to Paula on the phone, and she asks, "Will you come and witness my execution?"

He's at a loss. "Oh, Paula. Oh my gosh." He tells her, once again, "Don't worry, it's not going to happen. It's not going to happen, Paula."

Of course, he has no idea. It is just something to say to the girl.

II

Seven

NIGHTTIME
IN THE CRANE

B ill Pelke has an awesome van. A silver Ford, it's upholstered in red-wine velour, with curtains in every window; a thin plastic strip of lights runs a loop of the interior, overhead, like a halo. It's a good party van—Bill's taken it to the Indy 500 twice already, with his girlfriend Judy and the kids' seventeen-year-old babysitter in tow. That was cool, stepping out of a custom ride, strolling through the park ground with a girl on each arm. Most days, however, Bill just drives the van the fifteen minutes through Portage, from their house to the mill. He is thirty-nine years old, and he started at Bethlehem Steel twenty years ago this month.

Every day, a few thousand tons of steel travel out of Bethlehem by flatbed, barge, and train—mostly coils for cars that, wrapped tightly as carpets, stand nearly eight feet tall eye-up. The mill is a complex sprawled across two thousand acres, and a couple years before Bill hired in, all of that had been sandy terrain thick with forest, right up to the southern shore of Lake Michigan. Parkland remains on either side, and the rolling expanse of the Indiana Dunes; even now, the massive warehouses and the rail lines interlacing them abut thousands of white oaks and maples that shelter families of deer. Inside the buildings, some a half mile long, the men and the machines churn out steel and give it shape. It is born molten, poured into the slab-shaped mold as fevered-orange and peak-hot as lava.

Passing along the rolls, it is blasted by industrial waterfalls that scour the black crust from its skin, run through a series of rollers that flatten the bar into a ribbon a hundred times longer, a strip that's cooled and then coiled. If you walk the floor where the coils are laid out in their rows, you can feel the heat each still gives off: more than one thousand degrees after cooling.

Of the thousands of men on call, Bill is among the few hundred who rotate through the hot mill. He's a crane operator, seated in a four-by-four box suspended fifty feet above the floor, in a warehouse swollen with the rising heat. With a large hook, he lifts the tons of materials into the air and steers them through the space, sliding the crane, braced against the walls, up and down the line as needed. Often he stops to hover over the roughing stands, where a kind of guillotine bears down on the slab to slice its edge straight. Then the crop drops down into a pit full of water, sending up a plume of steam, and Bill lowers a magnet into the pit to clean it out. If a slab doesn't go through straight, everything comes to a halt; men rush onto the floor, and Bill pulls crops out of the pit that look to him like the twirled ends of Christmas candy.

Lately Bill spends most of his days in the shipping area, where the trucks pull in. This warehouse was once an open field, and now it is a field of hot coils, each marked in chalk for its destination. A call on the radio sets off a game of numbers, Bill scanning the rows on the ground below and reading the figures on each coil's belly. He lifts the delivery, keeping it steady, and places it carefully on the truck's bed, the one it was always destined for, and it is driven out across the country. Sometimes, he's expected to load the trucks for hours, maybe eighty coils that day, and he has to get into the rhythm of it. He stays alert. When a guy down below gives a signal, the crane operator watches his hands closely: if he says *up* you go up, if he says *over* you go over. To tip the coil forward, even slightly, could mean the death of a man below. His focus is constant as he lifts the package of pure steel—the largest ever lifted by his crane was thirty-nine tons—and lays it down again, the driver standing just feet away, watching. To be able to do this, you need the disposition of a person who meditates—not that Bill looks at it that way. He just knows that getting stressed out won't help. It takes a lot to make him angry.

On this particular night, Bill has signed up for a three-to-eleven overtime shift, and he is asked to report instead to the roughing mill, to 509, the crane he'd started on at nineteen years old. Overtime is often the easiest—sometimes you get eight hours' pay for only an hour's work (union rules)—but he feels dried up. A few weeks earlier, he and Judy decided to part ways. She'd stayed with him through the hard months after his grandmother's death, and accompanied him to court on that bitter day: the sentencing of the worst of the girls, months ago now. But then they'd started fighting over *anything*, and it seemed to Bill that on nights when he wanted to stay home and be together, she wanted to go out and drink and stare at strangers. They both agreed they must not have enough in common somehow—the decision was mutual—but the breakup had brought him very, very low. Bill had stopped seeing friends or returning phone calls. He was so low that he'd started to pray again, maybe twice a day—something he hadn't done since his grandmother's death or, before that, his days at that Baptist college.

When he is alone at home and not needed at the mill, he feels as if he is praying nonstop—he thinks of this as his *anguishing prayer*. He cannot put words to the heaviness; he does not understand the hurt he is experiencing. And so these prayers always begin the same way: *Why?* Sometimes that is the whole prayer. It comes from a place of such despondency, so deep inside, he is afraid of it. Nothing remotely like this has emerged from him before, even when he was set on becoming a preacher. A few days ago, he'd been standing in his kitchen, and then he was crying, and then he was crying and hitting his head against the wall and praying out loud like that, hitting his head and calling out *WHY?* Maybe it was a kind of nervous breakdown.

The job had made it a little easier to move through his days: one coil at a time, with perfect focus. From up in the cab, the world below was mappable, delineated in chalk, and his role in that world required his full attention. But this shift is dead. Seated up high, parked over the roughing area, he stares and he waits. The guys have yet to call with instructions. He sits alone, looking down on the empty floor: the machinery is still; the space is strangely silent. And perhaps because the mill is private at this moment, he starts to pray.

And now he feels it: His cheeks are wet. He is crying hard.

Bill had been a sweet-looking kid, tall and skinny, as pale as his German name suggests, with narrow, high-set eyes and slightly bucked front teeth. His white-blonde hair had the kind of blunt-edged cut that a mother gives her small son, a look he would sport long past those first years in Lebanon, Indiana. They didn't have much then, but they were stable; his dad, who worked for a watch manufacturer, was proud that he never went a week without a paycheck. They rented, but they had good neighbors—including a couple that let Bill come over to watch *Superman* on their television set (they had put red Saran Wrap on one half of the screen and green on the other and called it "color TV"). When Bill was halfway through the third grade, his dad started as a foreman at U.S. Steel and they bought their own house, a place with a double yard just west of the Gary limits.

The Pelkes built their lives around the Glen Park Baptist Church, as did most of the congregation. Bill's dad didn't socialize with people from work—he wouldn't have anything to do with the drinking and hard language—and everyone else at Glen Park Baptist took the same approach. Bill could only go to the movies, maybe at the Palace Theater, if he snuck a ride on the bus (downtown Gary was still a destination then). He managed to go to a couple sock hops by lying about it; if his parents found out, he knew they'd get upset. One time, when Bill was in junior high, his father discovered a pack of cigarettes he'd hidden, and he made Bill sit at the picnic table and smoke every single one until he felt sick. *Now he'll never smoke again!* was the idea—though it didn't work. This was the first of Bob's misjudgments of his son's temperament.

In high school, Bill was president of the Christian youth group of about fifty kids. On Sunday nights, after evening service, different congregations would get together for "sing-spiration," and the younger people could get to know each other. Bill's one non-Baptist friend, who he'd occasionally get into trouble with, was Catholic. You weren't supposed to hang around with Catholics—the pope might well be the Antichrist.

Bill grew up assuming he'd become a pastor or a missionary—that was how he was raised to think. But he also had an interest in girls, which he'd later refer to, in almost biblical language, as his "downfall." He was handsome, with a long jaw and a strong brow and a look in his eyes, and he enjoyed the attention he attracted. At sixteen, he lived in a constant state of desire. If he had felt *called*, that would have made things easier. Maybe once a year, his grandparents hosted missionaries in their house, many in their twenties, just back from Africa or Asia, and these were people who knew what they were doing. They had a clarity he envied, and they commanded respect; everyone in church wanted to ask them questions. And so, in his junior and senior years, Bill made a real effort: he spent the summer at youth camp and rededicated his life to serving God. He improved his grades and impressed a lot of adults, and in 1965 he went off to a conservative Baptist college in Grand Rapids, Michigan.

His freshman year, Bill committed to a full course load of Bible studies to prepare to become a preacher. He got engaged to his longtime girlfriend Mary Jane, who was good-looking and a very nice girl. But now that he was living away from home, he could imagine a freedom he'd never had before—and he'd already forgotten why he'd decided theology was so important to him. Soon he and some old friends started getting together to smoke, and when he got caught, Bill came close to being kicked off the basketball team. To make life easier, for his second year he transferred to a junior college in Illinois: still Christian, but less hardline. Three months in, he and a few guys picked up some wine and Bill got drunk for the first time. After that night, he never went back to classes. He realized he did not have the makings of a preacher; he'd been trying to please his family. He felt the force of his parents' disappointment—but at least he was being honest with himself.

Bill was nineteen when he hired at the mill: November 11, 1966—a date he can recite without hesitation, like a loved one's birthday. Though his father was a U.S. Steel man, they didn't have an opening that week. Bethlehem could take him right away. It was one of many times he would allow his life's course to be decided by whatever fell in front of him.

At Bethlehem, he was introduced to the rhythm of the crane, the logic of it, steering through that massive space, following the steel's path along the hot conveyor, surveying the coils in their long rows. He liked the solitude of the crane cab; you were not *in* your life, but outside of it.

And this is how, in the summer of 1967, having given up his collegiate exemption without a thought, Bill got drafted into the army just before the peak of the Vietnam War.

At Fort Leonard Wood in the Missouri Ozarks, Bill crawled through sand on his stomach; he wriggled on his back underneath a web of barbed wire; he spent eight hours a day on the rifle range; he got yelled at. Unlike the draftees who bucked against the drill sergeant, Bill took his training seriously. He could trace a clear line from these ritual humiliations to the ability to save his own life.

At the same time, unlike a lot of the other trainees, Bill wasn't worried about where he'd land. He had some college and he could type; he was sure the army would give him a good job. And he was right: they wanted him to go to Officer Candidate School—but he would have to sign up for another year. When Bill refused, "those sons of bitches" put him in the infantry, and then it was straight to Fort Polk, Louisiana, where he was lined up with about four hundred other guys and some sergeant was shouting in their faces, *Every one of you swingin' dicks is going to Vietnam!* If before Bill had felt devoid of a path, a man without a calling, at this point he believed he barely had a hand in his life's course. He resolved to do his best with the situation, whatever that meant. At twenty years old, having traveled to exactly four American states (if you included basic training), Bill was heading to Vietnam with the 1st Air Cavalry.

On the first day of the company, at a base in the middle of the jungle, Bill, on a whim, volunteered for radio operator. He went into battle with an extra twenty-five pounds strapped to his back and an antenna that extended ten feet above his head like a flagpole. His job was to hang back, about fifth from the front, and maintain the line of communication, to keep tabs on their rations, to make sure the Air Force knew where they were positioned during a bombing raid. The only firing he ever did was into the trees from about a football field away; he never knew if he shot anyone. But the antenna made him a target. At times, gunfire hit the ground all around him—he thought it looked like the sand was dancing—and more than once a bullet slashed through the radio wire.

Bill carried the radio for the squad, then the platoon, then the squad commander. Some of the men were gung ho, *let's go get 'em* guys who wanted to be right up front. That was never Bill. He didn't really fear dying, but five from the front was close enough for him. Each day, he thought: *This is your job; do your job.* And he prayed—not in the strict Baptist way in which he'd been raised, but in simple, pointed words, whatever came to him in the moment, whatever needs he had or (pretty desperate) hopes. He'd recite the names of the people he cared about: his mother, his father, his sister, his grandmother and grandfather, Mary Jane, whoever else was on his mind that day.

The Battle of Khe Sanh took place during Bill's tour, and it seemed interminable. By early spring of 1968, the Marines there had been under attack for months. And so the 1st Air Cavalry was packed onto helicopters and dropped in.

The first twenty-four hours there, for Bill's unit, were a disaster. Immediately upon their arrival, bombs began raining down across the hillsides. In a single day, sixty-nine men were injured. That same night, seven men were lost and their battalion commander was badly hurt. The next day, the bombing began anew, and with few trenches dug, the men were scrambling for cover. Bill tried to share a foxhole with another soldier, but the guy kicked him out, pointing his gun at him. Still looking for a place to hide, Bill was hit; he felt a hot sting as pieces of shrapnel from a mortar sliced into his back. He knew it wasn't fatal; he called in the helicopters, and he was one of the last to be flown out. Bill ended up in the medevac with a guy who, at nineteen, only a year younger than him, seemed like a kid, and he was wailing, freaking out. The kid had lost it. He survived the injury, but Bill never forgot seeing a man crack up like that. It opened you up to the possibility of another response to those surroundings, another instinct that was just below the skin—the part of you not prepared to survive. In the weeks ahead, a number of his friends were killed, and many more had limbs torn away.

A few months later, eight months into his tour, Bill had a week of R&R in Australia—though some soldiers called it "I&I": Intoxication & Intercourse. He turned twenty-one on the flight back to Vietnam. It was a terrible birthday.

Wounded three times, Bill finally asked to be taken out of the field. He promptly came down with malaria—and during the first onset of malarial delirium, he wrote a note to Mary Jane breaking off their engagement. Bill hadn't been very faithful during this time overseas, and when he dreamt of his homecoming he saw not a sentimental reunion in suburban Indiana but maybe a solo trip to New Orleans for Mardi Gras. So in spite of the symptoms—the aching head and the fever, the vomiting and convulsions—perhaps the malaria was a twisted kind of blessing. He had rarely been one to face the truth unprompted.

With a few months left to serve, Bill was sent to Fort Riley, near Junction City, Kansas. That's where, at a bar called the Tavern, he met a cocktail waitress—a woman who, Kansas being as all-American as Indiana, was *also* named Mary Jane—and she was raising a baby girl on her own. Bill decided Junction City might be a good place to settle after his time was up. He became the Tavern's unofficial bouncer, and he applied to join the police force—one of the few jobs he was told the military made him uniquely suited for. Besides, it was a way to end his army service early. The shrapnel still lodged high in the right side of his back didn't bother him; he thought he could handle it.

Bill was accepted into the force. But a week before his discharge, he got into a fight at the bar. A staff sergeant had been drinking with a woman, and he started to give her a hard time. Bill stepped up to him; the guy took a swing; Bill hit the guy so hard that he cracked his jaw. In the process, Bill also broke his hand and needed a cast. When he showed up at the police department on Monday morning, he was told they couldn't hire him with an injury; he'd have to come back in six weeks.

But Bill had to work. He took Mary Jane and baby Chris back to Gary with him, cut the cast off himself, and returned to his job at the mill.

They got an apartment close to where he'd been raised, and they got married. Bill didn't know if he was good at monogamy, but he knew that Chris needed a father and he loved her instantly. He settled into long days at the mill; his first several years, he averaged seventy-hour weeks. Then he re-enrolled in college on the G.I. Bill, which meant nights in the crane so he could have his days free for class. By 1978, he finally completed his degree in pastoral theology, at the rigid, very fundamentalist Baptist

Hyles-Anderson College (when Jerry Falwell was invited to give the commencement speech, students complained that he was too liberal). But he'd pursued the degree only to see it through; Bill no longer had the vocation, if he ever did. He put aside thoughts of pastoral work and continued showing up at the mill. He moved the family to Portage to be closer to the job; he hoisted hot steel through the air according to instruction. He would not set foot in a church for the next ten years.

Time went by, and Bill and Mary Jane passed their thirteenth anniversary. Chris was a teenager, and they had two more kids: Bob Jr. and Becky, the youngest at two years old. They had also stopped sleeping together and considered that part of their lives *separate* from their marriage.

For this reason, Bill liked the three-to-eleven shift: When he got off at eleven, he could do whatever he liked—head to a bar, go dancing— without worrying about getting up early. Around that time, he and his coworker Wayne started spending time at Private Eyes, at the Holiday Inn down the street from his house. Bill thought of it as a nightclub, but it was more of a bar with a dance floor. It was there that he met Judy.

Bill immediately liked three things about Judy. First, the obvious: she was slim and pretty and twelve years younger than him, with big blue eyes and wavy, light brown hair halfway down her back. He loved to watch her cross the floor with the drink tray, in that short satin shirtdress and heels they had the waitresses wear. Then, after they'd talked a few times, there was the fact that she was so different from him: Judy was sort of bohemian, and she and her four siblings were raised by a single mom who'd taken them to church only a handful of times. (Not that Judy could see Bill's Baptist past on him: it was 1981, and he still had a strong 1970s vibe, with that silver van and his brown curls grown out thick and bushy.) And the third thing that struck Bill: at twenty-three, recently divorced, with three kids and an ex-husband who wasn't pitching in, this was not a woman who had her shit together—and that gave him a reason to get *his* shit together. He decided to rise to the occasion. Judy dealt with a lot of assholes every Friday and Saturday night, saying stupid things to her, trying to flirt—but Bill took no part in that. He kept it relaxed, presented himself as a gentleman. He'd come in a lot, order a couple of beers, and over the weeks, their short conversations added up. Finally, she let him take her out to a nice restaurant: it was the first time she had crab legs.

Things grew serious quickly. Within a year, they'd moved in together—Judy and her three kids, Bill and his wife and *their* three kids.

Bill and Mary had talked about the situation, and she said she was fine with it; looked at a certain way, this didn't change their arrangement much. Bill had a contractor come in and develop the entire basement level into an elaborate apartment for Judy, with track lighting and marble tile in the bathroom. At first, Judy wondered if she might wake up in the middle of the night to find Mary standing over her, like in a horror film—but they got along well, and the kids did too. The whole thing reminded Judy of *The Brady Bunch*. When she and Bill would go on vacation each year, they'd take all six of the children with them, leaving Mary at home to enjoy herself.

In spite of Bill's weakness for women, he also had a strong fathering impulse that had twice lured him into responsibilities that many men would not have accepted. More specifically, he had an *adoptive*-fathering impulse: He believed the real reason he married Mary was because of her baby, and when he fell for Judy, he was the one to push their families together under one roof. He was helping to raise six kids, four of them fathered by other men. He and Judy and Mary rarely discussed their situation with friends and relatives—because, Judy would later say, "it was too much." Some of them knew, others didn't, and they didn't make it a big deal; the unspoken understanding was that their arrangement would hold as long as Mary was okay with it.

One evening about two years in, Bill came home from the mill to discover a man leaving their house and didn't like the look of him. When he confronted Mary, a friend of hers who happened to be visiting shot back, "He can't say that—he's got some woman living here!" And perhaps that was when the peculiarity of the situation hit Mary, because a few days later she announced that she was filing for divorce. Bill refused to hire a lawyer and lost custody of their three children (Chris and Bob were teenagers, but Becky was only six at the time). He was also forced to admit that, between the basement renovation and six children, he'd been spending well beyond his means. He declared bankruptcy, and he and Judy and her kids moved into a one-story house rented on her credit. She wasn't too worried, but Bill felt he'd made some promises to Judy that he hadn't been able to keep.

Sitting up in crane 509 two years later, he is a man with no credit, one divorce, three estranged children, and two despondent parents (if leaving the church hadn't been enough, living with Judy certainly had), and now it seems that he has lost the woman for whom he rearranged his life. Bill had survived a war and been given work for twenty years, a chance at a marriage and then a good relationship, and a bevy of kids—and yet he'd managed to ruin himself. And now the last in this scattered series of very bad thoughts comes to him: If he hadn't gotten divorced, they would all still be living together in that big house, with Mary and their kids, and his side of the family would not have been shut out of Bob Jr.'s birthday party that afternoon in May. Then that's where his grandmother Ruth would have been—not alone on Adams Street, for those girls to find her.

He knows this is not healthy thinking, but he lingers on these notions, letting them blossom like black ink in water.

High up in the dim warehouse, with its faint smell of sulfur, Bill is crying and cannot will himself to stop.

The night shift on this side of the warehouse is the same as the day shift—save the absence of that thin slit of sunlight that runs along the spine of the roof. Otherwise the rhythms are the same; the dark is the same, and the dark soot that covers everything. That splinter of sky is black now. Leaning back in the chair, Bill returns to his anguishing prayer, asking the same question over and over, like somebody dense, like a child: *Why?*

What is the logic of his god, if someone like *him* is still living while his grandmother took her final breaths pinned with a butcher knife to her dining-room floor?

It has been eighteen months—four since the last of those girls was sentenced. He pictures her, Paula Cooper, sitting in her death-row cell, probably no bigger than this crane cab, her back up against the wall. In this image, she is crying just as he is, and she is asking aloud, *What have I done?* But the girl is far more alone than he will ever be. Bill thinks of her sentencing, the only time he appeared in the courthouse. Seeing Paula Cooper in person, he was struck by how young she looked: Just turned sixteen, twenty-three years younger than him, she was a *girl.* And immediately after her sentence was read, that man, the girl's grandfather, the only grown family that had shown up—the way he had called out, the way he had *lost* it. And how a guard had escorted the old man down the aisle, right past Bill, still calling out about his *grandbaby,* wretched. Paula was led out next, the front of her prison smock darkened with tears, head bobbing, her eyes darting from side to side as if looking for the person who might appear, at any moment, to help her.

A single photo of Bill's grandmother was used in the press around her death. It is a close-up cropped from a church portrait of the Pelkes a few years back, taken against a velvety black backdrop: on the left are Bill's parents, Bob and Lola; seated down in front are Bill and his sister Dottie; and on the right stand Oscar, his shoulders hunched with age, and Ruth. The men wear freshly laundered off-the-rack suit jackets and wide ties; the women are in pretty, feminine blouses, their hair recently done.

Move in closer, and here is the familiar image: Ruth Pelke, with a ring of soft, silvery-white curls around her head, high cheekbones, a beatific half-smile. She wears pink lipstick, cat's-eye glasses, and silver earrings the size of coat buttons. Her collarless blouse is a pale Marian blue, and on its lapel she has pinned a "mother's crown" brooch, decorated with a rhinestone for each of her nine grandchildren. Ruth looks serene, her chin at an angle that suggests she is pleased. Bill thinks of how beautiful she is in that photo, the softness of her eyes (though there is no blood between them, he looks as if he inherited those eyes, dark and soft and high set). In the years leading up to his grandmother's death, he had rejected the rules he was raised with, down to rearranging the very architecture of his house to accommodate his lifestyle experiment, and his parents had been ashamed. But his grandmother never turned away from him. She continued to include Bill in her prayers, even after he'd stopped calling himself a Baptist; she had wanted good things to come to him.

At this moment, the image he holds in his mind begins to transform. His grandmother's eyes begin to shine—they are wet—and tears begin a steady, clear runoff down her cheeks. Her face remains still, frozen in that day in the portrait studio, but the photograph is weeping. Ruth Pelke has become like one of the weeping statues of the Virgin Mary, those figures discovered in so many countries leaking tears of blood or oil or scented water, receiving thousands of visitors desperate for a demonstration of Truth. Or else her tears are in the likeness of the Son, of Jesus in Bethany crying over the death of Lazarus: *Jesus wept.* This, too, is a lamentation. The photograph is weeping because here is a woman in pain. Ruth *hurts* from the memory of her death, from the final thirty minutes of her life.

But that's not it. No. It seems to Bill, in this moment, that Ruth's feelings are passed to him, that they flood his chest. And he believes he understands: she is crying for that girl. For Paula Cooper. For the girl's grandfather: she would not have wanted him to suffer the knowledge that his grandchild will be buckled into a chair and her body overwhelmed by electrical current. And she would not want this girl to be killed for killing her, to be killed in her name.

Bill thinks of what Jesus said when the Romans raised him up on the

Cross: *Father, forgive them, for they do not know what they are doing.* For the first time, he believes it is *possible* that the girl did not know what she was doing when she killed Ruth, that she'd been out of her right mind. That a blind anger must have propelled her forward. And now his grandmother is calling on him to forgive her.

His grandmother is calling on him. Is this a calling? Almost thirty years since he first dreamt of such a moment, Bill Pelke is being called.

At first, the revelation is a notion. It infuses no part of his body; it changes nothing about his instincts toward the girl—those remain cool and hard. Bill has decided to forgive her, to have compassion—but he has none to give. And he knows that if he cannot find that store of empathy sunk deep inside of him, then from this point on, whenever he pictures his grandmother, he will feel that he failed her. Eventually, he will shut her image out.

Bill begins again to pray, the way a desperate person forms words, unable to prevent them slipping from his lips. He prays for God to make him love Paula Cooper, to flood him with it—and he waits.

He waits. And inevitably, this comes to him: If that girl is worth forgiving—if even his grandmother can feel compassion for her, can wish for her protection—then he must be too. Though he has also, in his own way, fucked things up beyond repair, Bill himself must be worth preserving.

In the quiet of the mill, high above the dead machines, Bill considers what he will do. He will write Paula a letter, and in that letter he will tell her about his grandmother, and about God's forgiveness, and how Jesus loves her, just as He loves every person who ever walked the earth. And as he parses them out, the words he will write, Bill can see a way forward. He can imagine her, just maybe, writing back. And in his head this becomes a real correspondence, and he truly wants to know what she might say to him—not by way of explanation for what she's done, but as proof of humanness, of consciousness in a concrete box on death row. And Bill realizes he does not want to see this girl die.

There it is: compassion. This is enough to forgive. He has forgiven her already.

He will tell the story of this night for the next thirty years. For some with whom he shares it, the story will recall a passage in the Gospel of John, in which Jesus, upon learning of the death of one of his followers, begins to weep. And then he approaches the tomb and asks that it be opened, and he calls for the man to come out. Inside the tomb, the dead man sits up, and then stands, and then steps outside. His hands and feet are wrapped in linen; his face is covered. Jesus says to the crowd, *Take off the grave clothes and let him go.*

To be released from the threat of the death house would make of Paula Cooper another kind of Lazarus. And she and Bill, both: they would take off their grave clothes.

Eight

MEETING THE
"ANIMAL"

A young woman in a hippie dress steps out of her budget compact car in the parking lot of the Women's Prison and heads to the visitor's entrance. She is just over five feet, just over a hundred pounds, and just three years out of law school.

The facility, the size of a city block, is made up of a cluster of redbrick structures built nearly 115 years ago in the middle of a residential neighborhood close to downtown Indianapolis. A tall chain-link fence runs the perimeter of the grounds, crowned with razor wire.

Inside, the walls are cement, the floors are linoleum, and the doors are made of steel. Monica Foster hands her ID to a staffer and says she's there to see Paula Cooper, inmate 864800—though she hardly has to specify, as everyone knows about the girl on death row. This place is the first and oldest correctional facility for women in the country, home to a few hundred women. Before the girl's arrival, it had been a sleepy prison, without much drama. The women were offered cosmetology classes, the staff made their rounds, and little happened that was considered newsworthy.

Monica steps through the metal detector, then another steel door, and into the visiting area. She is led off to the left, into a private room for attorney meetings, and invited to take a seat at the table. A large glass window leaves her visible to the guards as she waits for her client.

While the state prison in Michigan City, for men, has a separate death row unit, the number of condemned women in any state is so low that the Women's Prison has placed their two death-row inmates on a second-floor unit used for disciplinary segregation. The doors are barred, like in the rest of the prison, but with a second, solid door that is shut at night. Paula is allowed out for one hour of recreation each day, and that's the only time she can interact with another resident on that wing—if there's anyone on lockdown for causing trouble.

A guard leads Paula to the room, steps outside, and locks the two women in. The residents wear their own clothes here, and Paula, now nearly seventeen, has styled her bangs tall and made up her eyes; she's identifiable as an inmate only by the yellow ID badge pinned to her sweater. As they begin talking, she quickly bursts into tears.

"Okay, we're gonna *breathe*," Monica says. "In through the nose, out through the mouth. In through the nose, out through the mouth." Paula will sob through most of the meeting.

If Monica is honest with herself, she had expected to meet someone more animal than human—because what type of person, what *fifteen-year-old*, would do what she's done? But the girl looks so young, and so very depressed. Monica realizes that Paula does not understand how the death penalty works—she thinks guards might take her off to the electric chair at any time, on any day. This is the state she's been living in.

Monica tells her that will not happen. They are filing an appeal. And *if* Paula were to be executed, that would be many years off. She has a whole string of appeals ahead of her, Monica says, not just one. And there are good and reasonable grounds why her death sentence may not stand. And if things start to look bad, Monica will let her know—but even then, her execution would be *years and years* away. She says, "Repeat back to me what I just told you."

She draws a chart for Paula that maps out the entire appellate process with boxes and arrows: "Here you were in the trial court, and then you would go on direct appeal to the Indiana Supreme Court; and if you lose there, we'll file for rehearing in the Indiana Supreme Court; and if we lose there, we'll petition the United States Supreme Court for cert; and if we lose there, we'll go back to the trial court and we'll file a postconviction petition, and we'll get a hearing there, evidence will be presented; and if we lose there, then we'll go back to the Indiana Supreme Court—" It is a long, long process. Monica promises her, "All of this is going to take many, many, many years. And nothing is going to happen until all of it is complete."

This finally calms the girl down.

But Monica can see she is truly depressed—not only because of her immediate situation, which would be enough to upset anyone, but on another, deeper level. Once Paula had started crying, it had been very hard for her to stop; and even now she remains overwhelmed. Nothing good has ever happened to her, she says, and nothing good will ever happen to her.

This is the story Paula is living. Monica is determined to disrupt it.

Six years earlier, during one of Bill Pelke's visits to the Indy 500 in his silver van, he might have seen Monica Foster if he'd known to look for her.

She was about to graduate from college, and she had two more weeks to decide whether to enroll at McKinney School of Law in Indianapolis. Her father was a men's clothing salesman and her mother a homemaker—Italian Americans, originally from New Jersey and Brooklyn—but Monica had known for years that she wanted to become an attorney. She was just nineteen; at sixteen, the age at which Paula Cooper was transferred to death row, Monica had started at SUNY Buffalo. She had grown up in Buffalo, New York—she has the hard *a*'s and *i*'s of that accent—and she'd never been west of New York State. And so she and a girlfriend drove the eight hours in her Honda Civic to check out Indy over Memorial Day weekend.

They arrived on what happened to be the day before the big race, and so they went to check out the track at the edge of town. It was the biggest party they had ever seen. The streets were closed, and the huge parking lots surrounding the two-and-a-half-mile track were packed with RVs and tents and motorcycles, people cooking and partying. Almost immediately, they were adopted by a large, tattooed biker whose crew was roasting a pig on a spit. They stayed out all night. And when they got back to Buffalo, Monica told everyone that Indianapolis was "the best-kept secret in North America!" This was how she chose where to get her graduate degree.

But when she moved there in the fall, there was nothing going on. That's when she learned the city's nickname: "Indianapolis, *Naptown.*" She eventually found her circle of mostly-guys to drink with—she wanted to talk sports and cases more than she wanted to have a "girls' night out." She also didn't mind going up *against* the guys at school or when she started working. In her profession, there were more men than women, but she never thought about it. She would describe her approach as: *Got a job to do, gotta do it.*

All she'd wanted to be was Perry Mason: righteous courtroom drama with every case. But Monica soon realized that lawyers don't win by pulling a confession out of someone on the witness stand. Where the stakes *were* consistently high for attorneys was in capital cases. While at McKinney, Monica got a job with the Public Defender Council, a research and training resource for Indiana's several hundred public defenders, and the month she passed the bar, in the fall of 1983, she subbed for the woman who'd been leading their new death-penalty project.

There were clear patterns in how the death sentence was handed down. At the time, Black Americans made up less than 12 percent of the country's population, but they were about equal to whites in their numbers on death rows across the country. A man was more than three times more likely to be given death if his victim was white than a person of color. And then there was the saying that critics of capital punishment liked to repeat: *Those without the capital get the punishment.* Few people with money have ever ended up on

death row. There was also the geography of it: the vast majority of executions were carried out in the South and in Texas—and that could not be explained away by presuming that far more heinous crimes take place in those regions than anywhere else in the United States. It was an incredibly high-stakes system that was fundamentally flawed: by this point in the country's history, 399 people sentenced to death had already been exonerated.

Executions had peaked in the United States in the 1930s and '40s, at between one hundred and nearly two hundred carried out per year, but they were down to the low double digits by the 1960s. With only a handful of people executed most years since 1977, that number spiked in the mid-1980s, to twenty-one; 66 percent of Americans polled said they were in favor of the death penalty for someone convicted of murder, edging close to the high set in the mid-1950s.

The Public Defender Council's death penalty project was created to better prepare attorneys for such complex cases with so much at stake. The state funds it because the less time a public defender spent on research, the less taxpayer money is spent—and death-penalty cases typically require twice as much time. They had resources to educate attorneys on ways to handle the various phases of a capital case, from pretrial motions to jury selection and final arguments. There is a video library of presentations by legal experts, and a file of experienced expert witnesses to contact. And then there is the research staff, including Monica. For Monica, it was support work, but in life-or-death situations. The challenge suited her. "The highest stakes is what I wanna do," she would say.

The first case on which Monica assisted was that of James Allen Harris, who had kidnapped a woman named Jane Brumblay from a parking lot at the Glendale Shopping Center and then raped and murdered her. When Monica met with Harris's public defenders, she realized they were unaware they were dealing with a client who was mentally unwell. He was hearing voices; he had stalked the streets and parking lots, believing he'd been sent on a mission, against his will, to humiliate women. Monica blurted out, "Well, don't you think you should have him *evaluated*?" She managed to find a therapist willing to do so, and the doctor declared him mentally ill. But because of how his plea had been entered, he remained eligible for the death penalty. Compounding the situation, his attorneys' performances in court struck Monica as pathetic; one of the men read his argument off a piece of paper, mumbling and hunched over. *Goddamn it!* she thought. *You totally suck!* To no one's surprise, Harris was sentenced to death.

A few years later, Monica decided to approach Rhonda Long-Sharp in the Indiana Public Defender's Office, one floor up. There the focus is on postconviction relief: working with people who've been convicted of a crime (or pled guilty) and trying to get them a new trial or have their sentence reduced. The two women had started out around the same time, and Monica knew Rhonda was doing good work. She asked her to consider taking on the Harris case, with the caveat that it was a complete mess. Rhonda would go on to have that death sentence overturned. This was the kind of attorney Monica aspired to be. *Oh my God*, she thought, *she is so fierce.*

It was in the earlier days of her work for Harris that Monica was brought aboard another capital case, this time as cocounsel. Her client was a teenage girl from Gary.

The lead attorney on that case is based in the Merrillville suburb, just south of Gary: Bill Touchette. He is the chief appellate public defender for Lake County, but sometimes Touchette (pronounced *touché*) still cannot believe he managed to get work that required no physical labor. A local boy, he was, like plenty of people in Lake County legal circles, the first in his family to go to college. He'd spent a couple of years working in construction (like his father) and at Midwest Steel (down the road from Bill Pelke's mill), but once he was able, he decided he might as well go to law school. His first job was at the State Public Defender's Office, where he was thrown into major cases right away. He would eventually rack up interviews with over a hundred people convicted of felonies, including many guilty of homicide. It never bothered him that his clients were guilty; he simply thought, *This is the way the system works.*

Touchette is a pragmatist, not a crusader. He does not overreact; he keeps his mind on the task at hand. This can be especially useful in his business—as it was the time a new client shuffled into the prison visiting room with his penis hanging out of his pants. When the man sat down across from him, Touchette simply scooted back a bit.

When he was assigned to Lake County, two and a half hours north, he didn't mind the travel: each time he went to court, it meant going home. The county has a large criminal court system, and he slowly got to know everyone through those after-work drinking sessions at the German Inn. He especially got along with Jim Kimbrough, who didn't act like most judges: the man was fun to be around, and he showed an interest in your life. Touchette also liked most of the prosecutors—something he felt the "ideological purists" in the Indianapolis office frowned upon. But when he found himself with job offers from both Kimbrough and Jack Crawford, he knew what felt most natural. He became an appellate public defender, a part-time gig that allowed him to also have a civil private practice, and he moved back to Lake County full time.

When Paula Cooper was sentenced, everyone in the building knew. Many could not believe Kimbrough had handed down the death penalty. Touchette and the judge had grown fairly close, and after the sentencing, Kimbrough pulled him into his office. He was incensed. He felt he'd had no alternative but to give the girl the death penalty, that he'd not been given an angle to work with. And then he said to Touchette, "I want you to get her out of this." He told the judge, "I'll do everything I can."

This was the first death-penalty case on which Touchette has taken the lead. But he believed he had a good shot: he'd lent a hand on capital cases before, and the State Public Defender's Office had a dedicated group of death-penalty opponents from whom he'd learned a lot. Personally, Touchette believes there are some very bad people out there, and he doesn't think it's completely out of line to call for their execution. He didn't hold it against Crawford that he pushed for death: the man is a prosecutor in a death-penalty state, and this crime was awful. Touchette's main complaint is that the punishment is unfairly applied.

As he began looking into the case, it didn't take him long to see that Paula's defense attorney had done an inferior job. He has never thought of Kevin as a "ball of fire," but to decide, like Karen Corder's attorneys, to plead guilty with no deal in a capital case? *Are you nuts, man?* And it simply did not look to him as if Kevin had done much work for the sentencing. When Touchette received the paperwork, he thought, *Look at this little bitty transcript.* A sentencing proceeding can take days, with a slew of experts called in, but Paula's had taken a few hours. Touchette can't introduce more mitigating evidence, not in the postconviction phase. He has to run with the existing record—and there's not much of one. Now it falls on him, and whatever team he can put together, to prepare for the uncertain road ahead.

Monica had met Touchette because the Public Defender Council was directly downstairs from the Indiana Public Defender's Office on

Monument Circle and everyone socialized. He wanted someone in Indy who could visit Paula more frequently, and since he trusted Monica, he'd brought her in for the earlier stretch of the appeal.

Judge Kimbrough now suggested Touchette take on Patti Wolter, the personal assistant he had kindly allowed to fib her way into a job in his office ten years ago. One afternoon, Touchette stopped by her desk. The two have known each other for years, and while Patti finds him to be a slightly nervous, nerdy kind of guy, someone who occasionally laughs at the wrong moments, she also thinks he's whip-smart. "Hey, how about doing me a favor?" he asked. "Come with me to the Women's Prison and see if Cooper will talk to you."

"Seriously?" she said. "*Then* what?" Touchette admitted that he does not know how to handle the girl's appeal if she continued to give him the silent treatment.

The next week, Patti makes the long drive from Crown Point to the prison. Her first meeting with Paula is very different from Monica's.

Patti has heard Paula described as a bully by her former classmates, and as the "ringleader" on that day at Ruth Pelke's house, and when they meet in person, she feels as if the girl towers over her. (To be fair, Patti is about as diminutive as Monica Foster.) One thing is clear: the girl can curse a blue streak. But they have no problem communicating, since Patti's got a mouth on her, as well—she shrugs it off as a habit born of working with so many men, all the years of off-color jokes. That first day, she finds Paula cold. Patti thinks she's developed a talent for reading whether or not someone is telling the truth, by the color of their eyes or a change in their skin tone—but she finds she cannot read Paula's eyes at all. They communicate nothing to her, and Patti thinks, *She's gonna be a tough nut to crack*. During this first meeting, Patti *does not care* for Paula. It will take the next several months for her to warm up to the girl.

Paula in a visiting room at Indiana Women's Prison

Touchette likes Paula, despite her resistance. And he does not think she deserves the death sentence—he's dealt with several criminals compared to whom the girls in the Pelke case are "stupid kids." He thinks, *How could they have appreciated the gravity of what they were doing?* Patti, however, gets the sense that Paula doesn't trust Touchette; that, perhaps, she doesn't trust men in general. Maybe it's a display of teen swagger, the girl wanting to let this guy know she can get by fine without him. And so, straightaway, Patti tells her: "You've got to be realistic here. You need these people. Pushing them away is going to get you nothing." Patti is also surprised at the pleasure Paula takes in making fun of Touchette's acne—the petty cruelty of a sixteen-year-old. "You can't do that," she says. "You need to have some decorum." This will be a recurring conversation.

Patti is trying to construct as full a record as possible of Paula's childhood, her abuse, her mental health, her life in the system. She has some experience with this: In a leap of faith, Kimbrough had assigned her to interview the backlog of criminally insane men on the jail's fifth floor, to help psychiatrists determine which facilities they should be sent to. Patti's job is to get Paula to speak to her about anything and everything in detail, and to accept the truth of her crime. They begin speaking over the phone nearly every day, and Patti travels to the Women's Prison two or three times a month. She records their conversations, and they talk for so long—three or four hours at a stretch—that she often runs out of tape. As the weeks and months go by, Patti becomes more of a confidante.

Monica asks far fewer questions. When she sees their client, she tries to keep Paula's spirits up, keep her sane, as she and Touchette continue trying to get her a new sentencing hearing.

As Touchette considers their options, he thinks about the girl. He is surprised by Paula Cooper. A young teenager from a lousy home, she was bounced around the system growing up, landed in juvenile detention a few times, committed this truly nasty crime—but she comes off as intelligent. Well-spoken, more poised than a lot of kids her age. That's how she had seemed on *60 Minutes,* and now that she's willing to talk to him, Touchette thinks she speaks, in person, like someone he might have grown up with in the suburbs. He believes that most people, if given the chance to meet her, would say, *Well, this is a regular teenager.*

With a little coaching, maybe they can help her to help herself.

Nine

LOVE, PAULA

At Bethlehem Steel, Bill Pelke sits up in the crane with an accordion of paper he pulled from the office printer, the kind with the perforated edges, and composes his first letter to Paula. He writes with a ballpoint pen, in large, neat handwriting, almost entirely in caps.

He introduces himself as Ruth's grandson, and says he was in court for the sentencing. He writes about his grandmother's faith, and tells Paula that he has forgiven her for what she did. He wants to help her however he can—speak out on her behalf, travel to see her.

He does not know what he expects in return.

Ten days after Bill posts the letter, he receives a reply—*Ms Paula Cooper 864800 IWP / IDOC* reads the envelope in his mailbox—and he opens it while standing there outside: pink sheets of paper, the handwriting a large and loopy script, immediately recognizable as that of a teenage girl. He starts reading before he even makes it back to his front door. The note begins with pleasantries: *Hello, how are you? fine I true-ly hope me I'll survive, I received your letter today & it was nice of you to write me.*

From there, Paula's tone changes swiftly. She's defensive: *Im not the mean type of person your family thinks I am.* She writes of Bob Pelke, who she doesn't understand is Bill's father: *Your cousin Robert was some thing else &*

what he said about not knowing if Ms Pelke would forgive me I've read my bible & I know it says the way you judge others the Lord will judge you the same way.

She describes life on death row as *a mental Hell because no one cares except for themselves.* She is now seventeen and in isolation twenty-three hours a day. That said, she writes with bravado, *It really doesn't matter if I live or die because Im ready any time they come.*

Paula tells Bill that she doesn't expect him to help her or testify on her behalf—*I really dont deserve it.* The forgiveness he's offered up is more than enough. Besides, *one day Ill be free even if its when Im dead.*

Paula seems unaware that, on her part, she offered up the thinnest of apologies to the Pelkes in court, because she writes, *I bet you didnt see any of the others look your family in the face & apologize because I have feelings.* She goes on: *I know all of you wanted to get even you may not be free until they execute me but you know Bill it wont help it wont help.* She is not a bad person; she cries whenever she thinks of Mrs. Pelke. She's misunderstood, she says, and full of anger.

After what she said about his father, it is hard to tell if she is being sincere when she writes, *No matter what you feel I will love all of your family.* She says she's been praying for them.

She tells him who to contact to try to arrange a visit, and she ends the letter with a challenge: *I dont mind talking to you I can face you no matter what you think of me or feel of me because I am still human & God loves me, he forgave me, can you?*

That's just what Bill had written to her to announce, his forgiveness. But Paula has taken his compassion under review.

Just after Bill mailed his first letter to the Women's Prison, he called Judy. He was aware that she'd started seeing someone else, but he had important news to share. In the only way he knew how in that moment, he told her about his recent revelation.

"So since you have someone else now, someone you care about and love, I've also chosen somebody new to care about and love."

"Oh, okay. Good for you, Bill. Who is it?"

"It's someone you know."

Judy started guessing, listing names. She recited the name of every attractive woman they knew in common—and each time Bill replied, "No, not her neither."

Finally, he put an end to the game and told her: "It's Paula Cooper."

There was complete silence on the other end of the line. And then: "What?"

"I have love for Paula Cooper," he said. "Love and compassion."

Silence again. Followed by a string of expletives. "You're *nuts*. Do you know you've completely lost it?"

Bill told Judy everything—about the night in the crane and the vision of his grandmother, about the image of Paula crying in her cell and his decision to forgive. Everything. But Judy doubled down. "I don't know, maybe it's the breakup—you've been so emotional. But Bill, you've finally lost it."

There was nowhere for the conversation to go.

After reading Paula's words over and over again, Bill sits down late that night to reply. He spends a long time at it; he prays over it.

He explains to her that Bob Pelke is actually his father, and that his father was the person who discovered Ruth. *Paula you must understand how hard it effected him. I am sure it is many times easier for me to forgive.* Bill would like to tell her more about his family as they continue to write each other—especially about his grandmother. He tells Paula that Ruth loved God, her husband, her stepchildren, her nine grandchildren, her great-grandchildren, her friends, and *all the many under privalidge children to whom she told flannel-graph Bible stories.* Of his family, he writes, *Nana was the greatest of them all.*

Bill is not a natural at putting his thoughts down, beyond the love notes he's written Judy over the years. But as he forces himself to think clearly about what to tell this girl, he becomes certain: he *means* these words; they have purpose.

> *You wrote in your letter that God forgave you. Paula that is true.*
> *It is probably the most important thing to keep in your mind. . . .*
> *Jesus forgave those who drove spikes into His hands and feet and*
> *then nailed Him to the cross. Surely Paula He has forgiven you.*

He tells Paula that he's been reading Matthew 5 and 6. *The end of Chapter 5 explains why I love you.* There, Matthew refers to Jesus's Sermon on the Mount:

> *You have heard that it was said, "Love your neighbor and hate*
> *your enemy." But I tell you, love your enemies and pray for those*
> *who persecute you, that you may be children of your Father in*
> *heaven. He causes his sun to rise on the evil and the good, and*
> *sends rain on the righteous and the unrighteous. If you love those*
> *who love you, what reward will you get? . . . And if you greet only*
> *your own people, what are you doing more than others?*

Bill is more specific now: *Verse 44 tells me that Jesus wants me Bill Pelke to love you Paula Cooper.* Verse 44 reads: *love your enemies.* Bill may have opened his heart to Paula, he may use the word *friend*, but some part of him still views her as his *enemy*, and this outreach as an act of charity. Though he agrees with her: no one will gain anything through her execution. He believes there is some reason for his grandmother's death—*I believe that <u>everything</u> happens for a reason*—but likely none of them will understand until they join Ruth on the other side. That is when, Bill writes, *we will know all the reasons why.*

He steps away to get some sleep, and in the morning he drives to the mill for his shift. When his workday is done, he sits down again and looks over what he's written: Yes. Good. *I just reread what I wrote yesterday Paula, and I mean every word I wrote.* He adds another page, and another.

He wants to help her, if she'll let him. *I really believe Nana wants me to do this and therefore I will.*

He signs off, *Your friend, Bill.*

And now Bill has finished his second message to the girl who killed his grandmother.

But he's not ready to mail it just yet.

Bill takes the letter in hand to Judy's house and asks if they can sit down together in the kitchen. He reads it aloud to her. And once he's finished, he looks up at Judy, sitting across from him at that Formica-topped table, and the two of them lock eyes.

She says, "You're nuts."

Judy stands, exits the kitchen, and slams the door behind her.

Next, there's a phone call Bill feels he has to make. Since Bob retired, just a few months before Ruth's death, he and Lola Pelke have spent their winters in Florida. After the final court date in his stepmother's case, he had invited Bill and the grandsons to go down with him—to check on their new irrigation system, but mostly to get away from everything.

Bill calls the Florida house and asks his parents to both get on the line; he has something to tell them. He's written to Paula Cooper, he says, and now he'll read them her reply. Then follows his second letter, which he plans to post right away—*Jesus forgave those who drove spikes into His hands and feet and then nailed Him to the cross. Surely, Paula, He has forgiven you . . .*

Silence.

His mother speaks first. "What is it that you're doing, Bill? And why?"

He repeats what is in his letter: that he has forgiven Paula, that his grandmother would have wanted him to, that she would have wanted them all to demonstrate compassion, he's convinced of it.

His father still has not said a word. Finally, he speaks up. "Son, we do not agree with this."

Bill says more of the same, laboring to find better words. Again: silence.

And then his father announces, "Well, do what you have to do."

Bill takes this statement as a kind of permission. It is possible, even likely, it was not intended that way.

A t first, Bill pictures Paula in a dark place; her cell on death row, in his mind's eye, is more like a cave. There she sits with her knees pulled to her chest and her back against a cold concrete wall. Something like that. He has little to go by.

As they write each other, however, Paula's circumstances begin to come into focus: she says her cell is like a bedroom, about eight feet by ten feet; it's painted yellow and is bright with fluorescent lighting. *I am very neat, I wash my clothes on my hands & I keep my table clean & every thing is fresh,* she writes. *its a big room but nothing to get excited about you know what I mean.* Sometimes her cell is cold, but in the summer it's achingly hot, with nothing more than a single fan to keep her comfortable. She has no desk or chair, only a bed—but she also has a radio and a TV set (thanks to Monica Foster), and she sometimes talks to the other women on her unit. She tells Bill that the residents cook the food, and it fluctuates between *really not bad* and *unidentifiable.*

She spends her days writing letters, maybe watching television— that's how *I try to expand my intelligence. The things I like are people, writing, reading, & to be relaxed, & I also like to talk, I dont dislike much except unhappiness thats all.* She really wishes she could go for a walk outside.

Paula has a Bible with red lettering in it sent to her by a friend; another sent her a study Bible for Christmas; a few from people in other states—*every one sends me bibles.* She has been praying more often, but she doesn't read the Bible with anyone at the prison because she feels the other inmates are disingenuous about religion. *I dont believe in playing with the bible nor God but they do.* In his last letter, Bill wrote that *God does answer prayers*—but here Paula writes that it was *unanswered prayers* that led her to lose her faith. *I love the Lord but we arent real close anymore.* She is *working* on her faith. But she will continue to pray for Bill's father.

She hopes that someday his father *will come to under stand me a little bit.* She tells Bill she is sorry. She tells him she will always write him back, anytime he chooses to write to her.

More letters from Paula arrive in Bill's mailbox in early December, and she is becoming more familiar. *Hello, my friend . . .*

She tells Bill she's convinced a guard planted matches in her cell just to write her up for it: ten days without her TV. That made her cry until her eyes hurt. Why would a person lie like that, punish someone for something they didn't even do? *I was so mad I finally realize what people really are.*

Paula tells Bill something she did not share in court: During the attack, Mrs. Pelke told her, "If you kill me, you will be sorry." *And she was right,* Paula says. She is full of regret.

Paula says she would exchange her life for his grandmother's if she could. Sometimes she thinks about killing herself—but then she might go to hell, and she doesn't want that. *Some times I hate my self, but then I realize that is wrong for me to do . . . I am a little lost . . .* Sometimes she lies on her bed and thinks about how it was a mistake for her to be born. When she's depressed, she can't bring herself to write either. *I feel like Im a no body & I dont even have a right to be writing to you . . . I dont deserve your kindness I dont know why you even give it to me.* She writes, *I really think you are beautiful inside.*

Bill included a photo of himself with one of his letters, and she tells him she's placed it in her album.

For the first time, she signs off with *I love you.*

———————⚜———————

The balance of authority between Bill and Paula shifts as they continue to write one another. Having never been a letter writer, Bill will not become one—only for Paula. Ultimately, he will write her a couple of hundred times, and in several letters he will mention his doubts about the direction of his life, his problems with Judy and the pain that's causing him. He doesn't have anyone else to talk to about that; he knows what most of his friends would say (*She's not worth it, move on*), and he doesn't want to hear it.

Paula, however, is a good confessor. She comes with few ideas about him, and she is a captive audience in the most literal sense, willing to discuss Bill's life in whatever detail he likes because the alternative for her is boredom. And she seems to *care*, a seventeen-year-old playing the counselor to a man more than twenty years her senior—a man she would have assumed, just months earlier, considered himself her moral superior. To his family, and to many who've read about his grandmother, Paula is a low creature, and now here she is, giving guidance to the old lady's grandson. Somehow, he trusts her to do that. There are times, she will tell Bill, when she'll be down for an entire month and not realize it until she's on the other side. She bets that's why he is this open with her: he knows she understands despair. And though every one of the letters they exchange is read by the prison censors, and Bill is aware of that, some part of him still feels that a letter sent to death row is private, separate from the world, a personal thought dropped into a dark container, a perfectly cutoff place—and there is Paula, sitting alone in that darkness, ready to hear him.

Bill spends more and more time thinking about forgiveness. He reads and rereads the Gospel of Matthew—particularly the passage in which Peter approaches Jesus and asks, "Lord, how many times shall I

forgive my brother or sister who sins against me? Up to seven times?"
And Jesus answers, "I tell you, not seven times, but seventy times seven."

A few days before Christmas, the Gary *Post-Tribune* publishes a letter
from Bill in which he announces that he has forgiven Paula and asks for
mercy on her behalf. The *Post-Tribune* is a paper that most people he
knows follow every day—everyone will read his letter or hear about it.
He signs off:

> *Paula Cooper is seeking a closer relationship with God and she has*
> *God's love and forgiveness. How about yours? She has mine. Ruth*
> *Pelke would want it that way. I am her grandson.*
>
> William R. Pelke
> Portage

He thinks about the people in his life—Judy, his family, his friends,
and for twenty years, the men at the mill. He has struggled through many
tensions with his family, and through plenty of heartache with Judy, but
he's given little consideration to the guys he's worked alongside for so
long. One man comes to mind straightaway: Jim, the assistant roller. Ten
years ago, while sitting up in the cab, Bill heard the guy say something
crass about him over the crane phone and it infuriated him. He steered
his crane to the landing and marched downstairs to find him, coughing
up a big "hocker" on the way. When he found the man, standing with a
group of half a dozen guys, Bill dared him to say the same thing to his
face—and he did. Bill spit that loogie in Jim's face, right between the eyes.
It was only their desire to keep their jobs that kept them from hitting
each other. And in the decade since then, they have refused to acknowledge each other whenever they have crossed paths.

Bill starts to think that forgiving Paula but keeping up this tension
with Jim makes no sense. He begins to think it makes him a hypocrite.

In the days before Christmas, Bill approaches Jim at work and tells him, "I'm sorry about my part in the event ten years ago. And I hold nothing against you."

"Apology accepted."

Not too much later, Bill turns his cart down an aisle at the supermarket and sees Jim. This would usually be enough to make Bill turn around and head the other way—but, instead, he heads toward the guy and says hello. Jim says it back. And each continues on his way. That bad feeling is gone.

Bill goes on to forgive three other workers at Bethlehem with whom he's had problems, cleaning house. How many is *seventy times seven*?

At the mill, Bill often works the same shifts as Wayne, another operator. Sometimes, during the lull between orders, they park their cranes alongside each other, pull down a window and talk. Whenever things get really quiet, Bill heads down to the landing and Wayne often joins him to play a game of chess or cards, or maybe cook a steak in the roaster oven they installed inside a locker. During one of these lulls, hoping for some kind of support, Bill shares that he's been writing to Paula Cooper.

Wayne says that, as a Christian, forgiving Paula is the right thing: it honors God, and it honors his grandmother. But he's not interested in any talk of saving this girl from the death penalty. For Bill, for the moment, that's enough. He's grateful to be able to speak plainly with his friend.

After the holiday, he visits his cousin Judi at her mother Ruthie's house in southern Gary. He is eight years older than her, but they have both been the black sheep of the clan, the two wild kids on behalf of whom their grandmother spent a lot of time praying—though Judi has since experienced a charismatic conversion back to Christianity. Judi has something she wants to tell him: She read his letter to the paper, and it expresses what she's been feeling but has not dared to say out loud to family. She, too, does not want to see the girl killed.

Bill decides to tell his cousin about the night in the crane—this is the fourth time he's told the story, and he's started to gain confidence in his ability to tell it. By the time he reaches the end, they are holding each other and crying in relief. Now, in their family, there are two.

After her sentencing, Rhonda and Mike began resigning themselves to the horrible fact that Rhonda's sister will be executed; it is just a question of when. Beyond her legal team, and a handful of relatives that does not even include her own parents, Paula has almost no support. This is why Rhonda is so surprised when she learns that Ruth Pelke's grandson has written to her sister to say he's forgiven her. More than that, he now wants to help—which, to Rhonda, seems a little late. And why has he turned around? This is the man with whom Rhonda exchanged withering looks in court, at whose family she'd shouted in the hallway. It sounds like he's had some kind of Christian revelation—but many of the people who turned on Rhonda and her sister were Christian. Many of the people calling for Paula's death at sixteen are Christian.

The Pelke grandson learned that the older man who cried out for Paula in court was their grandfather Abraham. And perhaps he is struck by the symmetry of it—he lost his grandmother, and here is someone else's grandparent thrown into pain by the same terrible event—but Bill Pelke is now asking to visit, to sit down and talk. Paula has even passed along Abraham's address and phone number.

Rhonda is not buying it. "I don't think that's a good idea," she tells their grandfather. "That sounds very *strange.*" Number one, Bill Pelke is a white man, and a slightly *older* white man. At one point, Black people had not even been allowed to cross the bridge to Glen Park, where Mrs. Pelke lived; they did not start attending Lew Wallace High School in that neighborhood until 1966. In Rhonda's experience, even the few white people who live in the Black areas of Gary keep themselves apart, do not talk to them. *They have their own little thing,* she thinks. *It's always been like that.* So why does this man want to come over to her granddad's house?

Mike is wary too. For him, Indiana will always be a place where the

Ku Klux Klan made a return, and flourished, during his grandfather's lifetime. In the late 1950s, when his father first joined the Gary police force, he wasn't permitted to arrest a white person. He wasn't allowed to drive a police vehicle until the 1960s; he and the other Black cops had to walk beats. So when a white man reaches out like that, Mike tells Rhonda, be careful. They both agree that Bill may be seeking some kind of vengeance.

"I think the man is serious," her grandfather says. "He wants to forgive her."

Rhonda cannot contain herself. *"Forgive?* Who does that? Who forgives you for killing someone in their family?"

Abraham does not listen; he invites the man over. And after the visit, Rhonda goes by her granddad's house to check things out. There, on the dining-room table, is a basket of fruit. It is *big.* She and her grandfather and a couple of his friends sit around and stare at it. And then Rhonda's announcement: "I am not eating that damn fruit."

It is snowing outside, but Paula would not know it. She's been on death row for five months now, but over the following weeks she will write about her future the way a senior in high school would, with that sense of possibility.

> *I am usually a very serious person when I write letters, usually people tell me that when I write them. I believe that if I would have made it on the outside world I would have been a successful businesswoman. . . . I believe that by the time I am able to face society again I will have enough talents to make it out there. I just need to get off death row so I can attend school all day instead of sitting up here doing absolutely nothing.*

She sometimes reverts to the cocky, defensive pitch of her very first letter to Bill—as in a note she writes just before New Year's, about forgiveness. *I forgive people faster than they forgive me*, she claims. *some times its hard but we all learn what happens if we dont forgive others.* She turns back, yet again, to Bob Pelke: *When your father was on that stand I knew what he had to say. all the pain & anger he felt. but he didnt realize I was the <u>only</u>*—she underlines the word five times—*one who really went through hell the lies, the court dates, every thing. I cried all the time. . . . I took all the blame & now I suffer the most. even though your grandmother died, I am dying inside also & also mentally.* At times like these, Paula does not seem to be thinking, with any care, about the Pelkes.

Paula asks Bill how his family is doing, a loaded question. She is trying to imagine how they would feel if she were executed, *when* she is executed. To witness an execution—that must be something a person would never forget, she says. She pictures what it would be like to sit in the electric chair and have someone throw the switch; sometimes she thinks about this for hours. She hopes never to be in that seat.

She turns to Bill for comfort. At times, Paula tells him, *I dont talk for days be cause I am hurt. but everyone thinks I am so strong.* That's when her thoughts fall into the dark.

> *maybe just maybe I wont be in this room 10 years if I would have to Ill probably hang myself . . . thats being weak minded I know but also its honesty . . . Ive been through enough & Im just about fed up. I dont know why it has to be like this if they want me dead they should just go ahead & execute me because I dont deserve all of this the same as your grandmother didnt deserve to go through what she did.*

Take care of yourself, Paula writes. *I love you.*

Ten

ENTER THE
ITALIANS

A pair of Italian journalists stands at the Hertz counter at O'Hare airport in Chicago, each with wavy brown hair and large eyeglasses: Anna Guaita and Giampaolo Pioli. She is from Rome, they tell the attendant, and he is from Florence. They are headed to Gary, Indiana.

"You're going to *Gary?* Then you'll be getting additional insurance," the man says, raising their total. "And remember: If you stop at a red light, your windows had better be rolled up and the doors locked. Because they'll pull you out of that car and steal it."

The Italians are at a loss for words. But once they're done staring at each other in disbelief—*America*, Anna thinks—they ask the man if he can recommend a hotel.

"There are no hotels in Gary."

They decide the attendant has an exaggerated view—maybe he lives in some sheltered suburb, maybe he enjoys frightening visitors from abroad—and they set off in their rental, east along Interstate 90. Anna has been a U.S. correspondent for *Il Messaggero* for two years now, and she likes to navigate, armed with an oversize road map. Giampaolo has been at *La Nazione* for the past decade, and he's an aggressive driver (years maneuvering high-speed Italian freeways), which works well in this country. They are both in their thirties, and they get along famously.

Anna had never intended to work for a newspaper; at the University of Florence, she studied Italian authors who had documented the freedoms of American daily life while they were living under fascism. But during a research scholarship at Rutgers University in New Jersey, she decided to stay in the States and began writing freelance articles on American cultural events for Italian papers. Within a few years, she'd given up on academia and become a regular contributor to *Il Messaggero*, a century-old left-leaning paper based in Rome and one of the largest regional papers in Italy. Giampaolo had more of a conventional start in the business: a journalism degree, and work as a junior reporter straight out of school. Just last year, he moved to New York to cover the long-running Pizza Connection trial, centered around a Mafia heroin and cocaine trade that had been laundering money through American pizza parlors. The trial, with its twenty-two defendants, is set to wrap soon—but Giampaolo has convinced his editor to keep him in the States indefinitely.

The previous summer, after Judge Kimbrough sentenced Paula Cooper to death, news of the teenage girl on death row in America was picked up by the international media. Kevin Relphorde, Jack Crawford's office, and the office of the Gary *Post-Tribune* received phone calls from journalists across Western Europe and Australia—all countries without the death penalty. When Touchette took over the case, he started getting calls too. It was extremely rare for the justice system in Lake County to be discussed abroad.

"To read the Paula Cooper thing to us is so unbelievable," a Dutch journalist told the *Post-Tribune.* "We are not saying it is right or wrong, but it is very interesting to us that a young girl would be put to death.... It almost seems like the motive is revenge." A segment about Paula aired on national television in West Germany, reaching six million viewers. West German *Stern* magazine ran a feature on the thirty-three juveniles on death row in the U.S. (up three since the Pelke murder first made news). A writer who covered the case for Rupert Murdoch's News Limited of

America, which services some three dozen publications in Australia, said that the idea of putting someone so young to death was "barbaric" to their audience.

But it is in Italy that the story has the most traction. In Rome, seventy-eight members of the Italian Parliament signed a letter to U.S. Ambassador Maxwell Rabb on Paula's behalf. And Italy's leftist Radical Party staged a protest on her behalf outside the American embassy, carrying signs that read DEATH PENALTY EQUALS BARBARITY, and IN AMERICAN JUSTICE, SODOMY IS PROHIBITED BUT THE DEATH PENALTY IS OK. The Radical Party represents only about 2 percent of Italian voters, but in a country deeply influenced by the Catholic Church, they're the force behind the movements that legalized divorce and abortion. Their protesters handed out leaflets about Paula's case, and they delivered a letter, addressed to the ambassador, explaining their position: her death sentence must be commuted. *A civilized society cannot respond with legal murder.* The protest, though very small (about fifteen people), was covered by the Associated Press and United Press International news agencies, bringing short items about the demonstration to Indiana.

The Indiana press began to pit Lake County against Europe. On August 3, *The Indianapolis Star* ran the front-page banner headline HOW A TEEN-AGE GIRL ENDED UP ON DEATH ROW, under which read "Crime stuns state; sentence alarms world." Paula's death sentence "so far has drawn only solemn headshakes from capital punishment foes in the U.S., where 32 teen-agers are on death row. But shockwaves were felt in many parts of the world where capital punishment is barred." When Jack Crawford was called for comment, he said of the Italians, "I just don't think they're in a good position to judge our sentence guidelines when, to my knowledge, they don't have anywhere near the crime problem that we do here." Judge Kimbrough told the *Post-Tribune* that he was not surprised by the protests in Italy: Italians have long been against capital punishment, "especially for children." At the same time, he admitted that the international interest in the case had surprised him. His hope, expressed through his sentencing statement, had been one much closer to home: that the Indiana Supreme Court would look more carefully at the death penalty for juveniles. But, he pointed out, there hadn't been any demonstrations for Cooper in Lake County.

Based in New York, Anna Guaita began pressing her editor in Rome to fund a trip to look into the young girl on death row, which would make her the first international journalist to do original reporting on the story. She called the local papers in Indiana; she called the office of the prosecutor; she tracked down Paula's new attorney Bill Touchette and eventually his cocounsel Monica Foster. Over the phone, Touchette sounded green but intensely committed to the case, and frightened of what could happen to his client. He insisted that Paula's trial lawyer had been inept, that the man had mounted a truly lame defense.

Around the same time, Giampaolo had drummed up interest at his home paper, *La Nazione*. The friendship between him and Anna was made easier by the fact that they were never in direct competition with each other: her readership was mainly in Rome, his in the northern cities. So they decided to travel together for the Indiana story and collaborate. It helped that they took the same approach to their work: rather than play up the relative glamour of their status as Manhattan-based foreign correspondents, they're both proud to be a little scrappy. This was the start of a working relationship that would last more than a decade.

And now they are turning off the Indiana Toll Road at Exit 14B, and they pass the Gary Works and turn right down Broadway. That is when they notice, just a few blocks farther, a huge hotel: thirteen stories high, overlooking the highway and the steel mill. "Look!" Anna says. "There's a Sheraton!" But when they pull into the parking lot, they can see: the place is boarded up.

As they continue along Broadway, through the downtown and into Midtown, many of the stores they pass have bars on their windows. They walk into a pizzeria and are surprised to find the cashier standing behind a bulletproof window; Giampaolo slides his money through the opening below (like in a bank, he thinks). They walk into a liquor store and talk to the owner through the metal bars he's had welded across the counter. "A bullet will get through this," the man admits, "but at least no one can reach over and grab me by the neck."

Eventually, they set out for Wisconsin Street in Marshalltown, to take a look at the house where Paula Cooper lived. They also have an appointment to see her grandfather Abraham. Retired from the post office, he keeps the television on and the windows of his clapboard cottage covered. He shares a family photo album with his visitors, as if to demonstrate that they are many, and none have done anything like what Paula did. Some of the images are of open-casket memorials, and Anna and Giampaolo do not know what to make of this display of the dead. The living room is packed with teddy bears that belong to his many grandchildren, most of whom Abraham has not seen in years. They get the feeling that he loves Paula, and that he did what he could to make up for her parents. "You know, I tried my best," he says. "I used my belt on her so many times." Anna is scandalized by this form of discipline, knows no one who was raised that way—but the old man is truly bereft. He was, and is, at a complete loss for what to do.

Anna was born into a family of intellectuals and activists with aristocratic roots; her parents had been devoted antifascists under Mussolini. She was not so much raised with religion as dropped off at church for Mass; Anna lost her faith early on, after realizing that people she considered good were "going to hell" because they hadn't been baptized. But she held on to the idea that truly being "Christian," at least in theory, required the same respect for human life and dignity that she was taught.

Anna believes that the only circumstance in which someone has a right to take another person's life is in self-defense. State-sanctioned killing, she will later say, is no better than "killing in a rage, killing for jealousy, killing for robbing, killing because you're an amoral beast." She has already written about the death penalty in the States, trying to explain to Italian readers why the country is in favor of executions, and she worked hard to see the issue from that perspective. She could empathize when a person would tell her, in an interview, that someone deserved to be executed for a particularly sadistic crime, of which there seemed to be more in America than in her own country. Beyond a desire for retribution, there could sometimes develop a common feeling that a perpetrator had committed a crime so out of bounds that they'd forfeited their place in human society. But to have that instinctive response to a *teenager* came with severe assumptions about how fully formed that young person was, how demonstrably beyond redemption.

This push to execute a teenage girl: the story has a natural dramatic appeal for an Italian audience. For them, the death penalty is un-Catholic—despite the Church's less recent past—and associated more with fascism and Nazism than the perceived values of the United States. With the exception of their fascist period, the Italian ban against capital punishment stretches back to 1889, and the philosophy underlying that ban reaches back to the Enlightenment. In his mid-eighteenth-century treatise *On Crimes and Punishments*, the theorist Cesare Beccaria, considered the godfather of modern criminal justice, used reason to advocate for penal reform. Torture, Beccaria believed, is dehumanizing to all involved: the tortured, their family, the torturer, the witnesses. The death penalty, he wrote, is a form of barbarism. *By what right can men presume to slaughter their fellows?* There was a limit to his reformist thinking—he suggested, in lieu of death, a life sentence paired with forced labor—but his resounding message was that a punishment should only be so severe as to deter the crime. His ideas are not foreign to the States: they informed the founding fathers—Jefferson, Adams, and Franklin, in particular—and their debates around the death sentence and the need to check the punishments the state can impose on its citizens. But with crimes of extreme violence, the God of retribution comes roaring back—the Old

Testament God who demands blood atonement, vengeance as first instinct. In such cases, only a dramatic intervention, a transformative event, can pull the crowd back from a call for death.

Anna and Giampaolo sit huddled around a speakerphone in Bill Touchette's office in the Lake County Government Center, listening closely. A small, girlish voice is being piped into the room, as the spools of a mini-cassette recorder turn slowly.

She sounds like a six-year-old, Anna thinks.

This is Paula's voice, from the Women's Prison. For many months, no one, save her family and attorneys, has been able to call or visit her. But today, for the Italians, Touchette has put his client on the line.

Anna, scribbling quickly on her pad, senses that the girl is completely untrained and unprepared in her remarks. She says she's received many letters from Italy—though, since they are mostly in Italian, she can't read them. More recent notes are written in English, and those voices keep her company. She would reply to every one, she says, if she could afford the international stamps. "Are you aware that you've become a symbol for the fight against the death penalty?" Anna asks. Paula says Touchette explained that to her. "It seems strange to me that so many people in another country care about me and want to help me in spite of what I did."

They speak for a half hour. And that afternoon and into the night, back at their hotel, Anna and Giampaolo sit in her room with their notes and some food and talk through everything they've learned. Then very early the next morning, their minds fresh, each sits down at their desk and writes up their piece. After a few hours and a few coffees, always aware of Italian time, they call their editors collect to dictate their work over the phone. And Paula's story is sent out across the ocean.

Because of her career change, Anna is already thirty-six, but she still feels young as a journalist; it's easy for her to become personally involved in a story. For Anna, the reporting of this girl's case is already becoming a kind of crusade.

Both papers tease the story on their front page. Both run the mailing address of Governor Robert Orr in Indiana and suggest readers write to him with their thoughts.

The reaction is immediate. In Italy, readers begin flooding the papers with letters, most of them incredulous that someone so young could be sentenced to die. While the prosecution had suggested that Paula being truant and a "runaway" might be evidence of a criminal nature, many Italian readers see her as the victim of a chaotic childhood. They write in with heated questions. The story of Paula Cooper makes it into the evening news roundups on Italian television.

Back in Lake County, Touchette, aware of the growing interest in Italy, makes a bold move: he writes to Pope John Paul II on Paula's behalf. He pleads with the pope to personally send a letter to Governor Orr, asking that Orr commute her death sentence: *I hope you find it in your heart*, he says, *to help Paula Cooper.* Touchette gives the letter to Anna, telling her, "A word from him would carry great weight in our state"—which is a bit of a reach, considering that Indiana is heavily Protestant, and Catholics have not always been welcome (as when they were a target of the KKK). His words are published as a letter to the editor in *Il Messaggero*. In Anna's and Giampaolo's stories, they mention that Paula has taped a photo of the pope (sent to her by an Italian supporter) to the wall of her cell. "I can't imagine him as a person, in flesh and blood," she had told them, "but I hope he'll be able to help me just the same."

Touchette has no idea whether or not the Vatican will respond, but the AP picks up the story, generating headlines like CONVICTED KILLER SEEKS POPE'S HELP.

This sequence—Paula's first death-row interview appearing in major Italian papers, and a direct appeal to the Vatican by an Indiana girl—gives new life and urgency to the story in the American media. But Touchette is concerned that there's still not enough momentum, and no guarantee that European interest will have a real impact. He knows how long the appeals process can take in a capital case, and Paula's teenage years are passing in isolation as she grows up in prison. "That's the sad part," he tells *The Indianapolis Star.* "By the time any execution is carried out, people will have forgotten that she was only fifteen."

Over the phone, Paula told Anna and Giampaolo that she feels as if she's "going crazy." She repeatedly writes Bill Pelke that she is worried for her sanity. *I think Im just falling completely to pieces but Im trying to get myself together . . . Ive been just sitting around trying to be able to control my mind.* Every morning at five-thirty, she takes medication, *but it doesnt help any none period.*

The worst, Paula thinks, is not having any kind of therapist or counselor. She'd rather be in a mental hospital, she says, so she could get some help for her head. When Rhonda brings Gloria to visit her, Paula wonders if her mother should see someone too.

She's tried prayer, but *I am confused because the more I pray I dont find peace & I feel awful just want to give up.* She sees how God has changed Bill's life but not her own. The only self-improvement she believes she's achieved is what she calls *a little self control.* In all other ways, she feels she's been sinking. *Im miserable & like a walking time bomb & its pretty bad to have to admit that to some one . . . very few people realize what I go through listening to screaming all day long . . . it isnt good to hold a lot of things in like I do because after a time you just explode . . . I dont want to have a break down or any thing but Im on my way to one.*

A piece of her wants to be strong, sees that as a kind of vocation. And so Paula sits on her bed, head bent over a stack of stationery, and answers her letters.

———————— ⚜ ————————

Soon an Italian friar will disembark from a plane in Chicago, wearing the brown robe of the Franciscan order, cinched at the waist by a length of white rope. And he will know Paula Cooper's name.

The original Franciscans, the Order of Friars Minor, were a handful of men brought together by Francesco di Bernardone early in the thirteenth century, gathered in a collection of huts just outside the Italian mountain town of Assisi. Monks committed themselves to life in a monastery, but the friars were often on foot, walking from town to town preaching the Gospel and the idea that all creatures are sacred. They lived on whatever was offered them. Begging for alms or for shelter was considered beneath the clergy; what the friars were doing was radical for preachers: on the surface, their lives resembled those of the indigent or the mentally ill. They wore nothing more than a hooded tunic made of the cheapest fabric available. They gave up all possessions, all claims to property, and they invited men from all social strata to join them; within the small group, some were once wealthy and others desperately poor. When a person chose to follow this lifestyle, it was said that he "left the world." In spite of all that set them apart, the Order of Friars Minor, or Lesser Brothers, would come to wield an outsize influence in the Catholic Church.

How the idea to join the Franciscans first occurred to Vito Bracone, in the small southern Italian town of Palata centuries later, is unclear. His parents were farmers with seven children, a two-room house, and a modest vineyard; Vito worked the land with them all day, alongside their mules, and attended school only in the evenings. They could not afford school supplies, and so he did his classwork with an "ink" that he made from red dirt and a rolled-up leaf as a stylus. Vito knew that, if he stayed in Palata, he would only be able to matriculate through the fifth grade; his own parents could not read or write. But somehow his family found a seminary in Sepino, about fifty miles south, where he could continue his education.

Vito was so young: he entered the seminary at fifteen—the same age at which Paula Cooper also, in a very different way, joined a community set apart from the world—and he does not associate that moment with a clear spiritual revelation, at least not one he shares with others. His time in Sepino was followed by studies for the priesthood in Assisi and Rome, then coursework in social psychology in Chicago. After he was ordained in 1969, just before his thirtieth birthday, he never returned home again, but he took with him bottles of wine from his family's vineyard to use when he gave out Communion. He had never been ashamed of where he came from.

Over the years, Father Vito gained a voice in the order, and in the summer of 1986—now forty-seven, thin-nosed, with a full head of gray hair and remarkably soft eyes—he found himself on a trip to New York City on behalf of their governing council. That was where he read about Paula's sentencing, in a local paper. He was struck by her age and how little her family had—that was familiar to him. He thought, *Someone must help her. And it will be me.*

Father Vito brought word of the girl's case back with him to Rome, where he shared her story with a colleague on a Church committee, Father Germano Greganti. At seventy-one, Father Greganti, gray and diminutive, had been a priest for almost forty years. In the late 1960s, after a colleague brought him to a prison in Rome to take confession, he made a commitment to help improve the lives of the incarcerated in Italy, and to support them as they reintegrated into society when their sentences were up. For that purpose, twelve years ago, he had founded the association Carcere e Comunità (Prison and Community), which has its offices on the top floor of an ancient building next to the Ministry of Justice. He receives letters from correctional facilities around the country, many of them requests for help, and he has a cadre of volunteers to answer them all. The priest has a dream of abolishing prison for women and juveniles entirely, and is a relentless advocate of rehabilitation without incarceration.

In speaking to Father Vito, Greganti took an immediate interest in Paula's case. And so discussions began in Rome about what to do on behalf of the girl on death row in America. The answer was the formation of a group called, in a nod to the Ten Commandments, Non Uccidere (Thou Shalt Not Kill)—a loose collective of Italian groups working to abolish the death penalty internationally, with Father Greganti as president. The collective includes, in a very active role, the Radical Party, bringing together the anticlerical, pro-divorce, pro-choice political activists in a truly counterintuitive collaboration with factions within the Catholic Church.

Non Uccidere decides to hold a press conference in Rome on Paula's behalf, and they offer to fly in her attorney. At this point, Bill Touchette has not received any explicit reply from the Vatican—but he was recently interviewed, long-distance, by Vatican Radio. Appreciating the momentum building in Italy, Touchette accepts Non Uccidere's offer and arrives in late March.

It's a bright Monday morning in Rome, and Touchette sits in a large hall, rearranging the papers in front of him as Father Greganti speaks. The priest announces that, thus far, their organization has collected thirty thousand signatures on a petition to be sent to Governor Orr, asking for Paula Cooper's sentence to be commuted. When it's Touchette's turn, he talks through a translator to the assembled reporters, their faces open and receptive, about the support throughout Europe for Paula—"but it is nowhere like in Italy." "The Catholic Church stresses the importance of the family and the upbringing of children," he says. "Italians realize how important parents are. When confronted with such parents as Paula's, they have no trouble understanding the background of her crime." He states, yet again, the oft-repeated fact of Paula's age at her sentencing and sees looks of shock across the room.

Protest in support of Paula Cooper in front of the American embassy in Rome, July 1986

When he has an audience with Agostino Casaroli, the Vatican secretary of state, Casaroli asks outright, "Are you Catholic?"

Touchette says he was raised in the Church but stopped observing long ago. Casaroli does not betray any particular opinion of this American's lapse in faith; he keeps it short and to the point. The attorney is distracted by their surroundings—he's been invited into the Vatican, beyond where the public can go, and they are strolling down hallways painted with extravagant murals on all sides—and at some point Casaroli stops short and asks something like, "Well, what do you want?"

"I want the pope to ask for clemency for Paula Cooper, ask that the death penalty not be imposed."

Touchette can see the man digest the message—but he does not promise anything. And then he sends the American on his way.

As with the rally in front of the U.S. embassy, the Non Uccidere conference had been small; not many papers had taken the bait and sent their reporters. But Anna's and Giampaolo's continuing coverage is enough. And again, the AP runs with the story, volleying Italian reporting back to the States. At the same time, a massive petition drive has mobilized in Italy, calling for Paula's life to be spared. Beyond the thirty thousand signatures announced by Father Greganti, the recent *La Nazione* features have brought in forty thousand more, and ten thousand high school students in Florence have also sent in petitions. The Red Cross International, Catholic Action, the Waldensian Church, and the Jesuits join in, as well as the Italian boy scouts of AGESCI.

The scouts are about the same age as Paula, and they've been collecting signatures at outdoor tables in front of Carrefour supermarkets and urging their troops to write to the governor of Indiana, somewhere in the middle of the United States.

In Indianapolis, Governor Orr remains unmoved.

Eleven

THE POWER OF
NUMBERS

While most of the Pelkes and their friends fled Gary nearly twenty years ago for the surrounding towns and suburbs, Earline Rogers's family has remained. For twenty-two years now, she has lived on a corner of a pretty block on the West Side where most of the homes are single-family, ranch-style houses with brick façades. There's a big window in the sitting room, set back from the sidewalk by a nicely kept lawn, and hedges and flower beds hug the house. Their home is just west of Midtown, in the Tolleston neighborhood, a German immigrant town before Gary was even built: U.S. Steel executives stayed there while drawing up plans for the new city. It was entirely white until the early 1960s, and is now mostly Black.

She was born Earline Smith in 1934, halfway through the Great Depression, when only about 18 percent of the city was Black—Gary was just twenty-eight years old—and life was strictly segregated. Growing up, she and her siblings lived a couple of blocks from the Gary Works, in one of the hundreds of units of the Delaney Housing Development in Midtown. Most of those residents had moved up from the South, like her parents (her mother from Georgia, her father from Tennessee). Her father Earl worked at the mill, as did many of their neighbors, and their family was close. Eventually, her father managed to do well enough to move them into their own house, a few blocks south. While Earl had given up a college scholarship to care for his sick mother, his children went on to get higher degrees, and three would go on to become teachers in the Gary public school system.

Earline attended Roosevelt High School, the first school built specifically for Black kids, in 1930. It was located close to the mill, and so everything she and her friends did was in that predominantly Black neighborhood, with beauty shops and restaurants and parks that had long been for Black residents. She liked that sense of community, but it hadn't come entirely by choice: up through the late 1940s, segregation was official policy in the city's school system, and attempts to integrate were often met with walkouts by white students.

She graduated from Roosevelt as an honors student and the first female president of a senior class, and she followed her parents' advice to enroll at Indiana University Northwest. For young career women of her generation, it seemed that the choice in the early 1950s was between becoming a nurse or a teacher; since Earline could not stand blood, her decision was made. Her first teaching gig was at the new Bethune Elementary—a school Paula Cooper and her sister would attend about twenty years later, around the corner from their house. "Mrs. Rogers" taught grades one through four.

She developed a sense of what she owed her community by watching her father. At the mill, Earl had a reputation for standing up for himself and his coworkers when there was a problem—which, more often than not, involved a white employee calling them the N-word. Rather than turn to their union representative, plenty of men went to Earline's father, and he'd end up suspended for a few days for being confrontational—a loss of income his wife sometimes had trouble justifying. In the Delaney projects too, Earl was the "go-to guy" for politicians looking for support from the residents. That was how he became close friends with Johnny Visclosky when he was Gary's interim mayor (his son Pete would later beat Jack Crawford for a seat in the Senate). The way people looked to Earl for help made a strong impression on his daughter. For years, whenever she'd encounter someone who knew her father, the best compliment they could give was to say she reminded them of him. And so when, in 1966, her former college classmate Richard Hatcher announced his candidacy for mayor, it felt natural for Earline to get involved.

Volunteering for Hatcher planted an idea in her brain that would take more than a decade to catch fire: to run for public office herself. It was not until she was forty-five, after twenty-two years as a public-school teacher, that she would feel ready. In 1980, she ran for City Council for the 3rd District (a big swath of the West Side) and won, with Visclosky as one of her first campaign contributors. Not long afterward, she became the council's first female president. And she wasn't afraid to stand up—as when she subpoenaed the patrol cars of the Gary Police Department for inspection, against Mayor Hatcher's wishes, because enough officers had complained to her about their condition. "Nobody has ever subpoenaed me," he told her. To which Earline replied, "You know, there is a first time for everything."

After two years on City Council, Earline was elected to Indiana's House of Representatives, as one of two officials representing Gary. Her rhythm became: teach the fall semester, have a substitute handle her classes when she went "downstate" for the session, then return to school from April through June. In Indianapolis, she found herself the only Black woman in Indiana's Congress in need of an apartment, and so she rented a place with two white colleagues—but they were also newly elected women, and teachers too. The trio would eventually develop a successful strategy of heading to the fourth-floor bar at the Columbia Club to get the Republicans to say too much over drinks.

In the summer of 1986, near the end of Earline's second House term, Paula Cooper was sentenced to death for a crime committed near her district. Earline was shocked. She told a reporter, "The state shouldn't be in the business of killing children."

Paula was the same age as some of her students and her own daughter Dara, and Earline immediately asked herself what the girl's home life must be like. She paid close attention to the coverage of Paula's childhood in the system—it made her think of a boy who'd been one of her fourth graders years ago. Winford was particularly dark-skinned, which she'd felt was held against him even within their own community, and so she'd called him by his school nickname Juice, as in "The blacker the berry, the sweeter the juice." Juice was always getting into trouble—but Mrs. Rogers loved teaching the boys who acted up, because she knew she had a gift for capturing their attention. She felt kids could tell when you really liked them, and they would rise to meet that. She would treat the rebels and the slow-and-behind students just like the others, assuming the best, giving them extra help until they did well in class. Once that happened, they often stopped misbehaving, and instead, she said, they became "braggadocious." She loved to see it.

With Juice, however, Mrs. Rogers got in deep: his mother hadn't been able to provide for her kids, and he and his siblings were being separated. So Earline asked to take him home with her; she intended to raise him just as she was raising her son, who was his age. It went well, she thought—but after about a year, Juice leapt at a chance to reunite with his family over on the East Side, regardless of what other opportunities Earline and her husband could give him. A few years ago, when he was in his twenties, she'd heard that he'd gotten into trouble and been sent to prison, she wasn't certain for what. And now Earline was full of *what-ifs*. She loved the boy—they still wrote each other—and it took her a long time to fully understand why he had chosen, as a child, to go home when that meant once again redirecting the course of his life. He had simply wanted to be with his people, to stay as close as he could. That was the longing, the pull of family, regardless of circumstances.

Based on experience, Earline firmly believed that you could not hold a child, even in their teens, accountable for their actions in the same way you would an adult. That way of thinking simply did not fly with her. Even a kid raised in a stable home would still be immature and vulnerable to whatever ideas their peers came up with, whether a gang or just some clique they belonged to. Her job gave her the opportunity to look into a child and see what kind of future they were likely to have, and then she did her best to help things turn out all right. She hates this fact, but whenever she runs into her students now, in the streets and the shops of Gary and Chicago, they have each turned out more or less as she would have predicted. There are forces bigger than any one individual.

Earline Rogers spoke up about Paula. Knowing she had relatively little clout, statewide, as a Black woman from Gary and a public-school teacher, she did not hesitate. Within hours of the girl's sentencing hearing, she made a public statement: she promised to introduce a bill to raise the minimum age for the death penalty in Indiana. Most of her colleagues did not realize that the minimum was currently set at ten years old—or, in school years, the fifth grade. "I wish I had proposed this legislation last year," she told the press. "We can't help Paula Cooper, but we can help other juveniles."

By the fall of 1986, Rep. Rogers had announced that her bill would be introduced in the upcoming General Assembly session. She was told by more senior representatives that eighteen, as a minimum, was too high—she would not be able to get a hearing—and so sixteen became the goal. While the first press conferences about Paula are being held in Rome, Earline prepares to present House Bill 1022 for its first vote.

———————— ☙ ————————

Five hours away, at Cleveland State University, another Indiana native prepares a document: a list. It is a catalogue of the youngest death-row inmates in the history of all fifty states—his pursuit for the past four years.

Victor Streib is a professor of criminal law and a legal expert on capital punishment. At forty-six, he looks every bit the academic: a man of lean stature, with a trim beard and small green eyes behind wire-rimmed glasses. He wore a ponytail for a couple years out of law school, but now he has a dome of a white head ringed with short, graying hair. Victor is calm and soft-spoken, but at school the students view him as a minor celebrity: he has appeared on *The Oprah Winfrey Show* in Chicago, and last year *60 Minutes* interviewed him on campus for a segment on those two teenage girls up for death in Indiana. Victor keeps a photo of him and Harry Reasoner in his home office.

Victor grew up in a small, mostly white working-class community in Marion, about two and a half hours southeast of Gary. His father had a machine shop, but Victor went away to Alabama for college. With decent grades, he soon latched on to the idea of law school, looking for a change. With little sense of what that line of work would entail, he enrolled at Indiana University Bloomington, a short drive south of Indianapolis. At first his focus was profitable—antitrust and corporate law—but it was the 1960s, and he was soon drawn to civil rights. He joined protests on campus, distracted from upward mobility by the possibility of improving the system. He loved the campus culture and hoped never to leave academia—so when he got his degree in 1970, he stayed at the university and began teaching criminal justice courses.

Inspired by a class he'd taken in family and juvenile law, Victor spent the next few years researching the system's treatment of young peo-ple. He was drawn in by the special status and the vulnerability of these defendants. In order to understand firsthand what he'd learned in the law library, he visited a friend who was a local prosecutor and asked if they'd hire him to work on juvenile cases. He was brought on board as their only attorney focused on teenagers.

He assumed that the purpose of juvenile court was not only to determine guilt or innocence, but also to make sure that each kid would get into the right correctional or treatment program; it wasn't about severe punishment. He knew that many other prosecutors disagreed with him; they leaned heavily on the assumption that certain kids were damaged and unlikely to change. But Victor made an effort to bring child psychologists into the courtroom whenever possible. They testified that juveniles were changing all the time. The idea that a teenager will not evolve, Victor would later say, "simply defies everything we know about how kids behave and think." He thought about some of the stupid things he'd done as a kid, his obsession with cars, how at fourteen he'd fantasized about stealing one. And what if he had? And what if he'd crashed into somebody? And what if he'd been poor and with little support from his family or school? What if he'd been Black? And *what if*, and *what if*—a situation could escalate quickly. This was when Victor first met teenagers who were charged with homicide, and was immediately struck by how ill-equipped juvenile court was to handle crimes that serious. But if you transferred those kids to *adult* court, the consequences could be tragic.

Victor struggled with being on the side of the prosecution, and defense work seemed just as much of a stretch. He had no personal fantasy of cutting a dramatic figure in the courtroom. He was interested in helping a jury come to a rational decision; he wanted to focus on the shape of the law. One way to do that was to become an academic, to dive into research and publish as often as possible. And so when he was able to get a full-time position at Cleveland State in 1980, he leapt at it.

He taught standard courses in criminal law and had enough time left over to write. *Publish or perish*: that mantra was regularly on his mind. The problem: he was almost forty years old and had nothing original to say. His interests were broad; he wasn't sure what distinguished him from so many other law professors around the country.

Then, in January 1982, the U.S. Supreme Court decided *Eddings v. Oklahoma*.

Monty Eddings was sixteen in 1977, the son of a police officer, when he and some friends ran away from home, ending up on a turnpike in central Oklahoma. After a highway patrolman pulled them over, Monty leaned out the window and, with his father's gun, shot the man dead. The justices ultimately found that the Oklahoma Court had not given enough consideration to Eddings's "difficult family situation" and stunted mental and emotional development—an issue of balancing mitigating circumstances against the violence of the crime. They did not believe Monty's age alone should disqualify him for the death sentence, but the Supreme Court, for the first time, debated the constitutionality of the death penalty for teenagers.

The newness of the terrain was evident during questioning: the justices seemed to lack a grounded way of discussing Oklahoma's minimum age for capital punishment, or the differences that might exist between a fifteen-year-old and an eighteen-year-old. At one point, Justice John Paul Stevens asked Oklahoma assistant attorney general David Lee if there was "*any* constitutional limit on the age of a person that could be executed." "Specifically, say, would it be constitutional for a state to execute a ten-year-old for committing this crime?"

Lee tried to skirt the question, as the only reasonable answer required that he admit the need for a minimum age. Inevitably, he caved. "I think it would be 'cruel and unusual punishment' to impose the death penalty on an individual who was ten years old."

He was referring to the Eighth Amendment of the Constitution: *Excessive bail shall not be required, nor excessive fines imposed, nor cruel and unusual punishments inflicted.* As was the case in 1972 with *Furman v. Georgia*, Eighth Amendment jurisprudence is often the crux of capital punishment appeals. But that language leaves room to maneuver. The word *cruel*, like the word *sociopathic* much later, is a label that carries great legal weight while remaining unfixed. Across the history of the United States, the definition of cruelty has been open to interpretation. While imagining a new republic shaped from their shared ideals, many of the country's founding fathers were also supporters and beneficiaries of slavery. During our first Congress's debates on the Bill of Rights, one representative (Smith, of South Carolina) said the Eighth Amendment "seems to express a great deal of humanity" while at the same time having "no meaning in it." That language had been lifted from the English Declaration of Rights—but how would it serve as a guide?

A century and a half after the drafting of the Bill of Rights, in the 1958 opinion for *Trop v. Dulles*, Chief Justice Earl Warren provided the modern-day method for parsing out the legal definition of *cruel and unusual punishment*. The Eighth Amendment, he wrote, addresses *nothing less than the dignity of man. While the State has the power to punish*, he continued, *the Amendment stands to assure that this power be exercised within the limits of civilized standards. . . . The Amendment must draw its meaning from the evolving standards of decency that mark the progress of a maturing society.*

Before the Court that day, arguing *Eddings*, Lee's response to Justice Stevens was based on principle, on the gut-level sense of a clear consensus, an accepted moral standard, that even the prosecution could not deny—our "standards of decency." But on what logic, history, science, or precedent was that consensus about juveniles based? And what made the execution of a ten-year-old or fifteen-year-old repulsive, but not (to some) a sixteen-year-old?

The constitutional debate gripped Victor right away. The questions surrounding the death penalty for juveniles were tough and layered, and he'd been wrestling with the age of liability for years. And for a professor looking to find his own niche, this discussion had scant research to prop it up. As his wife Lynn would later say of Victor's career (and he would enjoy repeating): He was the top person in the field because he was the *only* person in the field, and nobody can be better than the only guy.

As he began focusing on capital punishment, Victor realized he'd been a little naïve in his assumptions about why people support the option. He'd thought it was mostly as a deterrent to violent crime—logical enough, even if that view wasn't grounded in fact. But the closer Victor got to the issue, the more he saw that people's thinking on the subject was hardly *thinking* at all: it was emotional, a gut response to crime that was more on the level of *I'm going to kill the son of a bitch*. A slightly calmer version, though just as rooted in a desire for retribution, was *We have to do right by the victim*—but Victor could not see how to translate that into sound legal logic. He thought the victims and the public had a claim to their emotions, to a charged sense of justice, but a society could not build its legal system on raw feelings. "As a lawyer trying to argue logically, carefully, A then B then C," he would later say, "I found that they were just very, very angry. People on both sides were shouting at each other. I felt like I was speaking a different language." He was a believer in the power of data, facts, numbers: that was something he could contribute. *Eddings* might have made a bigger difference if the attorneys had empirical research to stand on.

He dove in, committing himself to a long historical hunt for juvenile death sentences across the country, state by state, trying to ground the issue in precedent. When he would tell friends, colleagues, or judges that he was researching the executions of teenagers in America, he would be met with some variation on "Oh, we never do that. We wouldn't execute children in this state." And he'd say, "I've found a long list of executions. *Look*." Personally, he was astonished. He believed that one of the reasons some people were comfortable with the death penalty, and did not question it, was that "we don't really know what we've really done."

And the list continued to grow. Early in the course of this new research, Victor learned of a man named Watt Espy. Watt, who was a few years older than Victor, was not an academic (he had a high school diploma) but a traveling salesman; he sold security systems at one point, cemetery plots later on. He lived in the rural town of Headland, Alabama, in the middle of the "Death Belt," the nine Southern states responsible for carrying out 90 percent of executions since capital punishment was reinstated in 1976: Alabama, Mississippi, Louisiana, Florida, Texas. In the seventies, Watt had begun collecting the last words spoken by condemned persons around the country—a hobby that quickly became an obsession—and the project evolved into an attempt to catalogue every death sentence carried out in the United States. Along his sales routes, he'd visit courthouses and prisons to gather information on men executed by that county. Without any credentials, based on the sheer breadth of his data-gathering, Watt received a grant from the University of Alabama Law School and was dubbed the director of their one-man Capital Punishment Resource Project. After more than a decade of research, his catalogue was more extensive than any in the country, and he was now preparing to publish evidence that the United States had legally executed 13,600 individuals thus far—nearly double the number presumed by legal experts. He projected an eventual total of about 20,000.

A few weeks after the *Eddings* decision, Victor, now an associate dean at Cleveland State's law school, wrote to Watt to tell him about his study of juveniles and to ask for access to his research. That summer, Victor took time off from teaching and drove seven hours south for a visit. Watt's office was packed with binders in different colors, file cabinets stuffed with index cards marked with the final words of so many condemned, court records, and microfilm of newspaper reports. But Victor's eyes were drawn to the walls, crowded with black-and-white images in thin black frames: photos of people who'd been executed in this country since the beginning of photography. Victor hardly slept for three long days. Through his own work thus far, he had identified about two hundred juvenile executions in several states, and here he was able to collect notes on nearly one hundred more: a windfall.

Once back in Cleveland, he continued to swap research with Watt. Victor realized that, more than whittling a legal argument to a fine point, he loved the feeling of discovery. He brought a childlike excitement to the process that might not have been in step with the gravity of death row, but it kept him going; he thought of it as the pleasure of a dog sniffing for truffles, or finding a shell on the beach. Watt let Victor know whenever he uncovered another teenager, though it upset him every time. Occasionally he rang the professor around midnight, when he and his wife were asleep. It was worth it: each time Victor double-checked Watt's stats, they held up.

With this vast amount of raw data in hand, Victor's work took off. In 1983 alone, he delivered multiple papers at conferences; published the law review article "Death Penalty for Children," his first on the topic; and persuaded the American Bar Association to adopt a resolution against capital punishment for juveniles, based heavily on his essay, making the collective stance of those 250,000 attorneys a public one.

Victor also served part time as supporting counsel on a string of juvenile capital cases. Because he was unique in his field, attorneys for juveniles who'd been sentenced to death reached out to him for input or help writing briefs—work he could do from afar. Victor would help with a brief, coach the local attorneys on how to weave his information into their argument, or fly to testify before a state legislature for a half hour before rushing back to the airport so he could sleep in his own bed. Throughout, he referenced the data he'd uncovered, making lawmakers aware of the state's—and the country's—history of executing adolescents. He was helping to shape a story that was bigger than any one teenager, helping to position each of these kids inside a larger legal narrative.

When testifying, Victor noticed a pattern in the kinds of arguments he was up against, about juveniles and violent crime: with judges and jurors, their point of reference was usually their own childhood, their own children, some kids in their neighborhood. When Victor was in juvenile court at the start of his career, one judge had told him "I know kids like this. My kid's sixteen," and Victor had said, "Your upper-middle-class community has nothing to do with this child's experience." It frustrated him to no end. *You need more than a sample of one or two from your own life*, he thought. *You need a real body of research.*

The cases were adding up. Each brief fed directly into something Victor was writing for a law journal or a book, and so he continued to publish, stacking up his bibliography—which led to more awareness of the issue and more invitations from teams across the country. State by state, legislature by legislature, appellate teams were gradually building up the argument that the juvenile death penalty should now be considered "cruel and unusual punishment" because the "standards of decency" had evolved. Victor saw that what was defined as *cruel* in America, legally, was a moving target, but he believed the way to change that definition was steadily, over time, through state legislation and the courts. Eventually, the Supreme Court would have to take notice of the shift.

Though he'd never moved back home, Victor continued to think of himself as a seventh-generation Hoosier, and in the summer of 1985, he got a call from an office in Lake County, Indiana. On the line was a young attorney, Kevin Relphorde, who had just caught his first death-penalty case. His client was only fifteen—and a girl.

Victor sent the lawyer some materials, and he emphasized: the last juvenile executed in Indiana was in 1920, and the last juvenile girl executed in *any* state was in 1912. *I hope you can bring the prosecutor to his or her senses before the case goes much further,* he wrote.

This case was singular, Victor thought. Something to keep an eye on.

I
n October 1986—three months after her sentencing and just weeks before she would first hear from Bill Pelke—Paula decided to write to the American Civil Liberties Union. She addressed her letter to the ACLU's headquarters in New York City, certain she was too notorious at home to write the Indiana branch. *To Whom it may concern my name is Paula Cooper & Im sure you have heard a great deal about me . . .*

Kevin, as a public defender, was moving on to new assignments, and at the time Paula knew nothing about who was going to take up her appeal. A few people had given her the ACLU's address, saying the group could help her. She had the idea that her case could be an example—*an example to show others how cruel society really is.* She wrote, *I was told I am past the point of being rehabilitated. well because of my intelligence I consider that a laugh.*

Within days, the head of the ACLU's Capital Punishment Project, Henry Schwarzschild, replied: They were definitely aware of her case, and they were eager to help. Write or call collect anytime, he told her. Henry had forwarded their correspondence to both the Indiana branch and the State Public Defender, neither of whom *for a single moment,* he wrote, *shares the bloodthirst of the state.* A new public defender, he said, would soon step up to represent her. Henry sent her information about the death penalty, and about other juveniles on death row. He wrote, *I will very much want to stay in touch with you.*

About a week later, Paula received a letter from a lawyer Henry had contacted on her behalf. It was Victor Streib.

Representing Paula, Kevin had not used any of the data Victor had given him a year and a half earlier—and Paula had received the worst possible outcome. Victor had read the coverage of her sentencing and been shocked. In his experience, women were rarely sentenced to death, and fifteen-year-olds were almost never sentenced to death; so he thought of her situation as a "never-never." Yet here she was, on death row. Now Victor wrote directly to her: *I want to join Henry in assuring you most emphatically that a large number of people are quite concerned about your case and the sentence you received. I have spent ten years researching juvenile death sentences and find your sentence to be absolutely outrageous.* He was embarrassed on behalf of his home state.

Victor told Paula that he actually had some experience at the Indiana Women's Prison: In the mid-1970s, he'd taught a college course there, and remembered it as *not too pleasant a place to be.* He hoped he could play a role in changing her situation. He would help her new attorney in any way he could. If this case went to the Indiana Supreme Court, it would be a chance for Victor to challenge a law he didn't like in its most extreme application.

Please keep up your spirits, he wrote.

Paula replied quickly. She contacted Victor on the same day on which, unbeknownst to her, Bill Pelke was writing her from his shift at Bethlehem Steel. Her letter was cynical and angry—as angry as her first letter to Bill would be, not long afterward. She said she was not surprised by her sentence, not really; she'd lost faith in the courts by the time she was twelve. At this point, she wrote, *I want people to know how Indiana really does youngsters when they are in trouble & abused.* She told Victor, *you can do all the research you want on juveniles but it all comes out to be the same we always lose . . . every one wants you to be a perfect angel for them to spare your life, I dont plan on begging anyone for my miserable life, not for one minute.*

She hoped Victor would understand her. Most people she's dealt with, she said, *believe they must talk to me on a juvenile level but they gave me an adult punishment & I cant seem to put that one together.*

Within days, Victor began helping with an amicus brief on Paula's behalf. He had already sent some notes on the federal constitutional issues involved to the ACLU: how culpable a juvenile could be, how very rare and therefore extreme the death penalty was for someone that age. Victor had also heard about a bill slated to come before the Indiana General Assembly in a few months, to decide whether to raise the minimum age for capital punishment, and he hoped to testify. Right at that moment, there were thirty-eight people on death rows around the country who had been condemned as teenagers. A decision had to be made.

Shortly after connecting with Paula, Victor was invited to appear on the first season of *The Oprah Winfrey Show*, in a panel discussion about teenagers on death row.

Victor, as always, played the part of the expert. *Here I am again,* he thought, *this dowdy, plain-wrapper scholar, while everybody else was pounding on the Bible and screaming and yelling.* He'd felt it in front of his students, could see their eyes glaze over when he insisted on sticking to the data. But he would rather it be him than what he thought of as the "instant experts" who sprung up around these cases, making uninformed statements to the media or injecting camera-friendly levels of emotion into their commentary. He tried to stay low-key. Over and over, he repeated the facts, the history, the law—these were his ammunition. And whether or not God wanted someone to be punished by death, or whether or not the defendant "deserved" it—those were not things he was going to talk about.

Among the others on the panel was Dorothy Thompson, a woman from Oklahoma whose fifteen-year-old son Wayne was on death row for killing his sister's ex-husband. When Oprah asked Dorothy about her son's crime, she described how the victim, Charles Keene, had a history of being abusive toward her, her son, and her daughter (Charles's ex-wife) Vicky. Wayne slit Charles's throat and shot him, and afterward he rushed to his mother's house and told her, weeping, that Vicky wouldn't have to worry about Charles anymore. Now, right in front of Mrs. Thompson—who to Victor Streib appeared to be a very simple country woman, completely unprepared for this arena—a debate was being had as to whether or not her son should be put to death. A debate on television. He would never forget the look on her face: she was devastated.

By the time of this appearance, Wayne Thompson no longer had an attorney. Oklahoma did not permit his appellate public defender to take the case to the U.S. Supreme Court, and he was having trouble finding the boy new representation. The appeal soon ended up in the hands of a then untenured, thirty-four-year-old University of Oklahoma College of Law professor named Harry F. Tepker (known to his friends as Rick), by virtue of the fact that his office was across the hall from Wayne's previous lawyer. "I was not their first, or second, or third choice," Rick would later say, "for good reason." He'd heard about the fifteen-year-old on death row—the "baby case," his colleagues were calling it—and he knew it was a rare opportunity to tangle with a major constitutional question. This would be his first capital case, his first *criminal* case, and likely his one chance to appear as first chair before the highest court in the country.

Rick rang up Victor—at this point, the national authority on the death penalty for juveniles—and was frank about needing help. He told him that he was familiar with basic constitutional law because he taught it, but that he didn't teach criminal law or criminal procedure, and he knew nothing at all about arguing a capital case, never mind one involving a juvenile. And so they began working together. Drafting his piece of the Thompson brief stirred up some excitement in Victor: five years after the *Eddings* decision, perhaps the Court would be ready to make a bold statement. Fifteen had to be too young.

In February, when Anna and Giampaolo's interview with Paula was just hitting Italian and Indiana papers, the U.S. Supreme Court announced that it would hear *Thompson v. Oklahoma*.

————— ⚘ —————

That same month, the Indiana House Courts and Criminal Code Committee—ten representatives from across the state—gathers in a room the size of a classroom to hear testimony about House Bill 1022.

Rep. Earline Rogers, as the bill's sponsor, steps to the lectern. She repeats the disquieting fact that Indiana has a minimum age of ten years old for the death penalty, the lowest any state has specified. Her bill would raise it to sixteen. "People vary on which age they would choose," she concedes, "but they think we should not execute children."

This is not only a feeling among locals: as a representative of Gary, Rogers says, she has been contacted by people across the country and abroad in the aftermath of Paula Cooper's death sentence. The spokesperson for the Department of Correction, Vaughn Overstreet, says the same: The DOC has received a lot of mail about Paula's case—mostly from Italy and West Germany.

Others testifying in support of the bill include the prosecutor for Marion County (where Indianapolis is located) and representatives from the Indiana Catholic Conference, the Indiana Council of Churches, the ACLU, and Amnesty International. But the featured expert is Victor Streib. He'd hoped to speak out in favor of the bill since first hearing about it months ago, and, as has become the norm for him, he was called in to testify. He's never before had business in his home state, and he had a good feeling driving in from the airport.

He speaks, strategically, as a local, in the first-person plural—*we* have received calls from people abroad concerned that *we* execute ten-year-olds. With personal investment, he says, "Indiana, I'm afraid, has become a worldwide scandal on this issue."

But, he offers up, this notoriety is unearned. "In fact," Victor says, "Indiana does *not* execute juveniles." There are three individuals on the state's death row right now for crimes committed under the age of eighteen—but the state, he points out, has executed only three adolescents in its history, the last way back in 1920. About teenagers, he says, "You don't let them vote, you don't let them drink, you don't let them serve on juries. You don't let them do all of those things because they're not quite mature enough, not quite sophisticated enough to make mature judgments." Altering the minimum age in the statute would better reflect the way adolescents are viewed in Indiana. And for the tough-on-crime in the audience, Victor frames the death penalty as a lame deterrent for teenagers, using language designed to cater to the crowd. "Seventeen-year-old punks are not afraid of death," he says. "They think it is *Rambo*, going out in glory instead of growing old." Prison, he argues, is a better threat.

After the committee meeting, Earline sits down with the Indiana Prosecuting Attorneys Council. To satisfy their demands, she agrees to allow the waiver of fourteen- and fifteen-year-olds into adult court—but those under sixteen will not be eligible for death. A clause requested by Jack Crawford is also worked in, stating that the bill will not go into effect until the fall and will not be retroactive—in other words, it cannot apply to Paula Cooper. In a collegial spirit, though with little love lost between her and the Lake County prosecutor, Earline announces that she will bend to "the present mood of the community" if it helps to pass her bill.

Over the coming weeks, she sits through more political grandstanding as 1022 moves forward. One conservative Democrat from Lake County, a longtime assemblyman, pushes for children ten to thirteen to *also* be eligible for adult court. Earline makes peace with the compromise—as long as death remains off the table for children under sixteen. The bill passes the House 89 to 9.

She is going to make this happen.

It moves on to the State Senate. But first there's yet *another* hearing, at which more amendments are proposed and dismissed. The meeting is memorable for Earline because of another white Democrat from Lake County who is emphatic that teenagers remain eligible for the death sentence. At the lectern, his gestures become increasingly passionate as he mimics the manner in which he believes Paula stabbed her victim. Earline is chilled by this horrific caricature, unbecoming of an elected representative; it strikes her, immediately, as racist.

Regardless, when the full Senate votes, House Bill 1022 passes 41 to 8. The first week of April, Governor Orr signs twenty-one bills into law, and 1022 is one of them. It will go into effect that September 1987.

In every piece of news coverage about the bill over the preceding months, Paula was mentioned. But the new law will not apply to her. When Victor testified, the bill had not yet been amended this way, and now, learning of its passage, he tells a reporter he feels it's "a little dodgy—it's not normally the way that we pass our statutes. People said, *Well, that is going to let Paula Cooper off.* And then they said, *Okay, we'll take her out and put her over in a corner and say nobody* else *can be sentenced to death at that age."*

He does not feel great about it. The girl's future remains wholly uncertain.

Three weeks later, Judge Kimbrough is killed just before midnight when his car, traveling east on U.S. 20 near County Line Road, runs into a semitrailer truck. The details of his death are not made public, but he had been out at a late-night bar with the bailiffs and his former partner, Fred Work, something they did often. The judge lived nearby, in Gary's Miller Beach neighborhood, and he'd been on his way home. He'd had a lot to drink (his alcohol levels were found to be at twice the legal limit) and refused to let one of the bailiffs drive him. Fred said he'd follow. And so his old friend was right behind him when the judge slid his car under the back of the semi.

Around two a.m., the court reporter starts making calls to Patti Wolter and the other staffers, and they rush to the court building. The tuxedo Patti had just picked up from the dry cleaners was in Kimbrough's car: he was supposed to chaperone his daughter to her prom that Friday.

His fellow judge Richard Maroc gets a late-night call as well, from the sheriff. "Holy shit. *No.*" He and his wife stay up all night, and the calls keep coming in. First thing in the morning, the judges hold a meeting to decide what to do; attorneys and staffers are crying. But people's lives are at stake; families are in court; there are defendants who have pled guilty, waiting for Kimbrough to sentence them. So an interim judge is appointed, and everyone tries to get through the day.

The following Wednesday, all Lake County government offices are closed to commemorate his death. The memorial service takes place at eleven a.m. in the Genesis Center, a large convention center in downtown Gary, before more than one thousand five hundred people. The body of the judge lies in state for two hours, several eulogies are delivered, and then everyone motorcades several miles, south on Broadway, to the cemetery. After the burial, many in the criminal law community go to lunch together: a long affair. People are stunned. At the same time, talk begins to spread—that the judge had never recovered from the Pelke case, that his drinking had gotten worse, that the sentencing of those four girls had led, in this way, to his death.

Paula had learned about the accident within hours, from Monica Foster. Soon, reporters contact her to ask what she thinks of the news. She tells them that Judge Kimbrough had given the public the sentence they wanted; that he'd done his job, and she doesn't blame him for it. She imagines that he must be at peace, that God has no problems with him.

To Bill Pelke, Paula confesses that she cried for a long time when she first heard. The judge had sentenced her to die, but she writes Bill that she *felt a closeness to him*—this man who stood in such stark contrast to Herman Cooper—*as if he were my father.* More than anything, Paula is shaken by the randomness of it, the feeling that none of us controls our own destiny. *we are all on death row & the last day of April his death sentence was completed & it should teach a lot of people we all have a date that is already planned.*

Twelve

THE
CHAPEL

A week after Kimbrough's death, Bill has his coming-out in the press: front-page stories about his support of Paula Cooper in the *Gary Post-Tribune* and *The Indianapolis Star.* He had recently received a call from RAI, Italian national television, inviting him to fly to Rome. Their Sunday talk show *Domenica In* wants to tape a segment about Paula Cooper, and on May 14, the second anniversary of Ruth's death, he will travel to Italy. Each paper runs a photo of Bill in close-up, with his very full beard and bushy 1970s hair. He looks, he thinks, like a terrorist.

Bill feels good about his comments, however. He told one reporter that, in Lake County, he believes "ninety-five percent of the people would like to see Paula burn and burn immediately," but "if you live as a Christian, forgiveness should be a way of life." To another, he described himself as "a loner" in all this—but not for much longer. His call for forgiveness, he said, would change his family's thinking.

As if challenging his hopes, the *Post-Tribune* soon runs a follow-up, SHOULD COOPER DIE? VICTIM'S FAMILY DIVIDED. In it, Bob Pelke, whom the journalist reached in Florida, says that he and his two sisters "are 100 percent behind the Prosecutor's Office and what they did," and that he wishes his son were not going to Rome. It also features two pull-quotes, just underneath the headline, pitting son against father:

> *My grandmother died a martyr for Jesus Christ, and Christ forgave his enemies. My grandmother would want us to do the same.*
>
> —William Pelke

> *I believe my son is one of the so-called new breed who doesn't feel you should have to pay your debts. That is contrary to my philosophy.*
>
> —Robert Pelke

With this new wave of press, coworkers at the mill who had been kind to him after his grandmother was killed now shout in Bill's face. They call him "crazy"; they call him a "bleeding-heart liberal" (*that's* a new one). Each time, he keeps his cool; he doesn't address them head-on. The mill becomes a harsher place, but he has always been alone up in the crane cab.

Other than Bill's time in Vietnam, this will be his first trip outside the United States, and he's elated. He has no desire to go sightseeing; he is consumed instead with the idea of bringing his new convictions to Europe, sharing them with a vast audience. In preparation for the trip, he begins fasting—his first fast since college—and these two weeks before the taping will be twice as long as he's ever gone. He sticks to only water and orange juice and relies on the old techniques: whenever they wash over you, your hunger pangs are a reminder to pray and to meditate on the purpose of your actions. He does a lot of praying.

On the way to O'Hare airport in Chicago, he stops at Ridgelawn Cemetery in southern Gary. A large relief by the wrought-iron gates shows two angels blowing their trumpets, and it reads *Blessed Are the Dead Who Die in the Lord*. Ruth Pelke is buried here, alongside her husband Oscar. The marker is simple, a stone plaque embedded in the ground, flush with the grass: his name and hers, linked by the sign of the cross. Bill takes time to pray.

His cousin Judi and her mother Ruthie (Ruth's stepdaughter) live near the cemetery, and Bill visits them before his flight. Sitting in the living room, he tells them about his trip. Ruthie, now sixty-one, is his father's sister—one of the two Bob told the press were in agreement with the prosecutor—and so Bill does not expect her to sympathize. But when he's done speaking, Ruthie tells him something: When Bob phoned her, two years ago nearly to the day, to say that their stepmother had been killed—Ruth, who'd let her follow her around the barn as a little girl, who'd let her bring the cows in from the pasture, whose name she shared—she forgave the killer before she'd even gotten off the call. At the time, she had no idea who that person might be, but she forgave them.

Now, among the Pelkes, they are three. And Bill and Judi and Ruthie bow their heads and pray together before the women send him off.

Bill is twelve days into his fast, and on the flight to Rome he is seated by the galley, where the food is stored. When the flight attendants begin warming up the meals for the dinner service, he feels ready to lose his mind. The hunger, for the next seven hours, is a reminder to keep praying. He knows he'll be fine; he is stronger, probably, than he's ever been. Just the day before, he'd told a reporter, "By being able to forgive Paula Cooper, I have realized that no one could ever hurt me again."

Together Bill and Father Vito step through the three-story colonnade and into the expanse of St. Peter's Square: here, across the centuries, millions of people have witnessed a string of popes appear at a window of the Apostolic Palace to bless the crowd. Inside that complex are the personal rooms of Pope John Paul II, one of the world's most recognizable men; even nonbelievers know his face.

Bill had arrived in Rome to find the cameramen on strike and the taping of the show delayed. Rather than return home, he decided to take more time off from the mill and wait it out. And this is how Bill, who was raised to believe the Catholic Church is the *Whore of Babylon* in the

Book of Revelation, finds himself at the Vatican accompanied by a friar in a hooded robe.

Father Vito leads Bill through the crowd and out of the square, and they walk slowly, winding along the edge of Vatican City until they arrive at the place. They pass through fortress walls, then one great hall and another, one galleria and another, and eventually into the chapel. He knows what every visitor wants to see.

And what Bill sees now arrests him: the tremendous human story, unwinding across the vast space. He is not a man who thinks about art, or who would go out of his way to visit a museum, but he is a man who responds to stories, particularly stories from the Bible. And as Bill walks through the chapel, staring upward, gawking, he knows the stories that span the ceiling. There is David straddling the giant Goliath, ready to cut off his head; and the prophet Jonah being swallowed by a great fish. There is Genesis: God with His hand outstretched, making the first man, Adam, his body laid across the new green earth. And all around there is God's justice: Adam and Eve banished from Eden for disobeying His law and eating from the Tree of Knowledge; the Great Flood, families fleeing from the rising waters; and largest of all, Christ's Second Coming and the Last Judgment. It covers the entire wall that stretches out behind the altar: so many bodies, clothed and unclothed; so many men and women standing before God to learn whether they will spend the afterlife in pain or in comfort, whether their faith was enough, whether their transgressions have truly been forgiven.

The church in which Bill was brought up has none of this pomp and circumstance, is suspicious of it. But he is deeply impressed by the situation in which he finds himself. The grandeur. This holy place. This is the world that has received him and his message.

While Bill is in Rome, Paula mails letters to his house in Portage anyway. She's anxious about his trip and the position it puts him in. Two nights in a row, she's had a nightmare about trying to reach him in Italy, a dream flooded with hateful feelings from his family. She says Touchette warned her that this time would be stressful for Bill, because of all the people who disagree with his actions. If he were to stop supporting her, she writes, *I will understand it for real.* She looks at the photo Bill sent of his grandmother and feels how inadequate her apology to the Pelkes was. She thinks about giving a speech one day, as a way to try to set things right—a speech addressed to his family. She doesn't know where or when or how that would happen, but she thinks about it.

RAI finally tapes the talk-show segment with Bill, to air that Sunday afternoon. The *Domenica In* hostess Raffaella Carrà, whom the Italian press often call "the queen of television," is also a hit pop singer, and her show is watched by nearly half the country. The program features a mix of current events and lighter segments—performances by Raffaella herself, popular Italian entertainers, or international artists like Duran Duran or Whitney Houston. Sitting beside Raffaella in his best suit and a fresh haircut, Bill feels more relaxed than he'd expected. He's never met a woman as glamorous as her, in a white silk blouse and cigarette pants, her platinum hair cut in a perfect bob. Bill tells her about his revelation, the moment he realized he was meant to forgive. The image of his grandmother crying in a plea for compassion: he describes this on Italian national television, with Raffaella translating. Father Greganti joins them, and he tells the audience that the petition for Paula Cooper now has half a million signatures.

Throughout his stay, late at night in his room, Bill has had several phone calls with the Gary *Post-Tribune* and the AP, which sent word of his trip back home and throughout the Midwest. The AP stories repeated comments from his father expressing his sadness and regret at what Bill is doing abroad. There is also, in the days just before and after Bill's return home, a string of letters from *Post-Tribune* readers in Lake County, most of which are sympathetic—questioning the death penalty for a person so young, debating whether or not the Bible, under any circumstance, permits the taking of a life. But the voice from home that Bill is most eager to hear is Judy's: the two have spoken on the phone most nights since his arrival in Rome. It has become clear, slowly, that she has absorbed the shock of his message. She no longer views him as radical, unstable. She is considering what he has to say, and she is relieved that others are listening now too, even if they are mostly across the ocean.

When his return flight lands in Chicago, Judy is there to meet him at the airport. It is not very long before they decide to get married.

Two hours north of Rome, the town of Assisi was built on the slope of Mount Subasio, surrounded by medieval stone walls and overlooking the Chiasco and Topino river valleys and their sprawl of olive trees. So much of the place retains the appearance it had when Francesco di Bernardone walked its streets, nearly eight centuries before Paula Cooper, before the death of Ruth Pelke, seven centuries before Italian unification. Francesco—the founder of the Franciscan Order, the Order of Lesser Brothers—would die in his forties, and less than two years later, in 1228, he would be sainted by the Catholic Church.

The son of a wealthy fabric merchant, and a playboy, Francesco believed that one night, when he was about twenty-five, he heard the voice of God, asking him to abandon his worldly values. And so he began to transform his life. He began praying in public, even in the town square; he gave constantly: cash, or his own belt, his hat, the shirt on his back. He sold his possessions and stockpiles of his father's fabrics, gave some of the money away in the street and used the rest to repair the run-down church of San Damiano. He camped out there, in the church just outside the city, bought materials, and set to work on the construction with his own hands. On the occasions when he would be seen in the streets of Assisi, the sight of him shocked people. Here was this young man who'd wrapped himself in fine stuff, now emaciated and carrying himself like a beggar. For what he'd taken from the family, his father Pietro asked the bishop of Assisi to command Francesco to appear before him and be accused of theft. In the presence of the bishop, Francesco handed his clothing to his father, one item at a time, until he stood naked before him. He renounced his inheritance, and then he renounced his father in favor of God the Father.

At about the same age as Francesco at the time of that first revelation, Vito Bracone, having completed seminary, arrived in Assisi to continue his studies to become a priest. He was assigned to the Basilica di Santa Maria degli Angeli (Saint Mary of the Angels), in the valley at the foot of Mount Subasio. The building is vast, boxy, baroque, with a great dome and triple-height doors—the seventh largest church in Christendom. But inside, at the crossing, directly beneath the dome, there stands a small stone building erected centuries before the basilica. It is awash in cool, clear light. This is the Portiuncula, the crude chapel in which San Francesco prayed and gathered together his brothers.

This is the chapel that Francesco was lent by the Benedictines, the place where men would travel to find him, having stripped themselves—like him—of their material belongings. They wanted to dedicate themselves to helping others—and so Francesco sent them out to wander the roads and towns, preaching. By the time there were a dozen of them, they were on their way to becoming an order and a movement. Within twelve years the Franciscan order, the Order of Lesser Brothers, grew to a few thousand, divided into provinces that came together at the Portiuncula. By the 1230s, after the death of Francesco, the brothers' missions had spread throughout Europe and the Middle East, and the order continued to grow. Four centuries later, the basilica was completed, built up around the modest chapel: one man's seemingly unhinged gesture now projected outward, become enormous. During that era, Franciscan friars followed Spanish and French settlers into the Americas and were eventually pushed back; in the nineteenth and early twentieth centuries, they migrated to the United States again, to minister to the country's new Catholic immigrants. In the 1980s, nearly eight hundred friars live in the U.S., across six provinces. Five precise replicas of the Portiuncula have been built around the country.

Many years after his ordination, Father Vito now flies to Indianapolis to visit Paula Cooper, and he stays with the American friars at the Sacred Heart parish, of the Sacred Heart Franciscan province, on the city's Old Southside. He knows one of the brothers there, Father Justin from Omaha: they met when Justin spent a semester as a novice in Assisi. He brings the younger brother along with him to the Women's Prison, as a guide and occasional translator.

For the prison staff, this is their first encounter with men in the long brown robes. This particular inmate continues to draw unexpected forms of attention.

Locked into a visiting room, the brothers sit around a table with Paula in plastic chairs. She is dressed in teen-formal style, in a dark, long-sleeved dress, with big clip-on earrings and a banana clip in her hair. Justin, an easygoing American, soon has her laughing. Having taught high school for several years, he sees her, in some ways, like Earline Rogers does: just another kid who was ready to blow up at nothing, to explode—and one day she did. He feels for the girl. *A single act*, he thinks, *cannot make her an evil person.*

They do not talk about faith or ask Paula any big questions, they simply let her say whatever comes to mind. Despite her laughter, Paula strikes Vito as struggling with a deep depression. A couple of days earlier, she tells them, the woman in the cell next to her attempted suicide and is now in a coma. She says she thinks it's easy to give in to that temptation in isolation.

Finally, the pair of guards returns: the visitors have run out of time. Father Vito asks Paula, "You know that I don't have the same religion as you—I'm a Catholic priest—but is there something that you'd like to ask?" And she grabs his hands and says, "I want you to pray for me."

As they grip each other, he says quickly, improvising, "Dear God, I entrust this young girl into your hands." She begins to cry, and asks, "Do you think that God can forgive me?" The friar tells her, very simply, "Even if men cannot forgive you, God is much better than them."

As the guards step forward and place the cuffs around her wrists, Vito thinks he sees a dark mood drop like a veil over the girl's face.

The priests' next stop is two and a half hours north: the Lake County Prosecutor's Office.

Jack Crawford is at his desk when his secretary enters: "There's a monk outside who wants to see you." It's Friday afternoon, and Jack does not need anything complicated at the end of his week.

"A monk? What do you mean?" (Not being cloistered, the man is, technically, a *friar.*)

"Somebody from the Vatican. A representative from the pope."

"Does he speak English?"

"He's got a translator."

She brings in the pair of men, and Father Vito presents him with some kind of credentials—Vatican credentials, Jack thinks. The prosecutor may be less devout these days, but he is impressed. The friar says that Pope John Paul II would like to express his belief that Paula Cooper should not be given the death sentence.

The message does not have the intended impact. If the head of one of the Black churches in the area had come to Jack this way, the visit might have swayed him more than the man before him. Instead, Jack asks himself, *What's this monk doing so far away from the Vatican?*

He is not receptive to this priest, and he is not happy with William, the Pelke family outsider. Back when Jack was weighing the death penalty in this case, he and his team made a solid effort to speak to Ruth's family members—he thinks he must have spoken to a dozen of them. Because no prosecutor or politician wants to see the victim's family complain in public later on—a nightmare. He needed their support, or at least their cooperation. So he sat in Bob Pelke's living room, and he'd done what he usually does in a murder case: he let the family speak for a while about their anger, their sadness, their immediate needs. Then he took his turn: he talked about "justice," and "process," and laid out their options. And, as always, he finished with "Is there anyone here who is adamantly against my decision to seek the death sentence for the killer? I want to hear about it *now*." And he did not leave until the more reluctant relatives had said, "Mr. Crawford, you do what you feel is right." *To a person*, they had been okay with going for death. They hadn't shouted, "We want her hung from the nearest lamppost!"—it was more modest than that. More like "We want the law to take its course." In his experience—of the seventeen death sentences he would win in his decade as prosecutor, this was his ninth—the victim's family members always sign off. They may not be *active* supporters of capital punishment, but they give their permission. All the Pelkes he met with, they signed off.

But here this man comes, speaking out with an authority that derives from—where, exactly? Jack sees Bill Pelke as an outlier. He is not someone Jack spoke with; he is someone on the edges of his family, now living a life separate from the clan. It irritates Jack that this comparative outsider should be pushing back in public against the wishes of the family, against the hard work the Prosecutor's Office put into achieving justice in a heinous situation—as if Bill has the right to go rogue. The Pelke grandson strikes him as someone enamored with his own brand of celebrity. And is it healthy for someone to be that interested in media attention, to crave it? What does that say about a man?

Paula reaches her eighteenth birthday. After two and a half years on death row, she is finally, legally, an adult.

She makes note of the day—but she also has another kind of birthday, one she marked in her mind last month: July 11, the date of her sentencing. She recently learned that Judge Kimbrough's replacement, Judge Richard Conroy, will not be granting her a new sentencing hearing. There will be no do-over in Lake County; she will have to transfer her hopes to the Indiana Supreme Court. Only a few weeks ago, she was lying on her bed, looking up at the ceiling, and thinking about the events of her life: *its like living in a story book with no ending to it. & it just goes on & on every day.*

The Women's Prison allows the residents in general population to invite a few family and friends to a picnic on their birthday—but Paula's request, coming from someone on death row, was denied (this, too, makes headlines). Instead, a rally is held for her in Rome: one hundred people gather outside the U.S. embassy to celebrate, holding signs that read 100 MORE BIRTHDAYS, PAULA and PAULA COOPER MUST NOT DIE. Caritas, one of the biggest charities in Italy, and ACLI, a major workers' rights group, both take part. The renowned antifascist writer Alberto Moravia sends a letter about Paula to Governor Orr. *Where there's no compassion,* he writes, *there cannot be justice.*

At the same time, Anna Guaita visits her in prison, alongside Monica: Paula now has permission to receive a limited number of journalists. She gives Monica a hug and asks a lot of questions about her life. Monica had wanted to surprise her with a small birthday cake—she'd planned to offer slices to the guards, like peace offerings—but Superintendent Trigg forbade it.

To Anna, the tone of Paula's voice is as babyish as it was months ago over the phone, and there is a childlike quality to her that does not feel like a put-on. In some ways, however, Paula seems older. The girl has become heavier-set from her sedentary life, and Anna thinks that she moves and speaks like an elderly woman, someone resigned to living at a slower pace, someone for whom time is relative.

Paula says she's learned to accept that, even if her sentence is eventually commuted, it may take months or years. She spends so many of her waking hours in isolation, but she insists that she can handle it—"I've always been alone, even before I was locked up." Anna does not believe her. But Paula recently mailed notes to Bill Pelke that read, *I am a special person & I know that I am & no one has to tell me it either*, and *Im just too strong to be knocked down & not get up.*

Thirteen

STANDARDS
OF DECENCY

On a fall morning thick with Florida heat, the streets of downtown Miami are being scoured by dogs. Handlers lead the German shepherds to manhole covers one by one, allowing them to sniff for explosives. Mailboxes along the route have been removed. Sharpshooters are taking up positions on nearby rooftops. Eleven miles of Interstate 95, the main artery of South Florida, have been shut down.

It is September 1987, and the city is preparing for the imminent arrival of Pope John Paul II. On his second tour of the United States, his first under President Reagan, the Holy Father will visit nine cities in ten days and give dozens of talks—on peace, poverty, materialism. He is the moral leader of the Church, its figurehead, and to see him in person, for a believer, is to glimpse someone who is living their shared principles completely: belief in the flesh. More than a million Americans will come out to see John Paul II, and many millions more will see him on television—the Catholic Church considers this well worth the cost of nearly $10 million. Its investment in the States has paid off handsomely: before the Kennedy era, the idea of a Catholic president was hard to imagine; now one out of four Americans are members of the Church, a number that has held firm for decades.

The next day, public schools are closed. A public Mass is scheduled to take place, in which a thousand priests and a thousand lay ministers, all in white, will hand out Communion—the wafers and wine that are "the body and blood" of Christ—and the pope will bless the crowd. The site of the Mass takes up a square mile of Tamiami Park, west of the airport. Three stories of stadium bleachers, carpeted in black, lead to an altar under a bright white canopy; above this platform, from which the pope will speak, workers have erected a massive white cross, one hundred feet tall and made of steel. Five thousand officers are on hand, some armed with grenade launchers. About a quarter of a million people have gathered in the park, sweating in the intense heat, many dressed in the Vatican colors. One group of locals crawled the five miles from their homes on their knees.

The papal motorcade begins to wind its way into the park, led by dozens of motorcycles, police helicopters overhead following its route. And soon, pushing gently through the crowd—people are frantically waving—the pope himself becomes visible, a figure in white, encased in a bulletproof-glass box atop a white jeep. He turns his head slowly from side to side, lifts one hand in greeting, then the other; he looks as if he were gliding through the masses.

Storm clouds have been gathering. It begins to drizzle, and the sky goes dark and it starts to rain in earnest. But few move. At the foot of the bleachers, the Holy Father disappears from view.

Soon the bishops in their tall mitres, all in white and gold, begin a procession—and behind them, in line, reemerges John Paul II, changed into his vestments, carrying his long papal staff. Slowly, he climbs the many steps to take his place under the canopy, beneath the steel cross. "Let us pray," he announces—and is met with thunder. He looks up and smiles. The rain becomes heavier and heavier, and now it is a lightning storm. Part of the sound system dies, and the live TV coverage is cut short. But the crowd remains, standing still. He continues speaking even as lightning strikes nearby. A great flock of priests stands ready to administer the Eucharist to the crowd in the downpour, should they make it that far.

For his flight to Miami, the pope had boarded a Boeing 747 the press dubbed Shepherd One. The sixteen members of his closest entourage, in dark clerical robes, had occupied the first-class cabin as always; in coach were the security guards and the Vatican media. Paying their own way were some seventy reporters. They will stay up until the early morning nearly every night of the tour, sleep a couple of hours (often in the air), then repeat—the next day, in the next city.

The papal cabin is upstairs. But on the trip from Rome, as he sometimes does on longer flights, the pope had strolled back through the press section, where the reporters jockeyed for his attention. Among them was Giampaolo Pioli, who had joined the entourage for the length of the tour. Somewhere over the Atlantic, he managed to ask John Paul II if he would raise the issue of the death penalty with President Reagan.

"We will see," said the Holy Father.

Then another question: The Paula Cooper case, will he mention it?

"Maybe it will be necessary," said the pope, "to talk also about her."

In Miami, he is unable to complete the Mass. But he meets with President Reagan that afternoon, on live television and then in private. And now John Paul II is airborne again, en route to Columbia, South Carolina. This is followed by stops in New Orleans, San Antonio, Phoenix, Los Angeles, Monterey, San Francisco, and finally Detroit.

While the pope is in Detroit, his press secretary Joaquín Navarro-Valls hands him a letter. The secretary, in turn, had received it from an Italian in their press corps, Giampaolo Pioli, who had gotten it from Bill Touchette.

Three pages written by Paula Cooper. They are mostly about remorse, a thread she has tugged at since her sentencing: *I believe if more people would look a little deeper maybe they will see what I really feel and how sorry I really am.*

She asks the pope to help her, if only through prayer. What she wants is peace, she says, and *to live even if its 60 yrs in prison.* She repeats what she'd said to Judge Kimbrough: *I've never really had a chance and that's all I really want is a chance.* Her words, written on death row, have made it into the papal cabin of Shepherd One.

Within a few days, the pope and his entourage have returned to Rome. In a Saturday morning news conference, Navarro-Valls tells the press that the pope has expressed a desire: that the death sentence of the girl in Indiana be lifted.

In D.C., the oral argument in Wayne Thompson's case is approaching, just a few weeks away. *Thompson v. Oklahoma* is a high-profile case for the Supreme Court, only its second hearing on the death penalty for juveniles in its history.

Wayne himself is now twenty and has been on death row for four years. Over the previous months, Victor Streib has answered the occasional letter from Wayne's mother Dorothy, tried to keep her calm and steady. At one point, she sent him a newspaper clipping that featured a photo of her son jogging in the penitentiary yard: he looked young and painfully small. Victor wrote back, *Wayne's picture looks like he is staying in pretty good shape! I am also a runner but haven't been as slim as he is for thirty years!* Repeatedly, he tells her about the many people working hard to prepare her son's case.

He and Rick Tepker played it both ways in their brief to the Court. Taking a page from the *Eddings* argument, they raised two questions related to the Eighth Amendment, one narrow and one broad: Was it "cruel and unusual punishment" to sentence this individual to death because of specifics in his sentencing? And, should the Court set a minimum age for the death penalty across the country? One of these questions, of course, has much bigger implications than the other. If Wayne wins this appeal, depending on the grounds of the decision, his case could spare the lives of thirty other death-row inmates and end the death sentence for juveniles entirely.

Since *Eddings*, the liberal-dominated Supreme Court era of Chief

Justices Warren and Burger has undergone a shift to the right, led by Reagan-appointed chief William Rehnquist. The last six years, under Reagan, have also boosted a newer strain of conservatism. In 1985, Attorney General Edwin Meese, in a talk at the American Bar Association, declared that the administration would be promoting a "jurisprudence of original intention"—that the Court should make decisions based on an understanding of the original intentions of the writers of the Constitution and the Bill of Rights. In its strictest interpretation, this is a view of the Constitution as having a meaning that was fixed in 1787, a view that not only does not allow for the concept of "evolving" standards but also seeks to interpret present-day standards through a lens two centuries old. In 1986, Reagan added Antonin Scalia to the Court, both a strong conservative and a staunch originalist.

The other Republicans on the Court are of a different profile. Sandra Day O'Connor, also a Reagan appointee and the first female justice, is a centrist and often a swing vote, while John Paul Stevens will go on to become a prominent voice for the Court's liberal contingent. Harry Blackmun, appointed as a "law-and-order" conservative by Nixon, had instead become someone far less predictable; he was the author of 1973's *Roe v. Wade* decision. The conservative Lewis Powell has just retired, and so they are down one member until his replacement is named and confirmed. The Democrats—William Brennan, Byron White, and Thurgood Marshall—have a history of voting to limit capital punishment and had voted with the *Furman* majority, but are only three in number. With this combination of minds on the Court, the outcome of Wayne Thompson's case is far from certain.

On the day of the oral argument, visitors file from the Great Hall into the Courtroom and take their places in the pews of the public gallery, behind the bar. Unlike in the average courtroom in this country, a person has a sense of smallness under this coffered ceiling, four stories high, the space flanked by Ionic columns and marble friezes. Rick and

Victor are seated at counsel table before the Supreme Court bench; across from them is Oklahoma assistant attorney general David Lee, who argued *Eddings* just six years ago. Rick knows Lee well: back home, he had arranged a moot court for him in preparation for that case. It's as if the man has become, by virtue of circumstance, the go-to advocate for the execution of teenagers.

The sound of the gavel: everyone rises. The eight emerge from behind red-velvet drapery and take their places on the bench. When Chief Justice Rehnquist announces their case, Rick steps to the lectern.

"Mr. Chief Justice, and may it please the Court . . ." He has thirty minutes to speak.

Rick begins by summarizing their points. But within just a few minutes, the justices cut in with questions: Would it be cruel and unusual punishment to execute someone who committed a crime at, let's say, "the age of seventeen years and nine months"? asks O'Connor. Rick says they are arguing for a minimum age of eighteen.

Blackmun presses, "Of course, sixteen would save Mr. Thompson anyway, would it not?" Like Earline Rogers, Rick and Victor are coming up against a reluctance to go any higher—and so they take what they can get. Rick says that every state with a minimum death-penalty age has chosen sixteen, so perhaps, he concedes, that's the clearest consensus.

They talk about mitigating circumstances in the case, and Rick refers back to the *Eddings* decision for support. But the discussion is, ultimately, a very high-stakes numbers game. In his brief for *Eddings*, Lee had challenged opposing counsel as basing his argument upon "human decency" principles, not the objective factors the Court demanded for any Eighth Amendment debate. One of Eddings's only amicus briefs, coauthored by the relatively small American Orthopsychiatric Association, had argued that juveniles are immature and lack impulse control and a grasp of moral concepts—but their statement was mostly supported by conceptual, data-weak breakdowns of adolescent development. (Adolescent psychology would not become a significant field until around the late 1980s.) Both sides in *Eddings* also lacked comprehensive numbers on the death sentences and executions of juveniles across death-penalty states. Eddings's attorney wrote that, *unfortunately*, little such information had been collected since *Furman*. But today two sets of numbers are woven into the arguments before the Court: the new data collected by Victor, Watt Espy, and the LDF; and the minimum ages state legislatures have set for the death penalty in recent years.

The state, as in *Eddings*, would like to avoid talk of numbers—as if such a thing were possible. David Lee veers away from words like "child" and "boy," referring to Wayne instead as a "young murderer" and juveniles convicted of homicide as "a significant class of violent criminals." But Blackmun immediately poses the same pointed question Stevens asked him during the *Eddings* argument: "Suppose Thompson had been ten years old? What would be your position then?"

Lee's reply remains what it was six years ago: a grudging admission that ten would be too young. He is forced to concede that "there is a bottom somewhere." Lee eventually floats a minimum age of fourteen, citing Blackstone's *Commentaries on the Laws of England*—the eighteenth-century treatise that influenced the development of the American legal system—as labeling that "the age of common-law incapacity."

Marshall, the first Black justice and a civil rights champion, does not sound pleased with this reliance on norms from 1765. "I would say that our educational system and our government and everything else has sure *progressed* from Blackstone. Has it not?"

"Well, yes, Your Honor."

Observing closely from counsel table, Victor thinks to himself: The state has no sound logic here; the prosecutor is going by his gut.

But the data grounds them once again. O'Connor asks when a state last executed someone fifteen or under at the time of their crime, and Lee can only think of someone sixteen, who was executed in 1948. As far as Oklahoma, he admits the state has *never* executed someone whose crime was committed under eighteen. He points to another number: over the past three years, across the country, there have been six people on death row for crimes committed at fifteen.

When pressed by Brennan as to *how many* of those six had their sentences carried out, however, the answer from Lee is none.

"None has been carried out?"

"No, Your Honor."

"Any significance to that, do you think?"

As the months roll by, Paula leans harder on, grows closer to, her legal trio: Monica, Patti, Touchette. With Touchette, she has finally let down her guard. When her cell is occasionally without heat in the wintertime, he rubs her cold hands during his visits, and now she is crocheting a blanket to keep *him* warm. He becomes easily frustrated when journalists write things about Paula that he doesn't like; in the middle of a particularly aggressive interview with her at the prison, he flew into a rage. Paula saw in him, in that moment, something very familiar: *He has a temper,* she thought, *just like I do.* And she realized that his anger had another dimension: the desire to protect her.

While Touchette begins preparing to take their appeal to the Indiana Supreme Court, Patti and Monica remain focused on keeping their client sane and steady. Monica found her a minister unaffiliated with IWP, who can come talk to her about the Bible, something Paula has longed for; and she found Paula a therapist, after nearly two years on death row without access to a mental health counselor who couldn't be called to testify against her.

Monica has another dimension to her life now: she recently eloped, to the Caribbean, with a man she'd known for just a few months. She met Bob Hammerle through her work at the Public Defender Council. He had been a Marion County public defender too, since the mid-1970s, straight out of law school. Bob was forty-two (thirteen years older than

Monica), and, unlike the Italian American girl from New Jersey, he was a real local—from Batesville, a very small, very white city an hour south of Indy. But they were both recovering Catholics who'd found religion in their work—attorneys known as crusaders, professionals who took their cases personally, large presences in the courtroom. And Monica was impressed when Bob began joining in talks with Paula on the phone and the occasional trip to IWP. He'd divorced young, and she had always sworn off marriage—the whole thing was impulsive. But each had a deep understanding of what drove the other, and he knew how to make her laugh really hard.

At the same time, Paula witnesses the toll Monica's work has started taking on her, with her growing load of death-penalty cases. She has less time to visit the prison, and when she does, she can seem anxious; her skin has been breaking out. When Monica's mood is up, Paula doesn't talk about her own depression. She wants to see her friend happy, not spoil it. She finds a way to shake off the dark feelings herself.

Paula is still being penalized after a series of write-ups by the staff. Since the start of her incarceration, she's regularly clashed with two guards in particular, and she claims she's been "jumped" by staff four times; *they* say it's been in response to her behavior. The write-ups have left Paula living an even more constricted life: she's not allowed recreation time, books, or use of the phone (except to call her lawyers), and her radio and TV have been confiscated. She often finds herself exhausted. She wants to set goals for herself, to study, but it's hard to have an accomplishment mindset when confined to one single room, twenty-three hours out of every day.

Superintendent Trigg and Cloid Shuler, the deputy commissioner of the state Department of Correction, decide to speak to an AP reporter about Paula. Trigg describes her as "very defiant"; Shuler says Paula "has not been a model citizen." Over the past year, he adds, she's been cited seven times for disorderly conduct and assaulting staff. He mentions a recent alleged threat with a pencil, and kicking—none of these records are made available to the press or to Paula's attorneys—and claims that this inmate

is "a very immature and aggressive young lady." "Someone facing death doesn't
have much to lose," says
Trigg. To a reporter for the
Post-Tribune, Shuler seems
to explain the staff's public
comments as pushback aga-
inst Paula's sympathetic
press. "I think our employees are tired of seeing her
portrayed differently than
they know her."

Paula being interviewed, summer 1988

Monica reads this cov-
erage and thinks, *This girl
is not making things easier for herself.* Mostly, however, she is furious. When
phoned by the press, she says, "People in the prison tell me some of the
personnel get upset when they hear a death row murderer is on the front
page of the Rome newspaper."

Patti had lived through Paula's wildness in her early months on death
row: in her opinion, the girl was loose with her threats. But Patti believes the number of citations is inflated. There are three legitimate write-
ups of which she's aware: one for assault, two for petty infractions. "I'm
not going to say Paula Cooper has been a total angel," she tells the AP,
but "they took her clothes, her books. No television, no nothing. She sits
there and vegetates." Paula knows the ramifications of her actions, Patti
thinks, but when she loses her temper, she does not care what might happen to her, and Patti worries about this absence of self-control.

She has gotten to know a more hardened Paula than Monica sees.
Whenever Patti has asked Paula to explain her write-ups, she's seen the
girl inflate: she pounds the table, rises up out of her seat, gets within a
few inches of Patti's face, and gets loud about how *that's not my fault and*

I'm not even gonna talk about it. At those moments, Patti tells her, calmly and firmly, "*Sit down*, Paula. Just sit down." But what's made her ease up and have empathy for the girl are the letters—because Paula puts so much more of herself into what she writes on stationery than she ever shows face-to-face. They are the letters, Patti thinks, of a vulnerable, insecure person who uses written language to reveal far more of herself. She must be some kind of natural writer, because she certainly did not learn it before her incarceration.

Paula has become serious about her education. In high school—the nearly two years she experienced, mostly skipping class—she could not sit still at a desk; she hated the teachers. But now she dreams of access to the prison library. Finally, studying feels like a way to form a plan. Just after New Year's, she receives her high school diploma in the mail: she passed her GED at eighteen, on the first try, and she's proud of it. Paula mails a copy of the diploma to Bill and another to Father Vito. Monica sends her flowers. When she sees Paula, she holds her and cries.

Monica offers to pay for college classes, and so Paula enrolls in some correspondence courses through Indiana University, mailing her work in to be graded by professors she will likely never meet. Soon, she homes in on psychology, because she believes it's the art of understanding one-self, something she would like to do. Her psych homework has been introducing her to new ideas about the ways in which parents shape their children and to the concept of *self-esteem*. She's also learning that a lot of psychological labels are open to interpretation, imprecise—such as the term *antisocial*, a word used in her sentencing hearing nearly two years ago. The categories in which we place people are sometimes little un-derstood, she discovers, and evolving.

That June, on the final day of its term, the U.S. Supreme Court gathers to announce nine decisions, a cumulative 443 pages of opinions. This is one of the busiest days in its history.

Second in line is *Thompson v. Oklahoma*. Justice Stevens reads the decision: Five of the eight justices—Stevens, Brennan, Marshall, Blackmun, and O'Connor—have voted to overturn Wayne Thompson's death sentence.

The two major reasons for the death penalty, Stevens says, are retribution and deterrence, neither of which supports the execution of a fifteen-year-old. The death penalty for those under sixteen, he pronounces, "involves nothing more than the purposeless and needless imposition of pain and suffering and is therefore an unconstitutional punishment."

But there is a catch: only *four* of the five justices who voted to overturn the sentence agree on this point. O'Connor has decided that it is unconstitutional for any state to sentence a juvenile to death without a minimum age in place—but she will not go any further until a clearer national consensus is established. And so this is a plurality decision, and not binding on the lower courts. There remains room for interpretation.

This is a modest result for those who fantasized that the Court would use *Thompson* to eradicate the death sentence for juveniles. Victor Streib and Rick Tepker have been more realistic about it—especially Victor, who knows well how often the country has seen fit to execute young people. But they have managed to spare their client and a very few others who had committed a capital crime at fifteen—and perhaps, looking forward, some untold number of young adolescents. They'll take the win. They have also, Victor feels, steered the conversation away from vague talk of delinquency and retribution and begun to map a way forward.

After the *Thompson* decision, major newspapers around the country speculate as to whether or not the ruling will save the life of the teenage girl on death row in Indiana, and this kind of speculation makes the front page of the Gary *Post-Tribune*. The paper runs comments from

Jack Crawford, who makes his disappointment in Justice Stevens and his plurality clear. He says that "biological age" should not determine a person's level of responsibility: "We have teenagers today committing adult crimes." Regardless, he tells the paper, the Court's decision was not a full majority, and so it need not apply to the Cooper case.

Victor and Touchette are determined that it will.

As Touchette educated himself on the history of the death penalty for juveniles, one name kept coming up in his reading, and that was Victor Streib's. He contacted him at Cleveland State and found the professor familiar with the case—in fact, he'd already been in touch with Paula. It was not a hard sell. And now Touchette and Victor are working in tandem, in their offices miles apart, on the legal brief for Paula's appeal to the highest court in Indiana. They have just been granted a sixty-day extension, and so they have until the first week of September.

They've divvied up the work based on experience. Victor is drafting the constitutional argument, a version of the *Thompson* argument that now presses the decision in that case to their advantage. Touchette is compiling the mistakes he believes Judge Kimbrough made during sentencing— a lawyer can never be certain what a particular justice might latch on to, what could create doubt about the soundness of Paula's sentencing. Each uses the proven turns of phrase of their profession, injecting a sense of urgency where he can while taking care to bleed any emotion from his prose. They agree that one of the worst things an attorney can do is insinuate that he believes he'll sway a justice through a clever turn of phrase, some personalized plea, beyond the letter of the law.

At the same time, Touchette's media strategy has been playing out as he'd hoped. From the beginning, because of how Paula's case was handled, he had very little mitigating evidence to reference and couldn't introduce more. And so, confident that most people would be surprised by how well she can handle herself when she chooses to, Touchette asked Patti to oversee Paula's press interviews, making sure she discusses her childhood. That was the way to get the larger narrative of abuse out there. He thinks, *The Indiana Supreme Court justices: they are human beings, and they read the news.*

In mid-January 1989, their appellant's brief submitted months ago, Touchette files their reply to the state's brief. He finished it at the very last minute, added Victor's signature himself, and raced to mail it at seven p.m. on the due date.

In the reply, Touchette countered the state's amicus brief from a trio of conservative midwestern nonprofits that contained a highly suggestive, lurid description of the crime and of Paula's intentions. Amicus briefs on Paula's behalf have been filed by Amnesty International, who had also come out in support of Wayne Thompson; the respected statewide Juvenile Justice Task Force, which monitors Indiana's juvenile justice system; and the Indiana Civil Liberties Union. It's a solid showing, though no one—and certainly no conservative opponent—would be surprised by this assembly of supporters.

Touchette writes Victor that they should soon receive word as to whether or not they'll be invited to present their case. He adds, straining to sound upbeat, that he believes oral arguments in this case will be *very fun and interesting.*

A few days later, he receives the notice: The Indiana Supreme Court will hear them out. They have five weeks.

Fourteen

A NORMAL PRISONER

In November 1988, Randall Shepard, after less than two years as the Indiana Supreme Court's chief justice, is up for a retention vote—a yes/no vote that decides whether or not he'll serve for another decade. Barely two weeks before Election Day, his fellow justice Alfred Pivarnik appears on local television and shares his frank opinion of his colleague.

At sixty-three, Pivarnik is more than twenty years older than Shepard, who's unusually young for the court, and he tends to be in lockstep with Richard Givan, the court's powerful conservative and previous chief. In contrast, Shepard is a moderate Republican, open to new ideas—and their differences run deeper still. Like Givan, Pivarnik had grown up mostly on a farm, working during his summers at a local steel mill, fishing in his spare time. As a younger man, he was the kind of judge for whom *the law's the law*; in circuit court his nickname had been "Big Al the Prosecutor's Pal." In stark contrast, in high school Shepard had been a member of the debate club and the star of a string of musicals; he performed in summer stock even through law school. Pivarnik had served in the military; Shepard had been 4-F for Vietnam because of migraines, and attended Princeton as an undergraduate and Yale Law School. On the court, the two men are strange bedfellows.

On NBC affiliate WTHR, Pivarnik accuses Shepard of having

"drinking problems," "drug problems," and a "personal social problem"—a coded reference (which he later makes explicit) to homosexuality. He does not offer proof to back up any of these allegations. He calls for an investigation into Shepard's conduct, claiming that Governor Orr and the Indiana Judicial Nominating Commission have been conspiring to shield Shepard's behavior from the public for years.

The governor quickly calls a news conference. "Never in all my years of public service," he says, "have I witnessed such a dirty trick as I have observed today." And Shepard gives the network an interview in response, calling the accusations "inexcusable" and "absolutely false."

Shepard, like Victor Streib, is a seventh-generation Hoosier. His family first came to the state in 1807, and his great-great-great-grandfather was a member of the Indiana General Assembly who voted to authorize the revision of the state constitution in 1851. They were a mostly Whig or Republican family, but almost none of his relatives had practiced law or held public office in generations. His father was an executive for Sears, and most of Shepard's childhood was spent in Evansville, then a struggling industrial city in southern Indiana, near the Kentucky border, known for manufacturing cars and refrigerators. Evansville had also been the site of the first chapter of the Indiana Ku Klux Klan, which flourished in the 1920s; at the time, about a third of white men born in the state were members. When Shepard's family moved to town in the 1960s, however, he joined a seventh-grade class that had only known integration.

At Princeton, Shepard majored in urban studies and wrote his thesis on Mayor Hatcher's election in Gary, which had just taken place. He spent the summer before his senior year working at home in Evansville and taking long drives to do research in Gary and interview the mayor's colleagues. He saw the story of Hatcher's career as another chapter in the evolution of Indiana and the evolution of American cities. At the time, cities throughout the country were run exclusively by white men, regardless of how large their Black populations might be, and Shepard wanted to look at the machinery behind that, and how this one city—Gary, Indiana—seemed to be clearing a path for change. He was twenty-one years old, white, and sheltered, from hours south—but he was made to feel welcome at each of his stops in Midtown.

Throughout the early 1980s, Shepard was a trial judge in Evansville, where he handled everything from murder to unpaid phone bills to child custody. In the spring of 1985—about a month before Ruth Pelke's death—a retirement on the state supreme court created the first opening in nearly a decade. A reformer on the nominating commission, Sara Davies, had an idea of who she wanted to push: Shepard, a young judge (just thirty-eight) who struck her as highly intelligent and forward look-ing. She later told a reporter that the justices at the time struck her as "all white, male, Anglo-Saxon Protestants between the ages of fifty and seventy. They weren't much interested in change, in progressive ideas, or anything of that nature." (No women, Blacks, or Jews had ever been appointed to the court.) She definitely placed Pivarnik in that group. When the commission later interviewed Pivarnik for chief justice, Da-vies would ask what his plan was to create a greater minority presence on Indiana's courts. His reply: "Why, there's no need to do anything. Anybody can apply; it's open." (He denied they had this exchange.)

When Shepard was being vetted, someone made a call claiming that he'd once seen the judge smoke a joint and flirt with men at a party in an Evansville motel room. No one could prove the latter, and the com-mission wasn't concerned over a dated story about a single joint. It all blew over—until, years later, Shepard was voted chief justice over Rich-ard Givan's man.

And so, in the fall of 1988, Pivarnik and Givan are once again making their acrimony known. (To no avail: Shepard retains his seat.) And by the following February, when Chief Justice Shepard gives his annual State of the Judiciary address, he cannot ignore how public the tensions within the court have become. He opens by acknowledging the "rumors of civil strife": "What's it really like down there? The short answer is: better than many might think. . . . And yet, courts are made up of judges, mere men and women with their own particular strengths and weaknesses. They usually work together very well, but they are not superhuman."

Privately, the chief justice is embarrassed to have to speak about this. He feels it degrades the court.

It is also a waste of time and energy. They have several cases to consider in the coming weeks. And one of them will be their most high-profile of the year: *Paula R. Cooper v. State of Indiana.*

On February 28, the night before the Indiana Supreme Court arguments, Mike, a volunteer with Amnesty International, stands waiting in Arrivals at the Indianapolis International Airport. A voice calls out to him: a reporter with one of the television crews gathered near the gate.

"Are you here for the Italians?"

The TWA plane from New York City has just landed. As the passengers file into the terminal, Mike sees them: seven men arrived from Rome, the contingent from Non Uccidere. Most visible among them are Fathers Vito and Greganti, a pair in Franciscan brown and clerical black.

Father Vito speaks to the media in the terminal as if they were gathered in a more intimate setting. He says:

> The first time I went to see Paula, I was, in a way, afraid—because in what I read she was described as a monster. But when I talked to her I found she was so good, so gentle, so smiling. I remember when she caressed my hand. The only thing she said: "Pray for me" and "Are you sure God forgives me?" She was not asking me to do anything for her. She decided to be forgiven by God. So how can you avoid to work with this child?

In a few hours, in anticipation of the Supreme Court arguments, about four hundred Italian citizens will begin fasting and praying for Paula Cooper.

That same night, Victor Streib checks into his hotel after an afternoon of prep with Touchette at an office downtown. Touchette had also taken Victor to the prison for his first visit with Paula.

Early on in his research, Victor was struck by how brutal murders by juveniles can be. But whenever he's met with young defendants or convicts, the visit has always been deep inside a correctional facility, surrounded by guards, nothing to fear. Besides, in Paula's case, he's never thought of the girl as frightening. That afternoon, he encountered someone subdued. Maybe she understood the stakes better than he knew, but Paula was mostly quiet, eyes fixed on the tabletop. After their meeting, they did not know each other any better.

There is also the fact that Victor does not see Paula as a repeat offender. Based on what he's read about her case, he believes that Paula, on that day in 1985, experienced "an emotional explosion" that was unlike her behavior before or afterward; the girl herself often says that she does not know what happened that afternoon, that something came over her. Her act was monstrous, he thinks—but if he's honest, the case makes him think that most people probably cannot predict the full range of acts they're capable of. None of us, he thinks, knows ourselves as well as we assume.

The halls at the Statehouse are crowded ahead of the one thirty p.m. arguments, and Touchette and Victor and Patti Wolter use a rear entrance to avoid the press. When the doors on the third floor are opened, about 120 people stream in—including a class of high school students on a field trip, many about Paula's age—and pack the courtroom to capacity. Though the courtroom is smaller and simpler than that of the country's highest court, it was still designed to convey the seriousness of what takes place here. The walls and the double-height ceiling are trimmed in gold, the arched stained-glass windows etched with olive branches. There is mahogany everywhere, and the space is decked with framed photographs of every justice to have served on the court. At the front of the room, flanked by a large American flag, is the bench, with five tall, leather-backed seats at twice the counsels' height.

The grand aesthetic is interrupted only by the sea of bright-blue stackable chairs that have replaced the traditional seating to make room for an audience of nearly twice the usual size. About six weeks earlier, the justices had met in their conference room to discuss the upcoming Cooper arguments and felt they had to acknowledge the obvious: this was a case that had attracted an extraordinary amount of attention—across Lake County, the state, the country, and abroad. Their administrator had boxed up several hundred letters and petitions to the court from all over Europe and Scandinavia (though the justices had not risked becoming biased by reading them). And so they agreed they would give the press plenty of advance warning of the argument's date and the bailiff enough time to rearrange the courtroom, bring in more seats, call in a couple of Capitol police officers to assist. This is one of the largest crowds for an oral argument that Shepard has seen—as big as there was for last year's debate over Evan Bayh's eligibility for the governorship. That decision had laid the groundwork for the new governor to be sworn in just last month, as Orr's replacement.

Victor and Touchette and Patti take their seats at counsel table. Victor likes a somber, quiet atmosphere, but this already feels more like a circus. Plus, there is the added surreal element of those monks or priests or bishops from Rome, seated in the front row, just behind the podium. They seem to be on a mission from the pope.

Victor welcomes their interest in the case, more or less, since they're on the same side. He feels the same way about Ruth Pelke's grandson Bill, whom he spots in the second row in a crisp gray suit. But their motives are grand and existential, Victor thinks, and do not fit into what he thinks of as the "little frame"—specific, pragmatic, precise—of these legal arguments. Through the press, they've been asking the American people whether or not they believe God wants the death penalty—and what is Victor to do with that? The answer to such a question is empirically unknowable to him, and it's unknowable to any lawmaker. So, for the most part, Victor keeps his distance from the Vatican contingent and any talk of what Jesus wants. Ronald Reagan had recently finished the second term—a president brought to power, in part, by the Moral Majority. Victor thinks, *Our systems should not work this way.* It's not right, he thinks, to insert religion into the law.

Gary Secrest arrives. At twenty-nine, he has been in Attorney General Linley Pearson's office for six years and argued before the court nearly a dozen times. If he were asked privately what he thinks of the Cooper case, he would admit this: for someone to plead guilty in a capital case without an agreement in place, to throw herself so completely on the mercy of the court and to receive none—to instead be sentenced to death—is horrible. But that phase of the case came to a close two and a half years ago; and here he is today, representing the state of Indiana, dedicated to preserving the sentence that was handed down.

In an unusual move, the court has allowed reporters in front of the bar, and they now swarm the defense table, pressing close to the attorneys, pushing microphones in their faces. *Where's Paula?* one man asks. *Why isn't she here?* In a few minutes' time, they will be required to leave the chamber.

Meanwhile, Paula is about two miles away at the Women's Prison, sitting with Monica Foster, who has allotted most of the day to spend with her. She buys them Fritos and soda from the vending machine and tries to distract Paula with talk about anything that comes to mind—stories about her fiancé Bob, Rhonda's new life with Mike in Minneapolis, the Italians who will visit tomorrow. Anything to keep the girl's mind off what's about to happen at the Statehouse.

The justices file in through a door behind the bench and take their places: a line of men in long black robes. Chief Justice Shepard glances down at the attorneys and looks out over the crowd.

Shepard has dwelled on the specific violence of Ruth Pelke's murder for some time now: the image of this girl holding an elderly woman on the floor, the number of times she stabbed her, the fact that Mrs. Pelke had been stabbed so hard that the knife went clear through her body and left a mark in the wood floor. He could not erase that from his mind. He thinks, *This was not a sudden fit; it took time for the victim to die.* He has tried to imagine the specific character a person must have to accomplish this act. At the same time, he continues to, as he puts it, "hold in suspension" his opinion on whether or not Indiana should have a death penalty. When he became a judge, Shepard never expected that his duties might someday include the signing of an execution order. But if Paula Cooper's death sentence is upheld, it will eventually be his signature on the paperwork that sets her date for the death house.

"Mr. Chief Justice, and may it please the court—"

Bill Touchette stands at the lectern, ready to deliver his half of Paula Cooper's appeal.

Like Secrest, Touchette is a familiar face to the five—in his case, because of his work with the State Public Defender's Office (they are, technically, his employers). He has long wondered whether some of the more conservative justices have a problem with him because he was associated with Jim Kimbrough, a man regarded as a staunch liberal. Lake County might be Democrat, but most of the state remains red, red, red. Touchette thinks of Pivarnik, in particular, as a "stone-cold conservative" and a "result-oriented" justice—as in someone who wants a case to turn out a certain way, so he works his way backward, interpreting the law and the facts accordingly. Touchette cannot recall a time the justice voted his way.

He gives the court a summary of the errors he believes were made during Paula's trial, and then Victor follows with the constitutional argument. *This* is what most of the justices have questions about: the Cooper case's relationship to *Thompson v. Oklahoma*, decided just eight months ago.

Victor speaks of how close the U.S. Supreme Court just came to banning the death sentence for those under sixteen. And he lays out the argument he has been sharpening for the past seven years: based on his own data, he says, "Indiana has never executed anyone as young as Paula Cooper." He repeats his research, included in their brief: Indiana, in its history, has executed 133 people, the most recent being William Vandiver of Lake County in 1985. Of those 133, just three were executed for crimes committed as juveniles, as far back as 1871, 1884, and 1920; they were each no younger than seventeen at the time of their crimes. Three juveniles have been sentenced to death since Vandiver's execution—in 1982, 1984, and 1986—and two of those were seventeen at the time of their crimes and have since had their sentences commuted. And here is the key: That leaves Paula Cooper *alone*, and the youngest among them.

While the court is not going to admit, publicly, to outside pressure—and they are led by a chief who's revived focus on the state's own Constitution—Paula's attorneys believe that the international attention has made a difference. Throughout, the men accompanying the Italian priests lean in and whisper in their ears, translating the proceedings. When Secrest has his turn at the podium, he feels they are so close behind him (those added rows of seats) that if he took two steps back, he might fall into their laps. Touchette believes that, at the very least, the court is aware their decision in this case will be heavily scrutinized beyond the state's borders. That has to count for something.

The arguments last for a little over an hour. And then months of prep for Victor, years of work for Touchette and Monica and Patti, have reached their culmination. The five justices file out in their long black robes.

Victor rushes to catch his plane—because he is efficient, but also because he wants to sleep beside his wife, with the five-year-old twins next door. It's too soon to celebrate, but he is hopeful. As he writes Paula once back in Cleveland, *We can't ever be sure in cases like yours, but I am quite optimistic that the court will decide it your way.* He signs off, *Take care of yourself and try to share my optimism about your future.*

That Friday, the delegation from Non Uccidere travels to New York City. Father Vito and Father Greganti ride in a taxi cab, a yellow Chevy Caprice. It's barely forty degrees out but a handsome day, and sunlight pulses through the windows as they make their way to Midtown East. The driver's foot volleys between pedal and brake, and every pothole produces a muffled thump—a reminder of the precious cargo in the trunk: three large, dented cardboard boxes, vigorously sealed with official tape that reads *SICUREZZA* over and over. The contents of those boxes: petitions, with more than two million signatures in total, that the delegation from Rome will deliver to the United Nations in support of the girl on death row.

The taxi pulls up at the curb in front of the long row of U.N. flagpoles: the flags of 155 countries. The driver pops the trunk, and the priests hop out—met by Ivan Novelli of the Radical Party and other members of their entourage. They struggle with the boxes, tugging on the twine handles to lift them up and out. The largest requires the work of two men.

The Italians carry their cargo slowly, proudly, across the grand concrete plaza and through the large glass doors to check in with security. They're in a festive mood.

With a cluster of journalists as their witnesses, the men deliver the boxes into the possession of Giandomenico Picco, special assistant to Javier Pérez de Cuéllar, secretary-general of the United Nations. The small crowd applauds.

Father Greganti's face is bright. In Italian, he announces, "Everywhere we have met friendship and openness. The power of good clears the way!"

Mid-July 1989: It is almost exactly three years since Paula's sentencing in Lake County Superior Court.

On the final Thursday of their term, the court publishes their decision in the Cooper case, as written by the chief justice. It begins: *The question is whether Paula Cooper may be executed for committing the grisly murder of Mrs. Ruth Pelke. We hold that she may not. This is a difficult conclusion to reach*, Shepard writes, *because of the gruesome nature of Cooper's acts*. Despite the many months of personal tensions among the justices, and despite their differences in ideology, their decision is unanimous: 5 to 0.

The court's opinion makes note of the *doubt* Judge Kimbrough expressed during his sentencing. It makes note of the *international attention that has surrounded the case*, citing several national newspapers. It makes note of the fact that, while Public Law No. 332-1987 (based on Earline Rogers's bill) was not intended to apply here, it *was popularly called "the Paula Cooper bill."* And with that bill's passage, and in light of Indiana's capital punishment history (as provided by Victor Streib), Paula would become both the first and the last person ever executed in Indiana for a crime committed at the age of fifteen. This, the court states, now makes her punishment *unique and disproportionate* to any other possible sentence for the same crime.

Later on, the assumption will be that the court had been left with no other option. But in writing the opinion, Shepard makes clear that the justices came to their conclusion independently and emphatically. The *Thompson* decision, he reiterates, was not a binding majority; had they been so moved, the five had enough space to uphold the Cooper death sentence. He also deliberately places the Indiana constitutional grounds first, when there is plenty of room to place the burden of overturning a high-profile death sentence on the U.S. Supreme Court, to frame the state's decision as top down, hands tied.

Years later, Shepard will say he made this choice because "I thought we needed to take responsibility for what we were doing, rather than to point at Washington. I just felt like we needed to *own* it and tell the people of our state that this is the way it happened, and we weren't forced to do it; we think it's the proper outcome under Indiana law given these facts. And so be it." Let there be no question: the state itself, through its highest court, had rejected the sentencing of a fifteen-year-old to death. Shepard would never have to sign the execution order for someone so young.

Paula Cooper's death sentence is commuted to sixty years in prison. On good behavior, according to Indiana law, she may be released in about half that time.

When Monica hears the news, she races to the prison—but Superintendent Trigg, who has had so little to say to Paula up until this point, decides to tell her himself. When Monica arrives, just fifteen minutes later, Paula is in a state of shock.

When the press calls, Bill Touchette tells a reporter that Paula is "looking forward to living the life of a normal prisoner."

Earline Rogers learns the news and is elated: she'd assumed Paula Cooper would remain the one adolescent beyond the reach of her bill, but she was wrong. A few weeks later, the state senator and the court's chief justice will see each other in the Statehouse, and he will stop to speak with her. "You know," he will say, "you saved a life."

Orr does not comment. Bayh does not comment. Crawford does not comment. His spokesperson says only, "He won't talk about it."

The new Lake County prosecutor, Jon DeGuilio, says he is disappointed and tempted to appeal—though how he imagines getting past a state supreme court decision grounded in the state constitution is unclear. Attorney General Pearson is plain with the press: the case is over.

Privately, Gary Secrest, though he argued the state's case, is not upset by the outcome. His job was to prove that the girl's sentencing was constitutional; that was the complete scope of his mandate. But Secrest had been troubled by the fact that Paula might be executed just after a state law passed that would save anyone *else* in her situation. That had not sat well with him. In addition, outside his role as a player in the system, he is personally against capital punishment. He has long thought that, for many lay people, the death penalty remains abstract; it does not disturb them to ask a fellow citizen to surrender their right to life. The mathematics of justice are too easily reduced to *You kill, you die.* But if these same people suddenly found their own son or daughter implicated in a murder, they would be unlikely to give up on their child. They would insist that justice be more nuanced; they would insist that powerful circumstances had contributed to that violent event. Of such people, Gary thinks, *Their hearts break—but only for their own.*

———— ⚓ ————

That night, Mike LaBroi is at home near Powderhorn Park in Minneapolis, watching TV, when a newscaster announces that Paula's death sentence has been set aside. Right away, he rings Riverside Medical Center, where he and Rhonda now work—she's on the night shift in the rehab wing—and is told by the receptionist, "Hey, you know you're not supposed to be calling."

"Put her on the phone," he says. *"Please."*

Rhonda gets on the line, and Mike tells her the news. No one had prepared her for this moment.

The two of them suddenly realize that they never understood that Paula had a chance. All along, they'd assumed that she *would be executed*, it was only a question of when. Rhonda had never expected she would get to keep her sister.

Bill Pelke is in his foreman's office at Bethlehem, on the phone with Judy, when she tells him to hold on for a moment—she has a call on the other line. When she returns, she says that a journalist from the AP wants to ask him some questions. She's gotten used to hearing from the press: she and Bill were married in the months before the oral argument, and now they live together once again, in a ranch-style house in Portage. Her husband must be the only worker in the entire mill getting these kinds of calls. He tells Judy to give the man the office number.

Within a couple minutes, the foreman's phone rings, and the reporter introduces himself. "Mr. Pelke, the Indiana Supreme Court, on the automatic appeal for Paula Cooper, has set aside her death sentence and given her a sixty-year prison term." Does he have a comment?

The first thing to come out of his mouth is *"Praise the Lord!"*

Judy passes out the foreman's number for the next hour and a half.

Over a dozen reporters call in from publications across the country, from papers, TV networks, and radio stations. To each one, Bill raises his voice about God. He is feeling good.

A month after the decision, Father Vito returns to Indianapolis to visit Paula. He is there to discuss her rehabilitation; he wants her to rejoin society as quickly as possible. He writes letters to Bill and to Amnesty International to map out a plan. He is uncommonly optimistic about the American penal system.

For now, Paula is still on death row. She dreams of being able to go downstairs with the other women, to take courses in the prison classrooms with real chairs and desks and a teacher who writes on a blackboard. She has been in segregation for over three years, allowed outside only twice last summer. This wait, for her, is another endurance test.

That fall, she is moved down into general population.

Now Paula, like the other women, is permitted to move around all day, only locked in her room overnight. She takes one class a week. She waits for a job assignment. The prison does not provide a counselor, but Monica continues paying for a therapist.

The reporters have stopped calling.

Paula writes to the friar, *I feel free even though I am not free.* She is twenty years old now. She can go outside, and there is grass. She looks up and follows the birds with her eyes as they arc over the courtyard.

She is free, she writes, *in & at heart.*

III

Fifteen

THE CARAVAN

The one-room church stood on Nickelson Hill in Miami County. The state was young then, in 1900, less than eighty years old, and that region of north-central Indiana was deeply rural territory. Good for wheat and oats and corn. Small mills, small churches—but this particular congregation had scattered. That summer, it was decided: the building, complete with a belfry, would be given away, transported five miles north to a dirt crossroads surrounded by farmland and open vistas.

For the journey, neighbors helped mount the church atop log rollers, so it could be pulled by steam engine over narrow roads and bridges. When they reached a creek, the moving crew decided to leave the building where it was, on the banks, until the Miami winter had grown bitter enough that the water froze solid and a team of horses could drag the structure across without falling in. By the time the church reached its destination, on a half acre of donated land, much of the plaster had been shaken off and the roof had collapsed. But the small congregation of twenty worked quickly to repair it. And by the spring of 1901, the Sunday morning after Easter, Center Chapel Brethren Church was dedicated for worship.

Stella Oswalt, of a farming family nearby, descended from German immigrants to Pennsylvania and Ohio, became a charter member. Two years later, at nearly twenty-eight, late for someone of that time, she married Ed Zimmerman, whose family had spent three generations in the county working the land. Stella had been penciled in as No. 30 in the list of members in the church ledger, and Ed became No. 68. In the spring of 1906, their daughter Ruth was born, and the congregation continued growing. Ruth Zimmerman, long before she was Ruth Pelke, would become No. 202.

Ruth's mother could trace her family back to the country's founding. They had come from Germany to the Pennsylvania colony, then the territories of Ohio and Indiana; there had been Brethren settlements in those places too. Persecuted for their beliefs, the Brethren had fled Germany and first arrived in the New World in Pennsylvania. Along with the Mennonites and the Quakers, they formed a movement: churches against violence, against war, against slavery, against the death penalty. Their convictions stood in tension with most other colonists' more punitive ideas of justice, ideas handed down from England. They refused to enlist in the military, even during the Revolutionary War, and it set them apart, forcefully, from their neighbors; nearly two centuries later, some would be imprisoned as conscientious objectors during Vietnam. This was one reason why many Brethren, early on, continued migrating to the south and the west, many to Ohio and Indiana. The Brethren steadily fanned outward, bringing their beliefs with them.

There is a Brethren ritual that demonstrates the closeness of the community, though it has fallen out of practice in many places because of its intimacy (the distance, so often, between tenets and how they are lived out). It is the rite of foot washing. The Center Chapel congregation would gather at tables in the basement and wait for their turn to be called: the men into one Sunday school classroom, the women into another, four and four at a time. And there the sets of four would each take their place on a long bench. The man seated on one end would start: He knelt before the brother beside him and washed his feet in a tub. And then that man, in turn, washed the feet of his neighbor, and it continued down the chain, and the next round would be sent in, until the whole congregation had been attended to. The place where each person's life had accumulated on the bottoms of their feet, what they had walked through: their neighbor touched that, rubbed it, rubbed it off, and the same was done for him. It was hard not to consider where that person had just been, where they had walked that day, how tired they might be. Their feet were among the most vulnerable, filthiest parts of that person's body, and of their neighbor's body in turn.

The ritual was inspired by a moment in the Gospel of John, on the last night Jesus spent with all twelve of his disciples. The men began arguing over which of them was more important to him—and so, to their shock and against their protests, Jesus wrapped a towel around his waist, poured water into a basin, knelt down and personally washed the feet of each man gathered there. "I have set you an example that you should do as I have done for you." The washing is a washing away of sins, of being forgiven and purified; it is also proof of a willingness to serve as well as be served, a reminder that we are all connected to and in need of each other. No man is greater than another.

The night in the crane, the night of Bill Pelke's revelation, took place nearly three years ago. And during those years he has told and retold that story numerous times—to family, to Judy, to a small number of friends, to a string of reporters, as the means for them to grasp his forgiveness of Paula Cooper. But this storytelling has mostly been intimate, one on one. He will soon begin to speak of his grandmother in public, to crowds of people. It will start out on the balcony of a government building in Macon, Georgia, on Mother's Day, on the anniversary of Ruth's death. Bill will go on to repeat his story, before assemblies of strangers, more than one thousand times over the next thirty years.

In the weeks after Paula's life was spared, in the summer of 1989, Bill is elated—but he also experiences a kind of withdrawal. Paula's appeal had given him a sense of purpose, and now what? He realizes that he may not have more opportunities to speak out; people may no longer have a special use for him. His days may be defined, once again, by his shifts at the mill, his weekends with Judy, a life bound to Portage, Indiana. Months pass without distinction.

And then he hears about an event scheduled for the following spring: a two-week march—a "pilgrimage," they're calling it—from Florida's death row, in the city of Starke, to Martin Luther King Jr.'s gravesite in Atlanta. Bill has little sense of the details, but he doesn't question it. For the past three years, he has followed his instincts, and that is what he does now. He lets Bethlehem Steel know that he plans to use his two weeks' vacation in May. This pilgrimage is something to grab on to.

When the time comes, Bill drives the silver van a thousand miles to Gainesville, Florida, where everyone is assembling, pulling over to sleep just once. As he crosses the state line, he turns on the radio: the first item is news of an execution in Starke. The man's name was Jesse Tafero—he'd been convicted of killing two police officers at a highway rest stop—and his was another electrocution gone wrong. Jesse had sat fastened into Florida's chair by multiple leather straps, wearing a headpiece from which hung a small black curtain to obscure his face. When the switch was activated, six-inch flames and thick clouds of smoke had burst from his head—and he did not die. As the room filled with an unbearable stench, the execution team sent two more rounds of electrical current through his body, until Jesse was pronounced dead.

The image will not leave Bill's mind.

When he arrives in Gainesville that evening, Bill heads to the gathering place: the office of Pax Christi, the Catholic pacifist association. They are about one hundred people, this starting group; more will join when the march reaches its final destination, in Atlanta. There are members of Amnesty International, from civil rights attorneys to shaggy college-age volunteers. There are members of the Southern Christian Leadership Conference, the African American civil rights group whose first president was King himself; of the National Coalition to Abolish the Death Penalty, started in part by the ACLU's Henry Schwarzschild after the death penalty was revived in 1976; and the American Friends Service Committee, the Quaker group for social justice. There are locals alongside activists from around the country, people of many stripes of belief—Catholics and Brethren and Hutterites and Jews and atheists as well. And in the midst of this is Jesse Tafero's mother: during one of her last visits to her son on death row, he had told her about the march and asked her to thank everyone on his behalf. Mrs. Tafero had few people to go to for comfort as she awaited her son's execution date, but she is welcome here—because of, not in spite of, her name.

Bill has never known any activists in his life and he wants to learn from them, to join in whatever work they are doing. He wants to be more than someone who puts in a couple of appearances on television; he wants to prove himself. A man walks up to Bill and asks, "How long have you been an abolitionist?" and Bill's face goes blank. He'd only seen the word *abolition* in American history books, when they read about slavery in school. He will need a little time to find his footing.

At this gathering, Bill falls into the most rarified category of all: murder-victim family member, of which there are very few out in public in abolitionist circles. He's a rare presence for another reason: he is wearing the carefully pressed suit he'd hung up in his van and carrying a Bible—the copy he hopes to give to Paula someday. There are not many strident Christians in the death-penalty movement right now, and not many men in hardly worn suits; he does not blend in. A college student with Amnesty later describes him as looking "like a Republican." But one woman has heard about Bill, and she embraces him: this is Sister Helen Prejean, a nun from New Orleans in a Dorothy Hamill bob and big eyeglasses, in her fifties and intensely animated. She is there to serve as the marchers' spiritual adviser. Father Vito, Father Greganti, Sister Helen—this recovering Baptist is growing accustomed to the company of Catholic sisters and brothers.

The next morning, they gather outside the state prison in Raiford and read aloud the names of the 315 men housed there on death row. Then they set off down the highway on foot, trailed by a string of rental vans. Bringing up the rear is Bill's silver chariot, pulling a trailer loaded with a pair of bright plastic porta-potties. This is the task for which Bill was chosen, his chance to prove his willingness to serve. He doesn't mind the job. It's not glamorous, but it has a purpose. Each driver in the cara- van has a CB radio through which they stay in touch, and it's instantly familiar to him, coordinating teams over the airwaves. His handle is "Porta-Pottie Bill."

The pilgrims march about ten miles each day, eat lunch on the side of the road, climb into the vans whenever a stretch is less walkable or less visible (the goal, after all, is to be seen). In the coming days this will add up to about 160 miles on foot: through Valdosta, Waycross, Albany, Americus, Macon, Forsyth, Jackson, Griffin, and Jonesboro, all the way to Atlanta. This plan had seemed like the only means of getting press: making a sunburnt, frequently exhausted spectacle of themselves.

Along the way, they talk. This is an education for Bill, who walks alongside the more experienced abolitionists, the death-row family members, the defense attorneys: he learns about the great disparities built into the criminal justice system, and how popular capital punish- ment is in much of the South. Sometimes they stop talking long enough to sing a few protest songs, mostly from the 1960s, and spirituals like "Down by the Riverside." A group of Hutterites from New York are the most gifted singers. They are Anabaptist, similar in lifestyle to the Men- nonites or the Amish; the women walk in long homemade dresses and dark bonnets, the men in workpants and suspenders. They sing in har- mony that is perfect, having learned to blend their voices, no one above the rest. The sound of them and the sight of them is a pleasant surprise to Bill, and he will remember their chorus for the rest of his life.

They make stops at churches, where they give talks about the death penalty. On a few occasions, the congregation makes them fried chicken; many times, they spend that night on the church floor. But they are in the Death Belt, and the pilgrims become more worried about safety after they cross the state line into Georgia. They receive a few death threats over their radios; a pickup truck follows them as they drive down a quiet stretch of highway late at night. When they reach Americus, the men of SCLC, accustomed to the dangers of political actions in the South, sometimes stay awake to keep guard. During the daytime, as the pilgrims walk through intersections, they occasionally notice men in cars parked nearby snapping photos or videotaping them; a rumor spreads that it must be the Georgia Bureau of Investigation. They are now down to thirty marchers walking alongside the highway with their signs, sometimes dazed and tired, raggedier than when they started out.

Bill's new friend Sister Helen has been giving spiritual counseling to a man on death row in Louisiana named Dalton Prejean, and he is scheduled for execution during the Pilgrimage, after ten delays. Dalton, who is not related to the sister in spite of his name, had killed a state trooper during a routine stop when he was seventeen; with a low IQ, he is considered borderline disabled. While the role of the spiritual adviser is to attend to the convict before his death, Dalton had asked Sister Helen to stay with the march, and she arranged for someone to take her place in the death house. But it's hard for her. On the night of his execution, the marchers are close to Atlanta, their final destination, and they gather together with the sister and join hands. In that moment, Dalton becomes the fifth person in the country to be executed within the past two weeks.

Beyond Bill, one other murder victim's family member is on the pilgrimage. Sam Sheppard's mother was murdered in 1954, and his father was convicted of the crime in a high-profile case—only to be exonerated a decade later. Whenever possible, the organizers send any journalists following the march to Bill and Sam. Their voices seem harder to discount.

———————⚹———————

Bill had begun connecting with others like him back in the summer of 1988, before Paula's case made it to the Indiana Supreme Court. Through an Amnesty event, he'd met, for the first time, someone who'd lost a loved one through violence but who was opposed to the death penalty: Elissa Schutz. Elissa was from Albany, New York, and her eighteen-year-old sister Suzette had been murdered in 1979. She soon called Bill at home to ask if he would help her start an organization of murder victims' family members against capital punishment. They decided to hold a brainstorming meeting at her house in a few weeks' time; Elissa knew who she wanted to invite.

Bill took off from work so that he and his cousin Judi could drive to Albany. There he met senior members of the National Coalition to Abolish the Death Penalty, Amnesty, Pax Christi, and the New York State Defenders Association. He met other victims' family members, including Pat Bane, a librarian from Syracuse whose uncle was killed in the 1950s, and Camille Bell, whose young son had been killed in 1979 in the "Atlanta child murders" that targeted Black boys. Bill also met Marie Deans, an activist whose mother-in-law had been murdered in Charleston, South Carolina, in 1972.

Elissa was convinced that Marie was the key to any group they might create. At forty-eight, she'd been on the board of directors of Amnesty International USA for the past several years, helping take the lead on the death-penalty fight, visiting death rows and reporting on conditions. Twelve years ago, Marie had started a small support group for murder victims' family members herself—mostly people based, like her, in Virginia—now called Murder Victim Families for Reconciliation, or MVFR. The members, who are all against the death penalty, write one another and share advice; they show up whenever a member gives a public talk or testifies before legislators. That support has made them each a little bit bolder.

Like Bill, the members of MVFR have been treated like pariahs, been screamed at in public or even by their own families. They are told, regularly, that they must not have truly loved the person they lost if they are refusing to call for the most extreme punishment the system makes available. To prosecutors—like Jack Crawford, who has seen Bill as little more than a nuisance and embarrassment—these are not model family members to bring before judge or jury in a high-profile capital case. They are advocating not for retribution, but for a more measured form of justice, and this is in direct tension with the role this administration would like victims of crime to play: someone who can be counted on to translate the prosecution's argument into an emotional plea, a "victim impact statement." The members of MVFR are prepared to give statements that challenge the state's approach, a fact that gives them a unique power to surprise and shock. And they have been seeking opportunities to make their impact statements—what they think of as their *stories*—independently if they have to, without the help of the state.

The discussions at Elissa's house lasted for two days, with Judi cooking for everyone. Marie talked about MVFR and how she wished she had the time and resources to expand the group. She also shared the list they'd compiled of additional murder victim family members, or *MVFMs*, around the country, as well as press about those who'd spoken publicly of their opposition to the death sentence. An AP story about Bill was in her packet.

It would be a little while before the group found its way, but common ground had been established. And Bill now had a phrase to define him: He was a *murder victim's family member.* Not the victim herself, but what some people called a "secondary" victim. In his case, an act of violence had not ended his life; it had not caused him physical injury or kept him from getting out of bed in the morning; it had not driven him into hard drinking or pills; it had not prevented him from feeling pleasure or tasting food or enjoying women. But it had redefined him. Those initials—*M-V-F-M*—gave a name, a diagnosis, to his invisible condition.

In Macon, Georgia, halfway through the Pilgrimage, Bill observes the fifth anniversary of his grandmother's death: a Sunday, Mother's Day. Sister Helen says he is welcome to share his story with the entire rally—his first time. And so, a few hours later, Bill finds himself in front of a microphone on the second-story balcony of a government building. Below, a crowd has gathered on the walkway and spills out onto the street.

He stands straight, hands behind his back, and he begins: "On May fourteenth, four girls from Lew Wallace High School in Gary, Indiana, decided they were going to skip class that day . . ."

A year later, in Texas, Bill is marching again—another week of vacation days. He drives the van over a thousand miles to get there, longer than his haul to Florida. Texas has nearly 350 people on death row, placing them first in the country in a dark category.

Once again, someone is executed during the march. Once again, Bill walks for miles of roadside with a few dozen comrades. Once again, they sleep in church basements. Between walking and van travel, they cover about 160 miles, from the death row in Huntsville to the Texas Capitol in Austin. Their diet is heavy on warm cheese sandwiches. They are only about thirty of them, but they will swell to nearly three hundred at their final rally.

Intense heat and they keep walking, blisters and they keep walking, thunderstorms and they keep walking. The trip includes several conservative towns. In the Custom Gun Shop in Brenham, two older cowboys watch the marchers head down East Alamo Street behind signs that read

TEXANS AGAINST STATE KILLING and AN EYE FOR AN EYE MAKES THE WHOLE WORLD BLIND. One of the cowboys says aloud, "I think these people fell out of a tree."

Bill and Sam are reunited on the road, and two other MVFMs join, including a Travis County judge who lost his brother. As they walk, Bill shares an idea with Sam, and then later with Marie Deans: they should organize an event like this one, but led by murder victims' family members. MVFR could be the main sponsor—they have about sixty members now. And they should do it in his home state of Indiana. He does not mind the discomfort that would stir up; he is not afraid. It does not mean much to tell his story if he cannot tell it at home.

Sixteen

THE JOURNEY

They were supposed to meet up in the park for a barbeque, but the rain drove them indoors. So here they are at Bill and Judy's place in Portage, about twenty in number, gathered on the large wraparound sofa, curled up in their socks on the carpet, squeezed around the table in the dining nook. It is June 1993, and they have arrived from across the country and a few from abroad: murder victim family members, Christian activists and Amnesty volunteers, death-row friends or family members, members of prison-reform groups and abolitionist groups and peace churches. Most sit in clusters, in sweatshirts and jeans, talking to the few people they know. Cousin Judi, in her apron, keeps emerging from the kitchen with plates of food.

Throughout the house are white lace curtains and doilies, fabric flowers and framed family photos. This is the life Bill waited years to rebuild with Judy, and he loves every inch of it. He moves around the place greeting the guests, making people feel at ease—he's good at it.

It matters to Bill that everyone feels comfortable: what gathers them here tonight is terrible. The nexus of the group is death; they have lost someone they love, maybe by a stranger or maybe by the state; or they are living with foreknowledge of such a loss on an appointed date. Most have a spouse, parent, sibling, or child who was killed, and they do not wish their killer's life to be taken in return. More than that, they are willing to stand up in public and talk about this. It's a gathering of people set apart from their friends and communities by extreme circumstance, and Bill, at this moment, is offering up his home as their own.

In a few hours, they will unroll their sleeping bags in the cabins of a state-park campground near Winimac. The committee has scheduled stops for the Journey in fifteen cities and towns, mainly in Indiana, over sixteen days: marches and rallies and 175 speaking events. Throughout, many in this crowd will retell, again and again, the story of the worst day of their life.

Bill had promoted the Indiana happening with a singsong slogan—*Indiana: The Place to Be in '93*—but they needed something real. A name and a message they could carry with them on a twenty-foot-long banner, print on flyers, repeat over and over to the press. That had come together when, during a steering committee meeting, everyone called out words to write on the board. *Tour. Pilgrimage. Journey. Healing. Hope. Compassion. Violence. Understanding.* A string emerged: *The Journey of Hope . . . from violence to healing.* That's what they would call it. It is abstract; people on the street might not know, at a glance, what they are about. But it sounds like a story of catharsis, of deliverance, of suffering and redemption.

A small stage is set up in a field across from the twenty-four-acre grounds of the state prison in Michigan City, where Indiana's death row for men is housed behind a succession of walls and fences. The oldest facility in Indiana, its best-known inmates have included the young John Dillinger and D. C. Stephenson, the former head of the state Klan; but many of the tens of thousands of men housed here since have remained largely anonymous. Of the forty-nine waiting for their death sentences to be carried out—some of whom have waited five, ten, fifteen years—many of their names dropped out of the papers long ago.

In the park, members of the Journey take turns onstage, their words pumped out by loudspeaker. About sixty people, mostly volunteers and perhaps a dozen locals, are spread across the lawn on blankets or seated at picnic tables. Every now and then a car approaches, slows down to look, continues driving past. But cameras for local television crews are fixed on the stage.

From among the murder victim family members, there is a woman named Marietta Jaeger, from Detroit: twenty years ago, she lost her seven-year-old daughter Susie when she was kidnapped from their family campground in Montana and killed. Now in her fifties, she has traveled here alone to speak about her child's terrible death, and how she kept a grip on her own sanity by choosing to forgive her daughter's killer. There is Lois Williamson, from Pennsylvania, who works in prison reform: as a Black woman, her focus has been on the damage the prison system has done to whole communities. She has lost two family members—her husband and her nephew—and her nephew's killer remains on death row. But, Lois says, she wanted to find a way to raise her children without bitterness, and with the belief that every person can change over time.

Not long after, Sister Helen Prejean takes the stage. She wears a large, simple cross around her neck, but she's otherwise not identifiable as a nun, in a wrinkled long-sleeved tee and striped pants. Twelve years ago, the chaplain at Angola Prison in her home state of Louisiana had asked the sister to write to a man on death row named Patrick Sonnier, and she eventually became his spiritual adviser. Two years in, she bore witness to his execution, and then took on the counseling of another of Angola's condemned men, Robert Lee Willie, executed just two months later. Each had been convicted of rape and murder, and the details of the crimes were repulsive. But even after their appeals were exhausted, Sister Helen had insisted on the humanity of both men; she had personally arranged for a proper Catholic burial for Patrick.

Today, across from the state prison, she speaks of how the justice system does not ask enough questions about the circumstances that led a person to commit a terrible crime. She talks about the time when she lived in the St. Thomas projects in New Orleans, among residents who, unlike herself, were "poor, Black, and struggling." What she learned during those years, she says, is that "I only look good because I've been protected from the day I was born . . . Given a situation where the protections are taken away from us, what would we be?" She puts it another way: "Our virtue that we supposedly stand on is made of sand."

When she speaks of the men on death row she's gotten to know, Sister Helen calls those relationships "a great privilege." She tells of how Patrick Sonnier's last words were an apology to his victims' families. She speaks of "the love that he was capable of," saying of her fellow activists, "That's the magic, and that's the secret, and that's the hope, and that's the depth of what we do, is that we know we are one human family."

This radical sympathy for those who have committed horrific crimes, as Sonnier's were, has become second nature for the members of the Journey. But for many others outside this circle, it is asking too much. Earlier, a half dozen women, some middle-aged and some elderly, had stood watching in a line behind the cameramen. In cotton pants and sun hats, they held up handwritten signs: *KEEP THE DEATH PENALTY. NO APPEALS FOR MURDERS. A Murder Ruined Our Lives.* The youngest, in a white hat and dark glasses, occasionally shouted out, "Send them to the electric chair, not Club Med!" Bill Pelke approached her, and photographers gathered around.

He tried to engage her in a conversation about the Journey. "But there has to be justice," she said to him. "There *has* to be justice."

"The death penalty is not justice," he said softly.

"People cannot know that they can get away with murder and live a normal life!" she said, shaking her head. "I'm sorry, Mr. Pelke."

"Absolutely," he said, placing a hand gently on her arm.

She took a step back.

———————⚘———————

Day after day, the Journey falls into a rhythm. They take up a block of sidewalk in front of a busy street and hold up their banners as car after car passes by. Some of their messages are straightforward: THE DEATH PENALTY IS RACIST; others are wordier, harder for onlookers to decipher: MURDER VICTIM FAMILIES FOR RECONCILIATION. A girl in glasses who looks about eight years old carries a handwritten sign that reads, in a tough sell, *Jesus Says Love Your Enemies.* Sometimes, as they march, they chant the classics, or variations on the classics. To the new, Democratic president, six months in office, they sing, *Listen, President Clinton, we shall not be moved / Listen, President Clinton, we shall not be moved / Like a tree that's planted by the wa-a-ter / We-e-e shall not be mo-o-o-ved . . .*

As they make their way down residential streets, people occasionally step out on their porches, smoke a cigarette, and stare. On one stretch of road, at a red light, a young guy in a baseball cap leans out of his car to shout, "Hey, they should *all* die! Child fuckers!" As the line of marchers walks past long rows of businesses, shoppers park and step out of their cars slowly, wondering what is happening and how to get their errands done. This is the response in South Bend and Lafayette and Fort Wayne—more or less wherever the marchers go.

At Journey events, they attract ministers, retired ministers, retired schoolteachers, local activists, high school students, college professors, paralegals. On the streets, however, it's not always clear who they are reaching. Theirs is a great but occasionally misguided effort, sharing these gruesome stories with random pedestrians who are going about their day, expecting them to stop and listen, to absorb what is being said. Whether the crowd they draw is a few hundred or a dozen, the press makes it worthwhile, regardless of the crowds they draw: coverage the day before their arrival in town, coverage the day of and the day after. By the end of the Journey, they will have stirred up coverage in over sixty newspapers and thirty radio and TV stations.

Some mornings at their campground, the travelers go around and introduce or reintroduce themselves. The number of MVFMs Bill sees in their circle of travelers is about thirty—from Alabama, Louisiana, Virginia, Washington, Florida, New York, Ohio, California, Texas. Among them is George White, who lost his wife and was wrongfully imprisoned for two years, in Alabama, for her murder; and Theresa Mathis, whose brother was beaten to death in Tacoma, Washington; and SueZann Bosler, who survived a home invasion that her father, a Brethren pastor in Miami, had not.

Their stories, in all their emotional and visceral detail, would be distressing for even a stranger to repeat. But each of the Journey members repeats them, aloud and in public. They speak—in churches and assembly halls, in university classrooms and on outdoor stages—in a voice that is as clear as possible. Each has their public way of describing the event and the details leading up to it, repeating precise phrases that make the retelling a little easier; some have spent years considering their words. Some try to give the listeners visuals to ease them into the terrible events they are sharing, links between the chaos of their experience and images or instructions in the Bible. They tell the story of their family's suffering, in a way, like Ruth Pelke told Bible stories as she moved figures across her flannelgraph board. They have each found ways—from Bill to Marietta and George and SueZann—to make their tragedies into parables, to be told again and again.

On the last Monday morning of the Journey, people rise from their bunks at the campground, about sixty-five of them now, and roll up their sleeping bags. It is raining like all get-out.

Since the Journey's start, they have marched through city streets and suburbs, given talks in churches and theaters, on corners and in classrooms. In Gary, Bill and his cousin Judi visited a class at Lew Wallace, once Paula and Karen and Denise's high school. At a Catholic church,

Bernice King joined the Journey to speak about the deaths of her father Martin Luther King Jr. and her grandmother Alberta by gunfire, and the family's insistence on nonviolence. In Indianapolis, Martin University— a school named in honor of King, from which Paula Cooper was earning her degree at the Women's Prison—hosted an event in a packed auditorium. The featured speaker was the Reverend Dr. Thomas L. Brown, a pastor whose son was killed in a carjacking in Texas.

Today is Bloomington, a university town a half-hour drive from their new campground in Spencer. An afternoon concert has been rained out, but the travelers can spend a few hours leafleting the Indiana University campus and parts of town, with a rally at five p.m. on the courthouse steps. And throughout the day, Journey members will speak in classes.

At midday, a panel sits at the head of an undergraduate criminal-justice course, "Victimization," in a row of classroom chairs with attached desks. Marie Deans has taken the lead. She's dressed hippie-relaxed, in dangling earrings and baggy pants, but she exudes the intensity of someone with a single-minded focus. Since the Albany meeting five years ago, she has been witness to twelve executions. Sister Helen will later say of Marie that she is someone next to whom, in the fight for human rights, "I'm a pale little wimp."

Marie tells the students how she ended up becoming her family's spokesperson after her mother-in-law Penny's death "because I've just got the big mouth, I guess"—everyone laughs. She tells of how, after she and her husband and oldest son spoke out against the death penalty for Penny's killer, they received letters and calls from other murder victims' family members who said they felt the same way. They shared their experiences with the Deans—of being made to feel "like pariahs in their communities or traitors to victims or . . . an emotional freak." They were so often seen, even by sympathizers, as outliers whose moral code was abnormal, saintlike, beyond what could fairly be expected of others. This was the impetus, Marie says, for the formation of MVFR: a way for these family members to connect with one another.

She mentions how a few years ago, at the NAACP capital-punishment conference at Airlie, they had asked the people in the room, about three hundred of them—lawyers, legal assistants, mitigation experts—how many of those who work full time on capital defense teams had lost a loved one to murder. And she guesses about two thirds of the audience raised their hands. "And it was kind of a revelation to us that there were murder victims' families all over the country, working quietly as abolitionists and not talking about the fact that they were murder victims' families."

Marie talks about how much of a second thought the victim's family usually is, except when they are needed by the prosecution. She and her husband watched as Penny was taken away in an ambulance, uncertain whether or not she'd survive; and they were given no update until hours later, when her body was about to be autopsied. Marie mentions cases in which the victim's family explicitly asked the prosecutor *not* to pursue the death penalty, and their wishes were not respected. The response is often that the punishment is on behalf of society—retribution on behalf of *all* of us—and not truly about the needs and desires of the victim's relatives.

Marie gives Mike Lawson a chance to speak. He's an alumnus of the school, with the look of a former athlete. In 1986, Mike had just started at IU Bloomington when his younger brother Scott, at the age of sixteen, was shot on Indy's Northside on his *Indianapolis Star* paper route by an elderly customer who'd grown paranoid. When the prosecution decided to pursue the death penalty, Mike was shocked: the idea that his brother, "who was extremely kind and would help anybody who asked," would want someone killed on his behalf was outrageous to him. "To have someone killed for my family, in my brother's name, was a complete insult."

Marie now turns to Tina Schnebelt, who is girlish and poised: her brother Timothy Bunch was executed six months ago in Virginia. Marie tells the students that Tina "lived for almost ten years being told, day after day after day, that the state was going to drag her brother out and take him to the death house." At least her own family, she says, did not anticipate Penny's murder. "My God, what if I'd known for ten years that this was going to happen to Penny, and yet I was helpless to do anything about it? . . . Tina never did a thing to us. Why did we do this to *her?*" Tina, in a relaxed voice, as if she's grown used to speaking about this, explains that her family spent that decade without any physical contact with Timothy, only conversations by phone through a sheet of plexiglass. It was not until the day of her brother's execution that they were allowed to hug one another, to sit at a table and drink sodas together. And within view, through an interior window, was the chair that would take his life within a few hours.

The widower of Timothy's victim, a forty-year-old woman named Su Cha Thomas, had written the governor in support of the execution— but Su's brother had written in opposition, on behalf of himself and his family. Tina says that Su's family members flew across the country, from California, to be with *her* family on the eve of the event. The governor had told the press he'd never received such conflicting messages from a victim's relatives before.

When it's time for questions, one student asks, "What do you think about a victim's family that *wants* the person who murdered their son or daughter or parent to be executed? . . . Shouldn't we have the death penalty for them?"

Marie immediately disagrees. "Because, you know, *you're* doing this. It's *your* act. It's the act of a society . . . *We* are dehumanizing people; *we* are killing people." That instinctive desire for revenge is human and recognizable, she says, but "it shouldn't be public policy."

Conversation turns tense in an appearance, later in the day, at a course called Corrections and Criminal Justice.

Marie takes part in this session, as well as Sunny Jacobs, the widow of Jesse Tafero, the man executed in Florida just before the start of the Pilgrimage. Sunny had been sentenced to death for the same crime, had her sentence commuted to life, and then finally, eight months ago, was released on new evidence. This is only the second time she has ever spoken in front of an audience. She tells the students that, although the death of her husband was legal, carried out by the state, it hurt for her and their children just as if he'd been murdered at random. In MVFR, she says, she has found people who understand her experience; they have become like family, a refuge.

The students seem respectful and receptive to Sunny. But when it's time for them to ask questions, the mood of the room changes quickly.

One young man offers up a story of a family friend in Florida who raped and murdered a real estate agent during a viewing. He is now on death row. The student tells Marie, in a tone that is slightly aggressive, "I just feel that there are certain crimes that are punishable by death."

"Why?" Marie asks, sounding a little worn out. "What is gonna happen that is gonna make something better if he's executed?"

There may be victims' family members, he says, who experience "a sense of restitution" through an execution. Marie says that victims' families that want and obtain the death penalty sometimes experience regret later on. "I'm just saying your belief in capital punishment is your own personal belief," the student says. "I'm not trying to speak collectively for everyone, and neither should you."

Marie, becoming confrontational, emphasizes that when she says *we* she is speaking for their national group of murder victims' relatives. For the members of MVFR, she says, the idea that the public can somehow pay back the victims' families "by taking *somebody else's* life" is offensive.

Someone raises the possibility that a person may be executed and later revealed to have been innocent. Of this concern, the young man says, "That's not my job."

"Well, it's *all* our jobs," says Sunny—who was exonerated herself—"because the state is killing people in our name."

"I don't feel my name is attached to every death-penalty conviction. I think that the people who are directly accountable"—the prosecutor, judge, jury—"*their* name is attached to it."

Another male student asks Marie, "What about guys like Jeffrey Dahmer and John Wayne Gacy, guys like that?"

"Do I think they ought to be executed?"

"Well, obviously you don't," he says. "But how can you defend somebody like that?"

"Wow." She laughs, taken aback. "You really made a face!"

He brings up the dozens of children Gacy killed.

"I don't *have* to defend Mr. Gacy," Marie says. "I am responsible for my actions and the actions that are taken in my name." The death warrants, she says, are issued on behalf of the citizens of Virginia.

The next day Marie leaves the Journey: she has an execution to attend in Virginia. It is the execution of a man who is certifiably guilty—and of a terrible act—but his guilt leaves Marie no less distressed.

On the final night of the Journey, the travelers gather for one more circle in the park lodge, a hot room with drop ceilings and a concrete floor. Tomorrow morning they head into Indianapolis for the last day of actions. There are about forty of them tonight, and everyone looks bone tired. Someone mentions that the execution Marie left to attend did indeed take place last night; a moment of silence follows. People talk about sending a statement to the governor of Virginia, maybe organizing a Journey there.

Pat Bane, the librarian from Syracuse, says penetrating the South, the Death Belt, should be the next step. And she asks people to sign up to start an MVFR chapter in their own area, even a small one, once they get back home. Someone requests they consider a Journey in California, which had its first execution since the 1970s moratorium just last year; another suggests Ohio, which some believe will resume executions soon.

A college-age volunteer gives a big smile and says, "I don't wanna leave." Everyone laughs, so pleased; people on all sides clap him on the shoulders. Marietta says she feels as if she should take off her shoes here, at their gathering place, "because it's holy ground."

These past sixteen days have been defined by the creation of a singular network. This is a network based on pain and loss, one whose membership no one covets, one defined by an emotional shorthand through which only they can communicate. Only when in this circle can they go without explaining themselves; there is no dark preamble to understanding where Bill or Marietta or George or Sunny is coming from. And for the strangers who see them stand together out in public and decipher that their connection is one of immense grief and uncommon beliefs, they are witnessing a significant event.

Tomorrow there will be three rallies, two marches, and a concert, culminating on the steps of the Statehouse, with about three hundred people in attendance. Mike Lawson says that this coming Monday would have been his brother's twenty-third birthday. "Let's go out and do the best damn march this town has ever seen." Everyone applauds.

The rallies will be smaller than they'd hoped; the march will wind through downtown streets that are desolate on the weekend. But there will be press. And they will try their best again, in the next state they descend upon.

Seventeen

HER SISTER'S KEEPER

The following year, 1994, is Paula's fifth since stepping down into the general population at the Women's Prison.

When she was first placed on death row in the summer of 1986, the residents had talked about how vicious the girl must be. Not yet seventeen, she was a kind of celebrity. But she was kept apart, in her cell upstairs on the locked-down wing, twenty-three hours a day.

Paula was separated from the other three-hundred-odd women in the facility, but she could often *hear* anyone who might be cycled through her wing for bad behavior. This was how she met Donna Stites. Donna is seven years older, a tall, skinny white woman from Evansville—but she had also entered the system as a teenager, for theft, and eventually been sentenced for murder the year before Paula. For all the hype about the new girl, Donna found her childlike in a way that seemed borderline peculiar. But over the course of weeks spent talking from their adjacent cells, the two grew closer.

Once off death row, Paula was moved into one of the dorms, alongside two dozen other women, with a shared rec room, private quarters, and doors that are only locked at night. The staff does not worry about physical violence here the way they would at a men's facility; a resident is allowed to borrow a pair of scissors, take them back to her room to cut her hair, and return them later. Paula was assigned a job: up at five a.m., climbing ladders to clean the walls.

She had gone from living in isolation to living in a community for the first time. Even as a kid, for her last several years on the outside, she had been moved again and again, to temporary housing, to different schools; this was the start of her first long stretch rooted in one place. A lot of the women chose to be kind to her; they had been aware of Paula not only as a high-profile resident, but as a very young person in a harsh situation. Many were ready to show her how to navigate the system, a couple of the older women in particular, and Paula listened and learned. After a settling-in period, Paula knew how to handle herself. Now she is on her own; she's managed to stay clear of complicated relationships. Some of the residents find her controlling; others respect how she carries herself; she writes Bill that she is starting to feel more relaxed around *so many people that are different from myself.* Paula enrolls in college courses like Psychology of Freedom and Introduction to Civilization and gets high marks; she maps out a plan for her degree. She has a free day on Thanksgiving and spends all those hours writing papers: she's surprised to find how much she enjoys it.

For those three years upstairs, under sentence of death, Paula had tried, whenever she had the spirit or the will for it, to work toward a new incarnation of herself: a person who could exist on the outside, who might do *well* on the outside. She studied, she responded to letters, she listened to the radio and watched programs on television that she hoped would teach her something she didn't know. She had regular conversations with her minister and went to church service on Sundays; she listened to Bible-study cassettes that Bill sent her in the mail. She started speaking to a therapist, got her high school degree, enrolled in college courses. She was looking ahead to a life that few others believed she would have the opportunity to live, while at the same time turning the guilt over and over in her mind. A year before her appeal was heard by the state supreme court, she had written to Bill, *I cant say if they opened the gates today I would walk out because I wouldnt walk out. I just have not payed the price . . . I could not live with my self being free because the person I am I would not be free inside you understand dont you.*

But once she became a long-termer, Paula's desire to improve herself began to buck up against the reality of the time stretching out ahead of her. Not long after her sentence was commuted, she had written to Father Vito: *Im not gonna stay here 30 ys father, because I dont believe God would allow me to be down & out that long . . . Man is negative most of the time but Im not gonna be because I believe Ill be out of here.* But with a sixty-year sentence, it will take effort to get out in thirty. And it will take powerful focus and powerful luck to be released in less time than that.

To Donna, her friend seems no less angry than when they first met. It did not take long for Paula to find the system infantilizing. *We have a hard time here with the rules that are like a children's camp,* she writes to Bill. *Every one acts like children instead of like women & it makes me really sick.*

It does not help that, even after a few years in the general population, Paula feels some of the guards believe she belongs on death row, that she has it too easy. There are so many chances to write up a resident for some small infraction. A guard might say *I want you to go in there and clean that wall for five hours today,* and if the woman protests, she might be written up for "insolence." It does not help Paula that she is forceful in how she expresses herself. She almost always pushes things further, demands that an officer file a formal complaint against her. Which means more work for the guard, and then a few days' wait before the Conduct Adjustment Board reviews the write-up; in the meantime, the officer may have to spend the week watching Paula walk around undisciplined. A grudge would have plenty of time to blossom that way, on both sides.

Rhonda is aware of the need for her sister to keep steady while inside. It will be the difference between them spending their middle age together or just their elderly years. And so she does everything she can to help, to keep Paula lifted, while living some four hundred miles away.

Rhonda and Mike left Gary about eight years ago, when she was still a teenager, and now she is twenty-seven. They have since gotten married—she no longer has to use the Cooper name—and they have a five-year-old son, Parish. She is as close to happy as she's ever been.

After Paula's arrest, Rhonda was dogged by reporters, and she tried a few times to speak to them, to be useful. She knew the impression she made had some chance of helping her sister in court. And so when *60 Minutes* reached out for their Lake County shoot, she agreed to an interview at the apartment she and Mike had been sharing with some friends. As the crew wrapped up in the living room, the couple talked with Mr. Reasoner; they said they hoped to leave town soon, to regain some privacy, they just didn't know where to go. Reasoner told them an old fraternity brother had recently relocated to Minneapolis, where he himself had grown up; he thought they'd love it there. After the segment aired on CBS, they thought, *Why* not *Minneapolis?* They packed their things and got on a bus. At nineteen, Rhonda was starting her third life.

Paula had been nervous at the thought of her sister leaving a second time. But Rhonda told her, "I can't do this anymore here. I've taken this part as far as I can take it. I have to go and get some air and breathe." Paula understood. She asked her sister to promise to visit.

When Rhonda and Mike first arrived at their new town, there was nearly a foot of snow on the ground, and it was freezing cold. They couldn't believe it. She imagined this was what Antarctica looked like. Neither of them had good boots or down coats or any of that—they'd thought Minneapolis would be like the movie *Purple Rain*.

In a way, it was: Prince was there. On one of their first nights in town, Mike took Rhonda out to First Avenue, the nightclub. There were over a thousand people inside, but the crowd parted: two large men were carrying someone through. That's when Rhonda began hollering, "Oh my God, *Prince!* Do you see him? That's *Prince!*" Nobody was shouting but her; she had no idea he was there all the time, sometimes playing for hours for a cheap cover. She followed close behind his security until one of the men whipped around and told her, "Get *back*, lady." It took her awhile to calm down.

They arrived in Minneapolis with a single trunk, but within two years they had bought a house and furnished it. Between Mike's gigs playing jazz guitar and their shifts at the hospital, their entire focus during those months was on working and saving and moving forward. Eventually, her father Ron joined them, offering to take care of Parish while they worked, and Mike was happy to have him around. Maybe, Rhonda thought, she had finally gotten out.

At first, no one knew about her sister—she was careful which of her new friends she told that part of her story. Her schedule at the hospital was flexible, and her employers were aware of her situation, so she would travel to see Paula in Indianapolis about once a month, whenever there was the money for it. There were also the times, before Paula's sentence was commuted, when Rhonda got a call from one of the new attorneys, Monica Foster, asking to fly her to Indy to talk to some reporters. It wasn't that Monica *asked*, actually—she had a way of firing you up, making it nearly impossible to refuse, even when Rhonda was not in the mood to repeat the tale of her tragic childhood. Monica would say, "Rhonda, get a grip. Snap out of it! You're going to have to tell your story. We're trying to get your sister off death row. *Do you understand?*" Rhonda would fly into Indy—and Mike and Parish too, if need be—and she'd meet Monica and Patti at the Hilton. There Monica would become her coach, pumping her up, telling her to go in the bathroom and wash her face, do her makeup, do whatever would help her perform.

Rhonda had first caught sight of Monica during the motion for a new sentencing, and she was struck by the fire in the woman's voice when she spoke about Paula in court. They were only about seven years apart, but Rhonda, who was not easily impressed by authority figures, had instant respect for her. The woman's spirit was *Let's get it done, get it done, get it done. We are going to deal with this.* Rhonda also saw her, during that time, as a mother figure to Paula. And as someone very aware of her role as a big sister, Rhonda came to see Monica as *her* older sister. She and Paula, who had trusted so few people in their lives thus far, trusted her. While they were apart, her sister wanted to talk on the phone nearly every day, and the bill sometimes came to $450 or $500 for the month; Rhonda had to limit their conversations. Monica's calls and visits made up the difference.

When Rhonda traveled to Gary, she'd stay with Mike's parents in his childhood home and drive those two and a half hours south to Indy and IWP. The prison facility on Randolph Street was more than a century old and the visiting room so small that she often had to stand in a line that curled outdoors, sometimes in the freezing cold, because the place could not hold everyone. But once inside, she was treated as if she were famous. She would hear from the other residents, *That's Rhonda! That's Paula's sister right there!* This was how she learned that most times she'd sent Paula a package, or bought her something from the commissary, her sister had shared the stuff with as many of her friends as possible. Rhonda had no idea she'd been providing for these other women.

Beyond these visits there was also the annual family picnic, in an outdoor area of the facility. Residents could invite their relatives and have them bring in whatever food they liked. In Paula's case, Rhonda was always the one to organize it, to make sure everyone marked it on their calendar and knew their potluck assignment. Sometimes she'd buy takeout that she knew her sister missed: White Castle, McDonald's, barbeque ribs. On that day, they were allowed to sit outside together and eat and talk and take photos—photos that would look like normal life. They could sit out there for hours. On that day, they had time.

———— ⚘ ————

Just as Paula was leaving death row, Superintendent Trigg was moved to a men's facility, and Dana Blank, his deputy, became interim warden and eventually took over. Ms. Blank, as the women call her, is in her late forties, her blonde hair carefully coiffed—she styles herself more like a headmistress than the superintendent of the state's only women's prison. Back when she was in college, she had actually majored in recreation, with an eye to becoming a social director at a resort.

With Ms. Blank as superintendent, the tone of the place is beginning to shift. Since this is the only max facility for women in the state, the population includes Indiana's most violent female offenders. Most are single mothers, victims of domestic violence or child abuse; many are in prison because of things they did to support an addiction, from theft to prostitution. But Ms. Blank says the staff is not there to "warehouse" the women but to "nurture" them. For every inmate she oversees, she knows that person's name, the important people in her life, her level of education, whether or not her mother is ill. In front of the officers, she might say to a group of inmates, *If you need anything, you tell the guards, and I'll see what I can do.*

But she considers Paula Cooper a challenge. In the warden's experience, the women who committed homicide are actually the easiest population to manage. The long-termers understand that this prison is now their home, and they want to make it as peaceful as they can; they decorate their room to make it their own, and they settle in. Paula does not fit into this pattern. She refuses to "settle in" and accept the hierarchy inherent in this place, her home for the calculable future. For Ms. Blank and the officers, her behavior is difficult and unchanging. In her first nine years in prison, Paula is written up for thirty-five rules violations—many of which she disputes—including fifteen confrontations with guards and six with other inmates. Just before she was moved off death row, she had written to Father Vito, *I plan on adjusting my attitude so that I will be clear of any problems.* Her time, thus far, has not played out that way.

There are two Paulas: there is the Paula who is known to the outside, through the press and through activists, and there is the Paula beyond the public eye. For Ms. Blank, these two selves are far apart. Again and again, the warden returns to the same few words to describe this particular resident: *manipulative, devious, treacherous.* She sees Paula as someone gifted at making others believe she is a victim, whether of society at large or some petty conflict inside the prison. Someone who plays gentle and soft-spoken to get what she wants from people. Much of the staff watches her closely. Monica believes Trigg and Ms. Blank showed no empathy for the situation of a teenager on death row. The warden, for her part, believes that Monica was easy for Paula to manipulate during their visits. That Paula would go into the visiting room and cry and be "poor and pitiful," only to drop the performance once she got back to her cell.

One day, Paula attacks a staff person—a rare occurrence in Ms. Blank's facility. A close friend of hers is being moved to another housing unit, and Paula lashes out. She jumps a nearby officer—someone with whom she's repeatedly had friction. When Ms. Blank sees the officer, she thinks, *She did some damage to this lady.*

With the disciplinary board, a standard of punishment exists for a range of specific violations, with minor offenses like theft receiving one to sixty days in lockup, adjusted for mitigating circumstances. The maximum sentence is three years, though no one has ever received more than twelve months—already a painful length of time to spend in segregation. Ms. Blank makes a practice of telling the residents that if they are found guilty of a disciplinary offense and cause no problems while serving that time, she will release them from lockup early. And she makes good on this promise, because often a person simply needs a cooling-off period, time to settle down and regroup, and then they can rejoin the population. But there is an exception: If someone ever attacks an officer, she says, they will do every minute of their disciplinary sentence.

Paula receives the maximum: three years—more than a thousand days—in segregation. She left death row in the disciplinary unit at twenty years old, and she is now returning to that unit at twenty-five.

Years earlier, Paula had written to Bill, *there cant be an explanation about how prison life really is because its too much to be explained.* In this way, no matter how close she and her sister may be, no matter the ever-growing number of phone calls and visits, there is a limit to what even Rhonda is capable of understanding about Paula's days and nights.

But there is also a great deal that Paula does not know about her older sister. Shortly after Rhonda received the good news that Paula's sentence had been commuted, she had a reaction that no one anticipated: she experienced a profound nervous breakdown. She was severely depressed and received severe treatment: hospitalization and electroconvulsive (or "electroshock") therapy. *A mad breakdown,* she would later call it. This would be the first of several episodes.

Back when Paula was in jail and throughout her winding appeal, Rhonda felt she had to be on her best behavior. She was no longer *just Rhonda;* anything she said, the way she dressed, whatever someone might learn about her, became a part of her sister's story too. Whenever she got a call from a reporter, she knew she could never snap, no matter how intrusive that person might be—because she didn't want some news-paper to print that she'd been rude, another mark against Paula Cooper, more proof that her sister was contaminated and from a contaminated source. So Rhonda had to be *good,* she had to be *nice.* And when the case came to an end, when her sister's emergency was over and she was able to breathe more easily, Rhonda fell apart completely. She was comfort-able in Minneapolis, with a partner and a child she had always wanted, but she'd never had the time to deal with what was living inside of her.

Rhonda was seven years old the first time she was assaulted by Glo-ria's younger brother. Three summers passed that way, until Rhonda was nine. Paula was always nearby—just four, then five, then six years old—and her sister kept that in mind as their uncle continued to force himself on her, telling her to keep it secret. She was convinced that if, somehow, she managed to escape his attentions, he would turn to Paula.

Almost twenty years have passed, and Rhonda still has not told her sister, even though it is with her constantly. The smallest thing might summon up a memory—a scent, a song—and send her right back to that place.

About six years after her first breakdown, Rhonda and her small family moved to Atlanta, where they are now. There's more going on there than even in Minneapolis, and with none of that snow. But her uncle endures, a constant presence in Rhonda's mind and body. She knows that the man is now in prison in Illinois, and sometimes Rhonda calls the facility to make sure he is still inside. He is not doing time for what he did to her—she never reported him—and so she tells whoever picks up the phone what *else* he is guilty of. She understands this is not a logical thing to do, but it gives her a calm that lasts the rest of the day.

Rhonda has a new therapist in Atlanta, and she sees her every week— the beginning of years of regular therapy for her. She is also on medication for a range of mental illnesses including depression. They knew as young people that their maternal grandmother had been diagnosed with paranoid schizophrenia—mental illness, Rhonda thinks, must be hereditary on her mother's side. How else to explain Gloria's behavior? Otherwise the woman is *just mean, just bad*.

One afternoon, after several sessions spent discussing her uncle, Rhonda's therapist makes a suggestion. "When you're ready," she says, "I want you, because you've never addressed him before, to start out by writing him a letter and letting him know how you felt, and how you feel."

Rhonda writes the letter. She pours everything into it. She writes that she thinks constantly of the times he abused her, of how he infested her life. She writes as if to say, *This is what happened to me, LOOK at it.*

She hears back quickly. *I'm so sorry that I did that to you. I did do that. And I'm very sorry.*

She does not forgive him. And she does not ever want him to walk out of prison. But he had written back. He had apologized. And what means the most to Rhonda is: he had borne witness to her story.

Rhonda and Mike would probably have chosen to stay in Atlanta forever. But they now find themselves pulled back to where they came from.

Mike's mother, who long ago had been Earline Rogers's supervisor in the Gary public school system, is sick, and he has to be there to care for her. And so he and Rhonda change their plans. He looks for work in the health-care system in Lake County. They sell their house and most of the furniture. They move back into his childhood home.

Gloria had been living in Atlanta since Paula's arrest—but she was busy with her new marriage, and Rhonda had managed to keep some distance between them. Within a year of their move, however, her mother announces she is following them back to Indiana. Something about being closer to family—or, as her daughter puts it, "Blah-blah-blah, blah-blah-blah." But Rhonda sets her cynicism aside: She is now thirty-two years old and a mother herself, and maybe there is a way for Gloria to be a part of her new family. She thinks of the word *compassion*. She keeps an open mind.

As they spend time together again in Gary, Rhonda realizes that she needs to tell her mother. She needs to talk to her about their uncle. She arranges for them to be alone; she waits for the right moment. And when she is finished speaking, Gloria says to her, "You're lying. That's a lie."

And that is the end of their conversation.

It is one more dark story Rhonda must carry, with nowhere to put it down. It is one more way in which two young girls were failed by their caregivers.

Eighteen

A PEARL OF GREAT PRICE

After Paula's sentence was commuted, Monica Foster stayed in touch. She attended a couple of the annual picnics—but eventually, she stopped reaching out. She'd grown frustrated: Paula is not taking her advice. Her sentence will be cut in half if she acts right, but she does not seem to understand the importance of good behavior while serving time. *She needs to have absolutely stellar conduct*, Monica thinks, *and she is a really long flipping way from that.* Sixty years versus thirty: in Paula's mind, it seems, both are life sentences, so what's the difference? Later on, Monica will look back and think, *Of course she acted out—look at how she grew up, look at her age.* But at the moment, this girl—a *woman*, in her early twenties—appears to be squandering the second chance she'd won. When she is given three years in segregation, Monica is not informed; she has already taken a step back. The number of people on Indiana's death row has nearly doubled since Paula's sentencing, and she has clients in desperate need of her attention.

Over the past few years, Monica has become an established attorney in her own right, with a private practice in Indianapolis and part-time work as a Marion County public defender. Death-penalty appeals are her focus. The sheer amount of time each case requires can be overwhelming, the stakes cannot be higher, and the postconviction process can seem endless. But this is the work she's drawn to, and her time with Paula had made it personal. This gives her an unstoppable drive—what she thinks of as her best weapon against the prosecution. Years later she will say, "I always want to save my people more than they want to kill them."

Monica had gone into practice with her public-defender friend Rhonda Long-Sharp, the attorney she'd convinced to take over the appeal of her first client, James Allen Harris. In the spring of 1988, once her work on Paula's case was done, the two women went into business with Monica's new husband, Bob Hammerle. Monica thought that for the other attorneys in their shared office, guys Bob had risen up with, this new arrangement was a big deal—because she was younger than them and "a girl." But she knew she was becoming someone to contend with.

When Paula was charged with a capital offense, there were about 1,400 people on death rows across the country; now there are 2,890. Forty-one of them had been sentenced to death for crimes committed under the age of eighteen and have not been spared like Paula. This year alone, 1994, would bring nearly the highest number of individuals sentenced to death in the country's history. Support for the death penalty has become the ultimate proof of a political candidate's tough-on-crime stance, and its public support is now at its highest: 80 percent, up from 70 when Paula was sentenced.

And now Monica has two clients on death row—Gregory Resnover and Tommy Schiro—who are in the final stages of their appeals. The next execution will be the first in Indiana since that of William Vandiver in 1985, and prison officials are still uncertain what went wrong that time. In Michigan City, an execution team is rehearsing the procedure once a month.

There is a saying repeated over and over by attorneys who represent those accused of particularly heinous crimes, and both Monica and her husband put great faith in it: *No one is defined by the worst thing they have done.* For some this is another way of saying *No one is better than anyone else.* No one is a lesser person; we are all shaped by our circumstances.

Monica is drawn to representing the guilty, the *demonstrably* guilty, like Schiro; she'd rather argue for mercy than innocence. She sees it as a nobler cause to convince people (judges, jurors) to recognize their own faults and failings, to see her clients as fellow human beings. Years later, she will explain it this way: "I'm not a religious person, but I think that we are all sinners. We're all fuckups. And how much punishment are we entitled to extract from them?"

In the fall of 1994, Gregory Resnover's date is set: December 7. Chief Justice Randall Shepard signs the order. The execution team begins practicing weekly.

Gregory had been convicted of taking part in the shooting death of an officer serving a warrant to a house in Indy in 1980, and though Gregory had not fired a gun, a poorly mounted defense at trial had allowed faulty evidence into the record. All his appeals have failed; there is little room left to maneuver. December arrives, and the governor denies clemency. Monica, Bob, and Rhonda continue strategizing, but the window is swiftly closing.

The work is changing the rhythm of Monica's days. The personal clarity with which she approaches the job does not prevent her from living with profound anxiety—anxiety around even the smallest decisions she makes on behalf of her clients. Paula saw the beginnings of this, saw Monica break out in acne from the stress, saw her cry during their visits. The anxiety wakes her in the middle of the night and leaves her staring at her ceiling, listing *all the reasons why I suck*, all the reasons her decisions were wrong. And then she argues the other side, and then she takes another angle and another, and then the sun is coming up and it's time to go to the office, and Gregory Resnover's date is growing closer.

When Paula is about a year into her time in segregation, Bill and Judy Pelke celebrate their eighth wedding anniversary, hundreds of miles from home. It is their third consecutive anniversary on the road caravanning with the Journey—there was Georgia, then California, and now two weeks in Virginia.

When they return home from the Virginia Journey—a nonstop, all-day drive in the van, taking shifts—they are both exhausted. But they always have a day set aside after a big trip to sleep it off. With Bill now forty-nine and Judy thirty-seven, their relationship has been solid for years. After the long time it took Judy to earn her nursing degree, Bill helping out at home, she has swapped cocktail waitressing for a good job in the nursery of a nearby hospital. They take turns picking each other up when their shifts are done. Bill can finally see them, in his mind's eye, growing old together. He can see her as his wife, his partner, his confederate.

Bill has managed, after years of resistance, to fold Judy into his new work. He was aware, early on, that Judy had told her friends the rallies were "Bill's thing." He was aware that she held on to an instinctive feeling that anger was natural, human, as was the desire for retribution when someone harmed someone you loved. She did not believe the state should be allowed to kill—but sometimes she read the news and thought, *There are individuals who should not be allowed to live.* Bill let Judy know how badly he wanted her to join in, and over the past few years, she'd begun making an effort. She started using long weekends or vacation days to travel to whatever rally he might be taking part in. And when Bill was organizing the first Journey, through Indiana, she was as supportive as she could be, while still working a full-time job and raising three teenagers. She brought the kids along on the Journey, stuffed in the van with all those duffel bags and their Great Dane Trixie. Throughout the trip, Judy shot videos with their camcorder, and each time she caught Bill in her sights, he'd wink or blow a kiss. He introduced her to family members of people on death row who were maintaining their innocence, and the chance they might have been wrongfully condemned gnawed at her. She met a woman whose brother *had* committed murder and was sentenced to death for it, and for the first time Judy thought, *Isn't there a possibility one of my brothers could mess up like that?*—her brothers, whom she loved power-fully. After hearing these testimonies for days and weeks, she was left with the certainty that capital punishment was terribly wrong.

Since that night in the crane at Bethlehem, Bill has been praying again, in private. In a way, it brought his childhood faith back to him. Judy had never felt comfortable inside a church. She was always struck by how much they talked about the money you should give, never a week without that collection plate. He and Judy tried a few churches together, but they couldn't find a place that felt good to them, a place they wanted to take the kids. She settled on a looser idea, something more New Age: God is within you. She didn't push much harder and deeper than that. Some-times Judy wonders: If she'd been raised more religious, like Bill, might she be better able to bend herself toward a cause?

In the long lead-up to the Indiana Journey, after Bill sent out infor-mation about the event to death rows around the country, he was con-tacted by the wife of a condemned man in Michigan City. Beverly had seen an ad in a prison paper and was asking the Journey organizers for support. She claimed that her husband, Perry Steven Miller, had been sentenced to death for a crime he had not committed. And so Bill and Steven, two forty-five-year-old working-class men from Northwest In-diana, struck up a correspondence. *In my particular case,* Steven wrote, *the conviction was all that mattered. Seeking the truth never existed and still doesn't.* He suggested that MVFR lend financial support to men on death row—for expenses such as, for example, the cigars he liked to smoke. They might also give his wife a job.

Bill did not know the details of Steven's crime, and he did not have an opinion about the man's guilt—he *might* be innocent, he thought. Bill was more interested in him as a soldier for the abolitionist movement. He suggested to the rest of the Journey committee that they find a role for Steven, and he spoke about the man's case during a promotional ap-pearance on local radio.

Judy knew very well why Steven Miller was on death row.

A year earlier, she and Bill and the kids had taken a road trip to D.C. for the annual conference of the National Coalition to Abolish the Death Penalty. The group had cosponsored the Pilgrimage from Florida to Georgia, and Bill was able to reunite with many of the marchers at the 4-H conference center, some of whom were Journey organizers. Plus, Marie Deans was being honored, and she and Judy had immediately loved each other: Judy has always appreciated a woman who speaks her mind. That weekend with Bill's abolitionist family felt good to Judy, as if she and Bill were into something righteous together.

A few days later, when they were back at home, the story of a horrific crime flooded the local news: a high school senior had been kidnapped during her night shift at a White Hen Pantry convenience store a short drive away, in Judy's hometown of Valparaiso. A police officer had stopped into the store around one-thirty a.m., as a lot of local officers did on their late shift, and noticed that the clerk was missing—a pretty, freckled girl with feathered hair, a little young for her age. She had been abducted only twenty minutes earlier. A mercifully abbreviated account of what happened next: The young woman was taken to a construction site miles away, brutally raped, beaten, tortured, and shot in the back of the head. The next day, as he walked the site, the contractor discovered her body.

Her name was Christel Helmchen. She was going to start college in two months and had been babysitting and working at the White Hen to help pay her way. She was good at planning ahead and saving money: at sixteen, she waited tables to cover some expenses when her parents allowed her to study abroad in West Germany (her father had emigrated from Berlin). She was very close with her brother and sister; she played duets on the violin with her father.

Two young men were arrested on the Thursday morning after Christel's killing: they had driven south to Kentucky in her car and a stolen pickup, and the plates gave them away. They were Billy Harmon, nineteen, who was Steven Miller's stepson, and Rodney Wood, sixteen, Billy's friend. Both lived with Steven and his wife. Steven, a delivery man for a LaPorte bakery, was arrested next; he had been out on parole after serving nineteen years of a life sentence for kidnapping and rape. By the following spring, Steven, as the ringleader, had been sentenced to death. By the fall, he had the attention of the Journey organizers.

In D.C. with the Journey members, Judy had been so focused, so much against the right of the state to kill, and now she was saying to Bill, "We need that death penalty, because that guy Miller has got to die. He took this little girl and tortured her." That girl, just a few years older than her daughter Taniya, her mother's name also Judy, snuffed out. Judy could not imagine forgiving Steven Miller, and she could not imagine fighting to save his life.

G regory Resnover's date arrives, and Monica, Bob, and their team gather at the death house.

That afternoon, ahead of the late-night execution, a judge orders the Department of Correction to install a video camera on a tripod in the back of the witness room. An attorney had filed a request, on behalf of six Lake County men sentenced to death, to videotape the proceedings to study the impact of electrocution on the body. She'd been denied—but the ACLU had succeeded. Death-penalty abolitionists believe this footage will shake the public out of acceptance. It is a year and a half since the Journey traveled through Indiana, and Bill Pelke, identified as the grandson of Ruth Pelke, tells the press, "When people see someone strapped into a chair and electrocuted, it's going to turn their stomachs and make them sick."

At six p.m., the execution team leads Gregory to a holding cell. At seven, the defense attorneys realize their job is done: the execution will proceed as planned, at midnight. At nine, about twenty of his relatives are permitted to enter the prison grounds; some of them crowd inside the outdoor guard shack to avoid the December cold. A crush of people stand on the other side of the gate: some hold signs cheering on the execution; some shout out "Fry him!" and "A life for a life!" Then there are the abolitionists. Among them stands Bill, under the bright light of a camera crew. "I can understand the pain," he tells a reporter. "There is a healing that needs to take place, and an execution has nothing to do with healing."

A half hour passes, and the Indiana Supreme Court blocks the taping. There will be no visual record. Only once has such documentation been allowed—of the execution of Robert Alton Harris, two and a half years ago, in California's San Quentin prison—and never again. In modern times, this process remains as veiled as possible, far from the "public executions in the town square" that so repulsed Jack Crawford. Gregory Resnover had written a direct invitation to Evan Bayh—*Come witness the fruits of your labors*—but the governor will not be attending.

Monica and her partner Rhonda are just arriving, having sped for three hours along the highway from Indianapolis. There they'd spent the evening waiting for word, by fax, of their last, unlikely hope—a federal appeal—only to have that effort fail. They have about twenty minutes left to spend inside with Gregory, before they are asked to leave. The moment has arrived.

Gregory's seven witnesses, Bob among them, are escorted by guards into a waiting room, through a metal detector and a series of steel gates, and eventually outside again, down a short path and into the small viewing room. There, rows of plastic folding chairs have been set up to face a large window covered by venetian blinds. Everyone sits in silence. Without warning, in a single gesture, the blinds are drawn all the way up, and here he is: a hooded man strapped into the chair. And it happens: Gregory is jolted upward. A light cloud of smoke rises from the hood. At some point, Gregory's body loses all tension—only to buck again, then fall still. He was strapped into the chair at 12:08 a.m., and he is pronounced dead at 12:13. The smell of burnt flesh sweeps into the viewing room. The blinds descend.

On his way out of the death house, Bob is crying. He tries to collect himself, but he cannot. When they reach the gate, where the press is waiting, a pair of friends grabs his arms and escorts him to a waiting car. They drive off the grounds without looking back.

Monica, Bob, and Rhonda stay in Michigan City that night, at a motel. A cluster of supporters keeps them company. Someone goes out to pick up a bottle of Jack Daniels, and they drink to anesthetize themselves. Among their team, Bob had been closest to Gregory—but Monica feels nauseous most of the night. She does *not* think about Paula and how she might have lost her, how she might have had to sit and watch, through a window, as the state took her life.

No one sleeps much at all.

The next afternoon, Gregory's family and attorneys and attorneys' friends meet with the mortician to pick up the body for transport. Then the caravan sets out for Indianapolis, a hearse followed by a string of a dozen vehicles.

It is sometime during this three-hour drive that the idea occurs to Monica: It is the night of Governor Bayh's big Christmas party. They will drive this caravan past the governor's home. "If Evan Bayh will not come to Gregory Resnover," says Bob, "Gregory Resnover will come to Evan Bayh." After what he has just experienced, Bob agrees to the plan. Monica has a cell phone, and she starts calling the press.

The mansion is a grand English Tudor, set back from the curb about 150 feet, and across that distance stretches a manicured lawn and the half-moon of a paved driveway. But from the road, where the caravan stops that evening, you can see the windows of the mansion, lit brightly from within. Reporters are also here now, scattered across the grass. Bob lays on the horn, and soon the other drivers do the same, and they can make out the silhouettes of maybe a hundred guests flooding the windows.

They do not step out of their vehicles, they just keep that noise going.

The police stand watch, and after a long-enough moment of that sustained shitty sound the lead officer steps up and motions for them to move along. The street falls quiet. Slowly, the crowd falls back from the windows. The cars drive on.

When Bayh was elected governor, the influential Democratic attorney Ed Lewis threw a party for him at his house in Brown County. Every Democrat of note was invited, and Bob and Monica were among them; they watched as the governor arrived by helicopter. And now they are on the outside, having escorted a corpse to that same governor's annual Christmas gathering.

They see their allies differently now—and they are fewer in number. The players in the state Democratic Party keep their distance from Monica and Bob, and the couple accepts that price. The realities of their work have transformed them.

But this is the beginning of living with the trauma of what Bob witnessed. He often wakes up screaming, in a cold sweat; he reminds Monica of men who have seen combat. And one night, in the months after the execution, while Bob is actually asleep, *Monica* wakes up—or she *feels* she woke up—to see Gregory sitting at the end of their bed. Their house is haunted by Gregory Resnover. Monica thinks: *This is a consequence of the work.* Sometimes she imagines her job is to stand in front of a high-speed train, delusional enough to think she can stop it from tearing through people.

Her husband will need years to recover from the shock of that execution. He has one more death-penalty appeal, which he sees through, but he will never take a capital case again. He cannot. For Bob, it is hard to even describe his experience in the death house.

Monica, however, keeps on. Bob admires her for it, even though it is a divergence between them.

Among her clients, still, is Tommy Schiro, who has yet to receive an execution date, and she continues to fight on his behalf. After another year and a half of work—including an unsuccessful argument before the U.S. Supreme Court—Monica wins the appeal. Schiro's sentence is commuted. And a man is taken off death row.

A t the end of each June, some of the Journey members, along with other death-penalty abolitionists, carry out a tradition: a Fast and Vigil on the sidewalk in front of the U.S. Supreme Court. For the four days between the anniversaries of *Furman v. Georgia*, which ended the death penalty in 1972, and *Gregg v. Georgia*, which allowed for its revival in 1976, a small but growing number of abolitionists stand out in the hot summer sun, most with empty stomachs, holding up signs, sharing their stories with any passersby on First Street NE on Capitol Hill.

Bill is pleased to see Judy taking part. She's stayed engaged, she's kept trying. She joined him and many of the Journey folks in D.C. for the second Fast and Vigil, sang the chants, managed to fast for the whole four days—even spent the last night out on that sidewalk in a sleeping bag, as was the tradition, the Court's "temple of justice" façade looming over them, the Capitol Building visible across the way, the streets silent save for the rare passing cab. She could hardly sleep, but it was fun, that kind of togetherness. She drew the line during the fourth Fast and Vigil, however, at volunteering to get arrested for protesting up on the steps of the Court. Bill, against her wishes, joined the group that spent a day in jail. Judy could not have stopped him anyway.

That jail time in D.C. did not really bother her as much as the degree to which Bill's activism had come to permeate their life together. There was the anniversary spent on the California Journey, and her birthday spent in the audience of an *Oprah Winfrey Show* taping about the death penalty, and the Valentine's Day back on the West Coast for a panel on murder victims' families. Looking back, even their honeymoon, though made *possible* by his activism (travel to Italy with free lodgings), had been built around Bill's talks. For some time now, Bill has thought of it, this commitment, as *the pearl of great price* in the book of Matthew—when Jesus compares the kingdom of heaven to a merchant hunting for pearls: *When he had found one of great value, he went away and sold everything he had and bought it.* But Judy was not sure how they had come to spend so many of their holidays and vacation days protesting the death penalty; there did not seem to be nearly as much *us* time. His drive to save Paula Cooper had become an ambition that might never be satisfied in their lifetime: to save *all* the Paula Coopers.

Bethlehem Steel provided couples counseling, and Bill and Judy decided to sign up. They agreed to take it seriously, and they began looking more closely at their marriage. For their third meeting, the therapist asked them each to bring in a list of things they wanted in life: Judy wrote down *happiness* and money; top on her list was a Harley-Davidson. First for Bill was *world peace*, second *abolition of the death penalty*. The stark disparity in their life's desires did not give the counselor pause, and their sessions came to an end. But much later, Bill would look back on this as a defining moment.

Bill had known about Judy's dream of owning a bike—she'd grown up around Harleys. Her brother Mike, seven years older than her, built his first Harley in his bedroom when he was sixteen, and Judy had been so impressed. He'd driven her to junior high, and all her girlfriends loved him. And so when Bill bought Judy a Harley as a surprise, she flipped out. Each time she returned from a ride she told Bill she loved him. He thought it was well worth the cost.

About six months later, they found themselves celebrating their eighth wedding anniversary in Virginia, on a Journey. And when they returned home, the stores had Halloween decorations in the windows. And in a few weeks' time those displays turned to gourds and cornucopia and cardboard pilgrims: it was nearly Thanksgiving.

This is when, early on a Saturday afternoon, Judy gets the call: her sister Carolyn has just been shot by her husband Ron, and now dozens of armed officers are positioned outside their home in Valparaiso. One of Carolyn's children from her first marriage, nine-year-old Nick, witnessed the shooting before being forced out of the house.

At the police station, everyone is waiting. Talking to Carolyn's kids, they learn that she had left Ron about a week earlier, and then quickly gotten back together with him. He had carried a gun for a while now, unbeknownst to Carolyn's family or friends. Around midday, Carolyn had decided to bake cookies for Thanksgiving, so she'd announced that she was going to the store. She wanted to take Nick with her; "Leave him here," Ron said. When she resisted, he struck her. She told the boy to call 911. As her son rang the police, her husband drew his gun and shot Carolyn in the head in front of the child. Then he pointed the gun at Nick and ordered him to hang up the phone. "Get out," Ron told him. As Nick rushed outside, he heard more gunshots. When the police arrived, they found Nick hiding in the family car.

Now hours have passed. And the police have yet to enter the house, afraid that the man is still alive, armed, and on the attack. Judy's mother presses harder: "She's been shot. Nick *said* she was shot. You need to get in that house!"

No movement. It is late November, and by four-thirty the sky is already darkening, and soon there are no lights down that long driveway. Still the authorities continue to wait. Finally, at eight-thirty that night, they shoot tear gas through the windows and force their way in.

Of course, Carolyn is dead. So is Ron: he had shot himself not long after killing his wife.

The family buries Carolyn the day before Thanksgiving. And then they all—including their mother and Bill—head up to Wisconsin to Mike's house for the weekend. They want to get away, especially from the media. At the log cabin, Bill comes up with an idea: a retreat center for members of the abolition movement who recently experienced a tragedy; the Journey could run it. Judy thinks this is sweet of Bill—but at the same time, she asks, "Maybe you should just focus on *my family* right now? Maybe you should just think about *us* right now?" She knows he can't separate himself from the cause. *Anything that happens*, she thinks, *he brings it back around to the death penalty. Everything, everything.*

Judy tries to move forward. But her mother cannot go on. She keeps photos of Carolyn and objects of hers on her kitchen table—Judy thinks of it as a shrine—and she cries whenever she is around her other children. A year and a half later, at sixty-two and in good health, she will pass without warning.

Throughout all this, Judy occasionally asks herself, *What if Ron had lived?* She and Bill talk about it. For her, the answer is clear: her brothers would be on death row, because they would have killed him. Even if he were in prison, they would have found a way. It was a huge relief that Ron had shot himself. This way, no one has to consider the death penalty—not for Ron, and not for her brothers.

With her sister's death, it's as if Judy is catching up with the company she keeps. She tries to think like them—the Journey people—but Judy knows that she will never be able to forgive Ron for what he did. Not for her sister's death and not, later on, for her mother's. She understands that the act of forgiving would be for her *own* sake—she's heard the stories—but it is beyond her ability. Forgiveness is "some kind of trick" she cannot perform.

Years back, when Bill spoke to Judy about his vision in the crane, that image of his grandmother crying, she'd asked, "How do you know, Bill, that your Nana was crying for Paula Cooper? Because if I were her, those tears would be for *the way that I died.*" But Bill was sure. He will be sure for thirty years and counting.

The night they returned from the police station, after nearly seven hours of waiting for word of her sister, after so much terrible news—Judy will never forget it. It was late, and she remembers how Bill drove them home, and how they walked with heavy feet into the dining room and collapsed into their seats at the table. Judy could hardly think; her head hurt. Sleep seemed unlikely. And that was when Bill said it:

"Now you're a murder victim family member, too."

She loves him. But she will never forgive him for it.

Nineteen

A NETWORK
OF FINE THREADS

I n the late fall of 1999, Stephen Harper, an attorney in Miami, receives an email from the American Bar Association. The new year, it says—the new millennium—will begin with the executions, by lethal injection, of five individuals sentenced to death at seventeen years old. These are scheduled to happen back-to-back, over the course of two weeks.

The memo comes from Patti Puritz of the ABA's Juvenile Justice Center, someone Stephen has known for years, and it is very simple: a list of names accompanied by their execution dates and basic statistics as provided by Victor Streib. The message is a reminder that the country is still executing young people; that death, for teenagers, is not an empty sentence inevitably thrown out on appeal. More than fifteen years ago, Victor had drafted a resolution: a promise that the ABA, according to its core principles, would stand against capital punishment for anyone under the age of eighteen. Patti feels she inherited the issue, and here is the moment to strike: seventy people are now on death row who were sentenced as juveniles, with five scheduled for execution. And so her memo is also a call to action: to help assemble a network to finally end the death penalty for juveniles in the United States. Stephen is on board, immediately.

Patti approaches about a half dozen juvenile attorneys—and this makes innate sense to Stephen: they are the ones who best understand the urgency of the issue, who have seen how immature, uninformed, frenetic, and traumatized clients that age can be. He would later say, "Our attitude was: If you can kill a kid, then *all* kids' lives are worth less. If you do that, there's no problem locking a kid up for the rest of his life."

Stephen is a capital lawyer who was recently the head of the juvenile division of the Public Defender's Office of Miami-Dade County. He's in his late forties now, and he'd gotten into juvenile law sixteen years ago because he felt he had an unusual talent for relating to children—perhaps because he believed he'd never fully grown up, a kind of Peter Pan. But above all, he held the conviction that they were unlike adults, deserving of special lawyers and special attention. He'd taken case after case, pushing for better treatment for his clients, until a few years ago, when Florida revised its statutes to be far more punitive to children and wiped out all his gains seemingly overnight. Even for someone with his excess of spirit, it was a terrible blow. Once he regained his bearings, he thought, *I can't save a kid's life, so I might as well save an adult*, and he began taking on capital cases in criminal court. For Stephen, this memo gives him a chance to return to his work for young people—but beyond the state of Florida, and with the highest stakes possible.

The group begins tackling this larger project after hours or on weekends, alongside their full-time jobs. For three of the five condemned men, the effort comes too late—Douglas Thomas, Steve Roach, and Glen McGinnis are executed in January as scheduled, in Virginia and Texas—but the other two are granted stays. And so on behalf of them, and the nearly seventy others without execution dates thus far, this unofficial team begins to stir up publicity. They build a section of the ABA website dedicated to the history of the death penalty for juveniles, full of Victor Streib's research, and the latest information on ongoing cases. They begin writing op-eds and giving interviews—and they find that many Americans are unaware that the country is executing minors. Central to their talking points is one simple idea that neatly removes the issue from the politics around the death penalty: *Kids are different*. And these differences make them less culpable than adults.

That spring, Stephen and Chicago juvenile attorney Steve Drizin coauthor an opinion piece to give the public a sense of the history and the urgency of the issue, and the *San Francisco Examiner* runs it as a three-page feature. They write of adolescence as *a transitional period of life where cognitive abilities, judgment, impulse control, identity and emotions are still being developed*. For all these reasons, they say, teenagers are capable of rehabilitation. They write of how the United States was once ahead of the rest of the world in its creation of the first separate court system for juveniles—but now it is nearly alone in its application of the death penalty to young people. Their message is framed by a sprawling photo spread: mug shots of every person sent to death row under eighteen. Thomas, Roach, and McGinnis are included, their images stamped with the word *EXECUTED*. There is a chance, Stephen thinks, they will be the last.

In the fall of 2000, Patti and a contingent at Northwestern law school in Chicago organize a small conference. About twenty people are in attendance—a chance for the team to test their strategy with attorneys and scholars in criminal and juvenile justice, human rights groups, death-penalty abolitionists, and, specifically, Victor Streib. Many at the gathering look on Victor as the godfather of the young movement they're here to formalize; they've been following, and will continue to build on, the model of state-by-state work that he improvised fifteen years ago. They want his blessing and his counsel—and Victor seems happy to give it, though he's skeptical of how much faster they'll be able to make progress. *Many* in the room are skeptical: they're recovering from the past decade's approach to crime, with its view of adolescent defendants as "superpredators"; the past several years were often devastating for these attorneys and their clients. Two hundred thousand juveniles were tried as adults in the previous year alone, one as young as eleven, and the number of them placed in adult prisons has more than doubled since the mid-1980s. So Patti, Stephen, and the team emphasize that they have a strategy. And they do their best to sound hopeful. They dub the network the Juvenile Death Penalty Initiative (JDPI), and Stephen emerges as its co-coordinator alongside Patti. This is a project much broader in scope than anything he's done before, on a national scale, and so he takes a leave of absence from his job to step in.

In their strategy sessions, the group identifies a missing piece of their outreach: they need the voice of the scientific establishment, experts on child and adolescent development who can speak to the public and to legislators with authority. And so Stephen reaches out to the major medical associations. He starts on the smaller end of the scale, with the five hundred-member American Society for Adolescent Psychiatry, and he eventually corners the president of the thirty-seven-thousand-member American Psychiatric Association in a hotel elevator during a conference in D.C. One by one, he convinces them to fast-track the publication of policy statements against the death penalty for juveniles. From professional groups that have long protected their neutrality—in order to play the role of forensic psychologists and expert witnesses—it is a show of support that's unprecedented. Their statements explain adolescents and their development in digestible terms: they are cognitively and emotionally less mature, have poor impulse control, and are easily influenced by their peers. It is not hard to win press coverage, because this is new terrain for the general public. Stephen can feel a shift taking place: the argument against the death penalty for juveniles is transforming from "only a moral argument" to a scientific investigation.

Stephen eventually learns about a research network being funded by the MacArthur Foundation—the ADJJ, or Adolescent Development and Juvenile Justice network. A team of psychologists, academics, legal consultants, and a small army of grad students, they are conducting sprawling, multiyear studies of subjects within the juvenile justice system, and the psychologist Larry Steinberg, an expert on adolescence, is their director. Right now, the ADJJ is midway through a study on the criminal culpability of adolescents, involving 950 subjects in four states—the most thorough of its kind. At the same time, the JDPI becomes aware of a number of neuroscientists who are demonstrating the developmental differences between adolescents and adults using brain scans: functional magnetic resonance imaging (fMRI), a process developed in the early nineties.

These new images are visual proof that the brain, which was previously believed to develop only up until the age of twelve, continues developing until the midtwenties. The primitive structures emerge first, such as the amygdala, which is responsible for instinctive reactions; more complex parts only develop later, such as the prefrontal cortex, which reins in emotions and impulses and makes it possible to assess the consequences of our actions. The connections between the brain cells are still growing during adolescence, creating pathways between the brain's parts, and then those are "pruned" and become more distinct. White matter, or myelin, is also growing, reinforcing connections and refining communication between the brain cells. This seems to explain why adolescents are far more likely than adults to act impulsively, without weighing their actions.

At the same time, David Fassler at the University of Vermont is referred to the JDPI team—they'd been searching for a child psychiatrist to speak to legislators about the adolescent brain. He borrows a 3-D brain model from the school and takes it on the road. From state to state, he disassembles the model in front of elected representatives, showing them the part of the adolescent mind that has not yet fully matured. The performance is effective when he holds up these pieces of plastic, his audience can imagine specific pieces of the brain—of *any* teenager's brain, of *their* teenager's brain. The demonstration gives some of them the freedom to set aside politics in the name of science.

There are those in the movement against the death penalty who are driven by data and science, and there are those whose work is the telling of their own stories. Even as their role in the justice system remains alien, the members of MVFR and the Journey are adding to their numbers and their audience.

Since the Journey through Indiana, the concept of "victims' rights" has become more entrenched in criminal justice. It has become commonplace for elected officials to use the voices of victims to promote a "tough-on-crime" agenda—a once conservative approach to prosecution that was then embraced by Democratic president Bill Clinton. The crime-fighting one-upmanship between Democrats and Republicans has escalated.

In 1994, the most expansive crime bill in the country's history created harsher criminal sentencing, expanded the range of crimes eligible for death, and funneled billions of dollars into the expansion of local police forces and the building of more prisons. All states had at least one mandatory minimum law, but now they were emboldened to pass laws that led to more punitive sentencing. And the impact was skewed along racial lines: in many states, 90 percent of the people incarcerated for drug offenses were Black or Latin. When Clinton ran for his second term in 1996, the changes introduced by the crime bill were a key piece of the Democratic Party platform, which also encouraged states to severely limit parole and to try juveniles as adults. The agenda was built, in part, on the statements of victims, emphasizing the damage that had been done to them by *individuals* and pointing away from the systemic problems that might have played a part in shaping the perpetrators. Attorney General Janet Reno, at a victims' rights conference, spoke of victims as "my heroes and heroines," "little lower than angels." But these angels are seen as difficult when, like Bill Pelke, they are at cross-purposes with prosecutors.

MVFR claims close to one thousand members, and Journey speakers continue to caravan across the country, to make appearances at schools and churches and in public spaces, to take part in rallies and conferences. Over the past two years, the Journey has gone on speaking tours of several Western European cities and the Philippines, and traveled through

Texas, Louisiana, Michigan, Tennessee, and Pennsylvania. Their number will eventually include two men who have dealt with Janet Reno in cases of mass homicide: Bud Welch, whose daughter was killed by Timothy McVeigh in the Oklahoma City bombing; and David Kaczynski, who turned in his older brother Ted, known as the Unabomber, to the FBI.

There is also Ron Carlson. In Houston in 1983, twenty-three-year-old Karla Faye Tucker—an addict by ten, a prostitute in her teens—broke into an apartment with a friend to rob the place. They killed the two people inside, including Deborah, Ron's sister. On death row for the crime, Karla eventually became a born-again Christian, and Ron, an evangelical himself, decided to visit the woman who'd killed Deborah. He believed in Karla's transformation, and forgave her; megachurch pastor Jerry Falwell and televangelist Pat Robertson also believed and spoke out on her behalf.

Shortly before the first Journey, Bill had seen a TV piece about Karla and the story of Ron's choice to forgive; he reached out to Ron and convinced him to briefly join the Journey caravan in Indiana. When Karla's execution date arrived, just months before the start of the Texas Journey, Bill drove down to Huntsville to join him at the vigil.

That afternoon, several hundred demonstrators, on either side, had gathered across the street from the Walls Unit. There were also many reporters—including Anna Guaita, reporting for *Il Messaggero* in Rome. And flown in from Rome was a soft-spoken man named Carlo Santoro, a volunteer with the Catholic lay community Sant'Egidio; he and others from the Italian Radical Party's anti–death penalty group Nessuno Tocchi Caino (Hands Off Cain) held a massive sign that read FROM EUROPE, TEXAS DON'T KILL. Bill spent time with the Italians and watched the crowd as it grew. Some of the people in favor of the execution raised up slogans like DIE BITCH DIE—Bill thought they had been drinking. Ron was inside, in the witness room: possibly the first time a victim's relative was present on behalf of the condemned. When Karla's death was announced at 6:45 p.m., some people cheered and chanted as if they were at a stadium. The abolitionists huddled closer, sang hymns.

These gatherings were intended to make state killings visible, to apply an outsider's pressure to the justice system. But for Bill they were also a way to see his clan, the people who, quite possibly, understood him best.

When Judy decided to leave him just before the Texas Journey—they simply did not want the same things—the thought occurred to him to take his own life. Without his wife, without the rhythm of his shifts at the mill, he felt very much alone; each time he returned to his empty house in Portage, he cried until he fell asleep. But the planning for Texas connected him to his adopted family. He could look forward, again, to rejoining his caravan of survivors.

In the summer of 2002, as the JDPI continues its work, the Supreme Court issues its decision in a Virginia case, and a change occurs. An opening is created.

In *Atkins v. Virginia*, the Court, 6 to 3, finds capital punishment for the intellectually disabled to be *cruel and unusual . . . in the light of our evolving standards of decency*. In the majority opinion, Justice Stevens writes of *their disabilities in areas of reasoning, judgment, and control of their impulses*; how *they do not act with the level of moral culpability that characterizes the most serious adult criminal conduct*; and how *their impairments can jeopardize the reliability and fairness of capital proceedings*. In this way, the *Atkins* decision lays out a blueprint for the next move. Stephen reads the news and thinks, *Now we've got it*.

The following summer, in 2003, the Missouri Supreme Court cites *Atkins* when it makes a surprising decision in the capital case of Christopher Simmons. Chris had been sentenced to death for a kidnapping and murder committed in 1993, at the age of seventeen.

Through the appellate system, the case wound its way up to the Missouri Supreme Court, where something extraordinary happened. By that point, the U.S. Supreme Court had addressed the death penalty for juveniles three times. They first raised the question of a minimum age in *Eddings* in 1981; they chose sixteen as the minimum (with only a plurality) in 1988 in *Thompson*; and in 1989 they affirmed the death penalty as constitutional for those sixteen and seventeen years old in *Stanford*. Then, in the summer of 2002, had come the *Atkins* decision. A year later, Missouri, which had stayed Chris Simmons's execution while waiting for this very decision, does the following: They declare that *Atkins* renders the Court's *Stanford* decision invalid. And they use that logic to overturn Simmons's death sentence, 4 to 3.

Everyone in the state attorney general's office is astounded. Missouri's justices have never talked back in this way before, never gotten *ahead* of the highest court in the country on a criminal justice issue. It is more or less a dare.

When learning this news, Elizabeth "Buffie" Scott, a consultant to the ADJJ—not a psychologist, but a law professor at Columbia University—thinks to herself, *This will be the one.* The case to bring the issue back in front of the U.S. Supreme Court. She reaches out to Larry Steinberg. They are still a few years away from an official announcement of their findings in their study of the criminal culpability of adolescents. But Buffie suggests that she and Larry coauthor an article on that same topic, laying out their thesis: how kids do not meet the standards of culpability required to be treated as adults in the justice system. They should publish soon—this could add a critical piece to discussions of this Missouri case. Because it is bound to come before the Court.

In late 2003, they publish "Less Guilty by Reason of Adolescence" in *American Psychologist*. In it, they argue that juveniles are not as accountable as adults *because adolescents' decision-making capacity is diminished, they are less able to resist coercive influence, and their character is still undergoing change.* Each of these characteristics, they argue, should be given as much mitigating weight in sentencing as forms of diminished capacity in an adult defendant. And they send copies of the article to each one of the justices' clerks.

At the start of 2004, the Supreme Court takes up the challenge. They will hear arguments in the Missouri case *Roper v. Simmons*. It has been fifteen years since the Court heard a case on the issue, and there are now twice as many people on death rows around the country who were sentenced as juveniles.

Back in 1989, three weeks after he and Touchette appeared before the Indiana Supreme Court on Paula Cooper's behalf, Victor Streib had flown to D.C. to sit in on the arguments for *Stanford*, for which he'd served as supporting counsel. In their decision, the Court had determined that the consensus among the states was not yet strong enough to declare that "standards of decency" had changed. Victor had not been shocked—the very nature of an evolving standard, he thought, was that it took time to truly shift—but he was disappointed nonetheless.

In the sixteen years since the *Thompson* decision, seven states (not counting Missouri) had ended the death penalty for juveniles, and two others had reinstated capital punishment with a new minimum age of eighteen. In recent years, the JDPI network had made their argument in Arizona, Florida, Kentucky, and Nevada—and failed to make headway. They had come nearly seen the end of capital punishment in New Hampshire, winning over both houses, only to see the bill vetoed. But in the wake of their legislative campaigns, they saw wins in Montana, Indiana, South Dakota, and Wyoming. There has been solid movement away from this practice, but it remains unclear whether or not *Roper* has come too soon.

A consensus has been established in the scientific community. The brain imaging, though very new, demands attention. They have the logic of the *Atkins* decision behind them. Out of all these elements, some piece stands a chance of making the difference before the Court.

Twenty

WHAT THEY WERE,
WHAT THEY ARE, WHAT
THEY WILL BECOME

By 2004, Paula Cooper has turned thirty-four and is two years into life at a new facility an hour and a half west of Indianapolis.

After more than one thousand days in segregation, and another four years in general population, Paula's time at the Indiana Women's Prison came to an end. Rockville Correctional, the only other women's prison in the state, had recently been elevated to maximum security, and Ms. Blank took the opportunity to hand over her most difficult resident. IWP had been Paula's life for seventeen years, and she was being sent into the unknown.

Throughout her time at the Women's Prison, much of the staff had considered Paula a hostile presence. But in 2001, the warden honored her: Paula had finally earned her college degree from Martin University. She'd made slow progress while on death row and in segregation because her studies were solitary and through the mail. But when she was able to take classes in person, seated at a desk alongside other women—not *inmates* during those sessions, not *offenders*, but students—she stood out. She led group sessions. She knew how to express herself, perhaps helped by those years of correspondence with people decades her senior and around the world.

For their graduation, Paula and sixteen other women sat in black caps and gowns in the gym, family and friends looking on. Underneath, she wore a white suit she had asked Rhonda to buy, and her hair was sleek and carefully done, falling to her shoulders. At the podium, Ms. Blank told the women to be proud. She said, "The door is open to you"—even though the graduate set for earliest release would not leave the facility for four more years. Paula walked up and accepted her degree; her smile was enormous. Looking on, her older sister felt good. Rhonda had lived her life on the outside, but she had given up the pursuit of a degree, including her GED, not long after leaving the yellow house.

Also in the audience was Herman Cooper. Paula had accepted a few visits from him; regardless of her biting memories, she *wanted* parents. On that day, Herman behaved the way a father might be expected to. He told a reporter, "It means a lot to us," and he sounded sincere. Rhonda was polite enough to her stepfather; he did not stay for the reception.

In spite of Paula's hard-earned degree, Ms. Blank was not swayed; she did not suddenly grow optimistic about the woman's chances. She had to acknowledge that Paula was solid academically: she'd arrived as a sophomore in high school and worked her way up to an undergraduate diploma; she stood out among the other residents as unusually bright. But these same qualities seemed to frustrate Ms. Blank. *It could have been different for Paula*, she believed, *if the girl had applied herself and respected the law*. Her perspective evoked that of the judges Victor Streib had dealt with early in his career, in juvenile court: they had not allowed for what might be the yawning gap between their own childhoods and that of a young person absorbed into the system.

Months later, Paula was briefly returned to segregation for a minor infraction. There she was on that row again, alongside her friend Shirley Cooper—their third time in lockdown together. Ms. Blank, despite her podium talk of pride and potential, had reached her limit. While Paula and Shirley were on lock, the warden applied to transfer them both to Rockville. The two women saw this as a form of punishment, and a way to make an example of them to the other residents.

Paula and Shirley were brought to Rockville in the summer of 2002: two of the facility's first long-termers. Shirley had a lengthy sentence too, also for homicide, but Paula was the high-profile transfer. She still carried much of the notoriety of her teenage self; her international renown had mostly been held against her within the system, and she had a record of "conduct issues" the Rockville officers were acutely aware of upon her arrival. After an evaluation, Paula was found ready for general population and placed in 5K4: Dorm 5, Room K, Bed 4. Quickly, both she and Shirley felt the staff was taking an aggressive tone with them because of their sentences.

Rockville was designed to be more rigid than the Women's Prison. It is now the largest facility for women in the state, more than twice the size of IWP, with about 1,100 residents. At that scale, it is not possible for the superintendent to know every person's name, her family life, the amount of time she has left. The women wear orange jumpsuits. They are allowed far fewer personal items. They are not permitted to touch one another, and that includes hugging and shaking hands. They are not allowed gifts—only letters, photographs, and wired funds for the commissary. The women are also not allowed to decorate their area, so Paula keeps her postcard of John Paul II in the drawer under her bed.

The women live in one of five dorms, sixteen in a room, with four bunk beds on each side, no privacy. On about fifty-two acres, one mile outside of the small town of Rockville, the facility is much more isolated than IWP, but the place is newer: classrooms that are clean and bright, computers, video games, a church, a well-equipped gym with flat-screen televisions, a library with armchairs and views of the outdoors.

But none of that makes a difference if a woman is placed in segregation. At IWP, Paula had done the most time in segregation of any female in the state of Indiana; now, at Rockville, she adds more time to her state record. Battery once again, this time against another resident. It's a serious offense, but the sentences here are less extreme: She's given three months, impressive enough. The deputy warden, Julie Stout, knows nothing about Paula's childhood and can only guess at the source of her acting-out. She's had few women under her supervision with this level of notoriety; she wonders if all that attention instilled in Paula a sense of entitlement. Either way, she's angry and always kicking back, drawn to a group of residents who regularly disrupt the flow of the facility.

Now two years into her time at Rockville, Paula has about a decade left to her sentence—if she can hold on to her "good conduct" credits—and she is still pushing back hard. Whether her remaining time climbs or continues to drop, how soon she is able to live outside of an institution (for the first time since she was fifteen), how soon she'll be able to visit her sister's house—it all hinges upon how she responds, day-to-day and moment-to-moment, to the pressures of life within this facility. But the future remains a faraway idea. And it is hard to care about something way off in the distance.

The same month that Paula enters segregation at Rockville, the U.S. Supreme Court hears arguments for an issue few expected the justices to wrestle with again so soon. *Roper v. Simmons* is about to determine the fates of seventy-two individuals across the country who, like Paula, were sentenced to death for crimes committed under the age of eighteen. It will decide the future of the death sentence for juveniles.

On a Wednesday morning in the fall of 2004, counsel gathers before the bench.

Jim Layton, who has been in the Missouri Attorney General's Office for the past decade, will argue on behalf of prison superintendent Donald Roper. He is one of the more senior state solicitors in the country, but his two previous arguments before the Court had not addressed the death penalty. Seth Waxman will make the argument on behalf of Chris Simmons. For four years, under President Clinton, Seth was the solicitor general of the United States. Now fifty-two, he has argued before the Court thirty-nine times, and has taken on decades of pro bono work in capital cases. Many of the advocates who've been working on the issue consider it a windfall that he came on board.

In the audience are Stephen Harper, Patti Puritz, Steve Drizin, and other members of the JDPI. Bill Pelke is here too—as an abolitionist and as a voice included in one of the Simmons amicus briefs. The last time Bill was at the Supreme Court building was in early July, with other Journey members, to camp out in front of the Court steps. He had packed a sleeping bag then, and this time he packed a suit. Over the past eighteen years, he has learned to be versatile.

From the outset, it has been clear which of the nine the decision will come down to. Ruth Bader Ginsburg and Stephen Breyer are staunch liberals, and David Souter and John Paul Stevens, though Republicans, vote regularly with the Court's liberal wing (Stevens had written the impassioned opinion in *Atkins*). The three most conservative justices— Chief Justice Rehnquist and originalists Scalia and Clarence Thomas— had voted to uphold the death penalty for the intellectually disabled; they would not bend for this case. But, in spite of their support for the death penalty for juveniles in *Stanford*, Anthony Kennedy and Sandra Day O'Connor, both Republicans, had voted with the *Atkins* majority. Each has a track record of being a less predictable vote. For Seth and his team to win, one of them will have to cross over.

When the proceedings begin, Jim Layton is first at the lectern, and throughout his exchange with the Court, he tries to undermine the idea that adolescence can be clearly defined, dismissing the science in the Simmons briefs. At Seth Waxman's turn, he pushes back, speaking of the strong consensus established by the data. "The trend is very robust," Seth says, "and it is very deep." It's a consensus established by the decades-long decline of the death penalty for juveniles and bolstered by the latest science. This new research, he says, confirms society's intuitive understanding that those under eighteen are different. "We know ... that it is impossible to know whether the crime that was committed by a sixteen- or seventeen-year-old is a reflection of his true, enduring character or whether it's a manifestation of traits that are exhibited during adolescence." He goes on: "I'm not just talking about social science here, but the important neurobiological science that has now shown that these adolescents are—their character is not *hardwired.*"

Justice Scalia soon breaks in. "Mr. Waxman, I thought we punish people, criminals, for what they *were,* not for what they *are,*" he says. "To say that adolescents change—everybody changes, but that doesn't justify eliminating the proper punishments that society has determined."

Seth does not pause. "I think that there is an interesting question about, with respect to *death,* whether what they are and what they will become is totally irrelevant." He then repeats his previous point: An adolescent's character is not fixed. That person is highly likely to continue evolving.

He refers to the consensus created by the state legislatures, and the fact that the United States stands alone in allowing for the death penalty for juveniles. The international argument is aimed, in particular, at Kennedy, who is unique among the justices for his frequent trips abroad. And while the opinions of other countries had not gained much traction in *Thompson,* Kennedy now steers several minutes of discussion to this very topic.

But his vote remains uncertain. Because later in the argument, the justice says something that unnerves the Simmons team. Among the two sole amicus briefs filed in support of the other side was a document that Seth had considered a hack job, and the least relevant to any legal debate. This was a brief filed by the attorneys general of six death-penalty states, comprised almost entirely of graphic descriptions of a half dozen truly terrible crimes committed by sixteen- and seventeen-year-olds. It is a catalogue of horrors—and Kennedy draws everyone's attention to it. This is "chilling reading," he says, "and I wish that all the people that sign on to the amicus briefs had at least read that before they sign on to them." The justice seems to have set aside his legal mind and is speaking from an emotional place—and he now expects a response.

Seth says the brief, through its list of crimes, actually *proves* the point he is trying to make. The very first example, he says, "is a kid who went on a killing spree, including his father, because he felt he was unjustly deprived use of the family truck." Is this a person, he asks, "who a jury could, with a degree of reliability that the Constitution requires, say acted out of a stable, enduring character rather than transient aspects of youth? I think that's a poster child for us."

Their team has another response to the brief. They had filed an amicus that is even more pointed—from Murder Victims' Families for Reconciliation. Its perspective is unlike any other offerings to the Court, from either side. In spite of all the talk of consensus-building data and science, prosecutors would forever fixate on the horror of the crime. Implied is great empathy and anger on behalf of the victims, and a call for retribution in their name. But here were people intimately connected to terrible violence pushing back against the call for death, saying that it gives them nothing in recompense, that it causes them pain.

They occupy a wide spectrum of backgrounds and religious and political beliefs, and the members whose stories are shared come from throughout the country—from Texas, Colorado, Oklahoma, Illinois, Indiana, California, Tennessee, and Massachusetts. What they have in common, they write, is the conviction that their pain and grief and anger, as victims' family members, should not play a role in a constitutional debate. *Victims' emotions cannot justify the use of the death penalty*, they write, *because the legal system's purpose is not to heal emotional wounds*. It is the wrong place to turn for closure, and a gross manipulation of their experience for *the politics of crime control or law enforcement*.

They write that the death penalty cuts off any possibility of rehabilitation. And many of them still hope for, or have felt relief through, the remorse of the offender. That is how Jennifer Bishop-Jenkins feels, whose pregnant sister Nancy and brother-in-law Richard were killed in their Chicago home by a sixteen-year-old. And Azim Khamisa, whose twenty-year-old son Tariq was killed in San Diego by a fourteen-year-old gang member. And Linda White, whose daughter Cathy was killed by two fifteen-year-old boys in Houston. And Bill Pelke, whose grandmother was killed by a fifteen-year-old girl in Indiana.

Paula, he tells the Court, *is not the same person she was when she committed the crime.*

F ive months later, the Court's opinion is announced.

The decision has come down to Justice Kennedy. From the bench he reads aloud an announcement of the majority opinion. He states, in part: "When a juvenile offender commits a heinous crime, the state can exact forfeiture of some of the most basic liberties but the state cannot extinguish his life and his potential to attain a mature understanding of his own humanity."

The Court has decided, 5 to 4, that the Eighth Amendment forbids imposition of the death penalty on those under eighteen at the time of their crime.

Seth Waxman receives an email announcing the decision. He is in a conference at his firm, blocks from the White House, and he and a colleague rush out into the hall to steal a quick moment of celebration. He sends a message out to a number of people who worked on the case. The note is simple: *!!!!!!!!!*

Stephen Harper knows exactly what this means. He is back at his familiar desk at the Miami public defender's office, but he has never had a feeling like this. A breathing-out, an incredible release—and joy. Within minutes, as word spreads, he begins receiving email after email, text after text.

Seventy-two lives have been spared, and a piece of the system has been altered. The courts now have a broader definition of *cruelty*, a more precise definition of what is decent.

Justice O'Connor had recently announced her retirement, to care for her husband who is struggling with Alzheimer's. And six months from now, Chief Justice Rehnquist will die after more than thirty years on the Court, ending the longest period in which the same nine justices served together. The Court is about to shift much further to the right: Republican president George W. Bush will nominate John Roberts as Rehnquist's successor and replace O'Connor with the Court's third originalist, Samuel Alito.

Victor Streib's research was cited in six of the amicus briefs for *Roper*, and in the Supreme Court's decision; his work, at this point, has been cited in the Court's decisions twenty-eight times. That fall, in his home office in the Cleveland suburbs, he will complete the seventy-seventh and final edition of the report he's been amending for more than two decades. *During the last twenty-one years,* he will write, *these reports have been with us (1) through the intense litigation of the late 1980s, (2) through our society's near hysteria about violent juvenile crime in the 1990s, (3) into the era of the international pressure on the United States to abandon this practice, and (4) now at the end of this practice.* He will write that the *solitary goal of these reports is to collect in one place the best available data and information,* and that it *takes no position on the legality, wisdom, or morality of the death penalty for juvenile offenders.* But the numbers did take a position, as he is well aware. They had charted the reality of this practice—and mapped out a route to its end.

A month before the *Roper* decision, Paula is released from segregation. And in the weeks and years that follow, as if proving the underlying premise of that case, a slow transformation takes hold. She seems— at least to Ms. Stout, now the warden, and to her friends inside—to be gripped by a possibility. An idea of what could become hers. Paula Cooper is changing.

She has worked a string of jobs—dorm porter, maintenance, grounds crew, tutor. Eventually, she talked her way into the "honors" job program and began pressing metal parts for ice machines and doors for PEN Products. She doubled her daily quota. Now she earns $1.75 a day and has begun saving every cent for when she leaves this place.

Just before her last stint in segregation, she had been one of a dozen residents working with a service-dog program. Their goal is to teach the animals to help people with mobility issues, who often also have intellectual or physical disabilities—mostly children or teenagers, but occasionally disabled adults or veterans. Paula worked at training her dog, a golden retriever named Maddy, to eventually perform a long list of tasks: turning lights on or off, opening and closing doors, recovering dropped items, taking laundry out of the dryer, dressing or undressing her owner. Paula was constantly responsible for Maddy, even slept with the dog alongside her. Maddy came from an abusive home, and this bond was not lost on Paula. But because of her burned-in memory of how she was treated, the dog could not handle the presence of men. The retriever was eventually pulled from the program—in a way, her past was being held against her. Paula had decided then to leave the program too.

But now she tries again to find something she can throw herself into, this time in the kitchen. Years earlier, during the long months of waiting for the Indiana Supreme Court's decision in her case—a period of some of the greatest anxiety of her life—she had developed an eating disorder and lost thirty-five pounds. But this is a different moment for her: She decides to enroll in the "culinary arts" program and discovers she loves cooking. Now that the food in Rockville (as at IWP) is privatized, meals consist of rice and beans, and the women, if they have funds coming in, lean heavily on the commissary. (It's become like a grocery store: ramen noodles, peanut butter, beef sticks, little tubs of cheese, sugar packets, microwave popcorn.) But the culinary program is something else: Paula is trained to make complex dishes; she reads recipe books and improvises in the kitchen. The class serves the hundred or so officers a discounted lunch on Fridays, and Paula makes sure to have their favorite meals on offer. Word spreads of her talent, and the officers—some of whom, despite Paula's past record, have become friendly—look out to see if she's cooking. The supervisor lets her plan a special meal for the women in the college program who make the dean's list.

In the system since she was fifteen, Paula's never had the chance to cook for someone on the outside; it was her older sister who'd made the meals when they were young and alone at home. But she and her friend Donna, who transferred to Rockville about a year after her, have cooked together many times in their rooms, stuff from the commissary. With Rhonda's regular donations, they would always have something left over, and Paula would pick someone to give it to, telling them not to worry about paying her back. She likes being in a position to give, but it's also about trust—the trust someone places in the person feeding them. She relishes it. Whoever accepts the food you have prepared, whether an officer or a resident, accepts that you wish them no harm.

Twenty years have passed since Anna Guaita and Giampaolo Piolo first visited Paula in prison, on death row in Indy, and now the pair travels to see her again. When they meet with her, she's done a little to dress up for the visit, in hair clips and green eye shadow. As they talk, Anna feels that she could be speaking to another person altogether, far from the teenager she first met. Paula tells them how rigid Rockville has been, how she's been kept busy every day. How she has seven years to go, but it doesn't seem long, not when she's constantly preparing for her reentry into the world. She thinks a lot about money. She thinks a lot about work—maybe as a chef. Paula will later tell a friend that it was during this period that she began to see herself as "the common denominator in all of the trouble." She has stopped seeing the staff as a force to push back against; she believes they are treating her "like a human," and she has decided to treat them the same way. They treat her like a human, but also *just* a human, not special or set apart—and, somehow, this comforts her. "We're all the same here," she tells Anna. "We're all on the same level. There's no one that's more important than anyone else.

"We're all numbers," she says. "And I like it that way."

In the years to come, there will be only a couple more stays in segregation, of a week or less, for nothing much. Paula is weighing the time she has left inside and cutting it up into pieces she can make use of. When her death penalty was commuted, effectively, to thirty years in prison, it felt to her like a thousand years. But with great effort she began to divide the time, in her mind, into five-year blocks. And each time she reached the end of a block, she let herself feel she had accomplished something tangible. Each cluster of years is something she can process.

No one can be certain why Paula has started to change. Maybe it's the simple fact that she's older now. Maybe it's the number of programs at Rockville, the training, the work. Donna thinks it's the tightness, the strictness, of the place that's worked for her friend. Paula is still willing to take risks, but only with good reason. As a diabetic with damaged kidneys, Donna is constantly sick. One time, finding her ill and untended in her cell, Paula went to the laundry room window in their unit, waited for the supervisor to pass the dorm, and screamed to get her attention—a violation that could easily have sent her back to lockdown.

She has developed an instinct for extending herself to others. If a new woman comes in and Paula hears she doesn't have help on the outside, she may buy her an extra pair of shoes. She's thrown birthday parties for women who don't have anyone else to do it. When she has clothes that no longer fit, she gives them away instead of selling them. Another time when Donna was ill, Paula volunteered to watch over her, and noticed a hole in her panties when she rolled over in her sleep. Donna awoke to find that Paula had gone and collected *all* her holey underwear and was seated beside her sewing them up.

Rhonda and Parish visit Paula in the mid-1990s

A few times, Gloria has accompanied Rhonda on her visits to Paula, and her younger daughter has fed these encounters into her stubborn, long-running fantasy of a close relationship with her mother. She tells Anna and Giampaolo that Gloria is now in rehab for alcoholism, and that "the hope of hugging me again is keeping her alive." Paula's focus is sharpened during this last stretch in prison by the desire to earn her mother's praise. Rhonda, however, does not understand why her sister believes they will someday become like the families Paula used to watch on TV—*The Swiss Family Robinson*, the Cosbys. "That's not going to happen, sweetie. It just does not work like that," Rhonda would tell her. "You don't know your mom still—I'm out here with her. I don't know what she's telling you, but I'm honest with you. Listen to me: Your mom is not right." And Paula would say, "You're just being too hard." She understands why her younger sister thinks that. That is the personality Rhonda has cultivated for herself: being hard, not letting people in. That's been her armor.

Paula's dream of family extends to having children. Even if things go as well as possible, she will not be released until her early forties, which would mean not much time to try for a family of her own. Rhonda, however, sees her son as belonging equally to her sister. Parish knows his aunt, and is awaiting her release—he has grown up visiting Paula in the prison system. Occasionally, he even spends the day with her at Rockville, to help her take part in the parenting program. Sometimes it makes Rhonda nervous, her son becoming accustomed to the prison environment. But Paula is his aunt and the two want to spend time together, so she allows it.

On display in Rhonda and Mike's house in Gary is a gift Paula made for them while at the Women's Prison: a small-scale model of a white house, about the size of a toaster, with a bright green front yard and a dog like her sister's. When Rhonda first saw this, she thought, *How does she know? She's never even seen our house, and this looks so much like it.* It is an object that had required hours of care.

IV

Twenty-One

ANNIVERSARY

About eight years have gone by. It is the late spring of 2015, a Tuesday morning at the end of May. Paula Cooper has been out of prison for one year, eleven months, and one week.

The sun is just starting to rise. At the edge of a parking lot in northwest Indianapolis, beside an ash tree, Paula lies in the grass. She lies on her side, dressed in the clothes she bought just last night—a fitted shirt in black and white, gray pants; even her underwear is new, as if for a special occasion. She does not move. There is a terrible wound in the side of her head and a handgun in her lap.

It is twelve days since the anniversary of Ruth Pelke's death.

People are entitled to the way they feel." That is what Paula told the reporter who came to see her a year before her release from Rockville. The people who might not want her to get out, who would not sympathize with her situation no matter what she said, they had a right to those feelings.

A pair of major stories about Paula's case and her "second chance"—front page, banner headlines—ran in *The Times* that summer. Paula spoke about her "change," her rehabilitation, her culinary training. She said she was ready to prove herself however she had to, on the outside, working as a janitor or dishwasher or short-order cook, whatever. The reporter also gathered up the members of the Pelke family and published their memories of the trauma of Ruth's murder and their discomfort with Paula Cooper's release. Her name and her face were out in public again, paired with the story of the killing of the "perfect grandmother," the "elderly Bible teacher," that phrase repeated again and again like a mantra.

Those months were already filled with anxiety. Paula had been incarcerated—juvenile detention, county jail, the Indiana Women's Prison, and Rockville Correctional—for most of her teenage years and into midlife. She had spent over a thousand days in segregation as well as thousands more almost completely without privacy. The rhythm of her adult life had not resembled anything like that of an adult in the outside world. But now she was approaching the final countdown of her time in prison, the last stretch of days until she would be required to blend back into society as, in the DOC's words, a "returning citizen." She had seen fellow inmates who, approaching their release date, had protested that they did not want to go home, that what lay in wait was more chaotic than these fixed times for rising, showering, eating, sleeping, this uniform to wear, this collection of regular faces, this dearth of choices. On the other side was a job search and bills to pay, a foreign landscape, conversations with people who had never been inside, and, most fearsome of all, the likelihood of being asked to explain yourself again and again. But no one was permitted to stay in prison past their date. Once a person's sentence was up, they would be launched into the world.

The prison administered an eight-week reentry program: how to write a résumé, budget, reintegrate into family, manage stress, find resources in your community. Paula took it twice. Three times, she wrote the magistrate to ask permission for work release. *Prison already has the "protective" affect on each of us*, she wrote, *and mentally we dont have to prepare for much. I must prepare.* Bill Pelke petitioned the judge as well: *Ruth Elizabeth Pelke was my grandmother. I am trying to help Paula . . . reenter society in the near future. Her successful transition is very important to me.* She was denied.

As her date grew nearer—June 17, 2013—Paula began rocking herself to sleep at night.

By the spring, she was no closer to knowing where she would live come summertime. Paula had requested placement with a friend in Indianapolis, but the parole board did not approve. They wanted her to return to Lake County, to family, as was typical, which would mean living with her mother in Hammond. While Paula had for years nursed a dream of a closer relationship with Gloria, the reality of moving in with her mother began to trouble her. She mentioned her anxiety in an email to Bill Pelke and asked, without much hope, if he could find some way to help. Weeks passed without progress.

Bill had moved to Anchorage, Alaska, to live with his girlfriend Kathy, whom he'd met during the Journey through Texas in 1998. He traveled to see family in Indiana as often as possible, and he timed a trip to a visit from Carlo Santoro of Rome's Sant'Egidio community. Bill drove to Indianapolis to stay with Carlo at the home of an activist-friend, and together they followed the coverage of Paula's impending release. They were horrified to see that racist threats against her were being posted online—in some cases, specific threats to kill her once she was free. Carlo thought they should turn to an acquaintance of his for help: Joseph Tobin, the new archbishop of Indianapolis. During his twenty years in Rome, the man had celebrated Mass with Sant'Egidio, and his work for the Church in the States was giving him the reputation of a modest reformer, someone sensitive to social issues. Carlo reached out.

The next day, an archbishop of the Catholic Church appeared—an event Bill, in his days as a conservative Baptist, would never have predicted. Father Joe arrived in lay clothes, with none of the pomp and circumstance Bill had expected, and joined the men for lunch in the backyard. They reviewed the situation, and the archbishop agreed that Paula might be in danger. He would look into it. "I am sure," he said, "God will help us."

In the week before Paula's release, Father Joe reached out to the office of the new governor, Mike Pence, and explained the DOC's plans for Paula's release. *The mother allegedly has problems with alcohol*, he wrote, *and there are other conditions in the home which are causing great anxiety for Paula.* He told of the online death threats coming from Lake County, and how Paula's request to live elsewhere, Indianapolis, had been denied. The governor called the archbishop and announced that he was "a law-and-order guy" and wary of taking unnecessary risks. Send her to Indianapolis, Father Joe told him, and the Church will watch out for her.

At Rockville, Ms. Stout was unaware of these maneuverings. But on the Friday before Paula's scheduled Monday release, the warden received word that her placement with her mother had been denied and Paula was being assigned to Marion County parole, which she'd originally requested. With three days to go, Ms. Stout made some calls and found a halfway house that would take Paula, as long as her residence was approved by the DOC. They kept waiting.

That Sunday, the front page of *The Indianapolis Star*'s metro section was dominated by the story of Paula's case and her imminent release, under the enormous headline WHO IS SHE NOW? It replayed the best-known facts of the crime and described her *hard-to-shake notoriety as a heartless killer.* The reporter spoke to Jack Crawford, who described the murder in gruesome detail, still claiming it had been premeditated. Taking a stance that went against both the Indiana Supreme Court and U.S. Supreme Court, Jack stood behind his decisions in the case. His pursuit of the death penalty may have been "controversial," he said, "But if it was ever justified, this was the time. . . . It was so amazing that these girls could have killed so dispassionately and viciously." He added, thinly, "I hope she continues to try to rehabilitate herself and make some amends for the crime she committed some 30 years ago."

On Monday, after hours of waiting, the call came to go ahead. Paula met Ms. Stout in the visiting center, wearing street clothes for the first time in years. The custody supervisor stood holding her possessions in a clear trash bag. Paula signed her release agreement. It read: *I will make every effort to remain gainfully employed. . . . I must obtain written permission from my supervising officer prior to changing my employment or residence. . . . I understand that out-of-state travel will require written permission. . . . I will allow my supervising officer or other authorized officials with the Department of Correction to visit my residence or place of employment at any time . . .*

The staff knew that the media would be trying to cover her release—something they had never dealt with before, and something they did not wish on Paula. So they planned to exit through the rear door, usher her into an unmarked van, and have her driven out the back gate. But on her way out, Paula stopped and turned to Ms. Stout, crying. "Well, what are you crying for?" the warden asked. And Paula said, "I'm going to miss you guys."

Ms. Stout was taken aback. An unintended consequence of their work was a kind of world creation: these inmates lived, for the duration of their sentence, on a planet maintained by her staff. They put a great distance between these women and their former lives—and then they asked them to close that distance, to travel back home to uncertain country. But of all the women she had released from her charge, Paula struck her as the most hesitant to go.

The supervisor stepped outside with Paula, and a van pulled up. Paula paused again: a copper-colored bell, like a small Liberty Bell, hung from a beam to the left of the exit—the bell the boys used to ring on their last day, back when the facility housed juveniles. Paula asked the warden if she could ring it. Ms. Stout couldn't turn her down, she'd been there so long.

Paula tugged the rope, and the bell rang out.

Paula was placed in Spain's House, a two-story stucco and redbrick building that was a halfway home for women in recovery from alcohol and drug addictions. She wasn't in recovery herself, but they'd been willing to give her housing at very short notice. Her parole officer Denise Jackson introduced Paula to the other women as Renae, her middle name, and helped her to settle in. Miss Jackson was awoken at two a.m. that night to a phone call: it was Paula Cooper, shouting about how dark the place was. She had not slept with the lights out since she was fifteen years old. In the morning, Miss Jackson promised, they would buy her a nightlight.

For the time being, her parole officer wanted to make sure Paula had constant company, so she assembled a small team: the house manager at Spain's, a job counselor, a safety officer, a psychologist, and a volunteer from Catholic Charities. Sometimes Paula stopped by Archbishop Tobin's office to talk about her new life. And for the first two weeks, Miss Jackson visited with Paula each day, took her for walks around the neighborhood, sat on the front porch with her and people-watched.

She also introduced Paula to a woman named Kim Kidd who ran a prison ministry. Kim helped Paula to open her first bank account, buy her first cell phone, go shopping at the Walmart Supercenter. At the register, when asked to swipe her debit card, she would sometimes freeze in place and Kim would have to do it for her. When she eventually started shopping on her own, Paula, frustrated, would occasionally rush out of the supermarket before she was done. In some ways, she seemed to Kim and Miss Jackson like a young teenager—at times desperate for help, at times pushing back, demanding her independence. It had never been an option in prison to be seen as vulnerable or too dependent on the generosity of others.

Herman Cooper had died in 2010 and left Paula a modest inheritance. But to meet the conditions of her parole, she needed to find work. That August, she was hired as a fry cook at a Five Guys location, and she never missed a shift. They soon made her a cashier. For a while, handling money and customers during the busiest hours was a lot of pressure—but the restaurant chain had a mission of giving work to people who'd spent time in prison, and the management was patient. Soon, she was promoted to shift manager.

The first time Rhonda came to visit Paula at Spain's, they sat down in the designated smoking room, alone together. They sat and they stared, and maybe a half hour went by like that, in total quiet. And the whole while, Rhonda was thinking, *It's just the two of us again*—without a guard or all the other visitors, after twenty-eight years. Just two sisters sitting around and looking at each other. Then aloud she said, "Is this really weird?" Paula was feeling something too. Rhonda had to light a cigarette.

Paula called her sister about twenty times a day, and Rhonda didn't mind that she needed to lean on her, to hear her voice. But she did not agree at all with Paula's desire to reunite the family: the two of them and their mother, together again—ridiculous. She watched as her younger sister reached out to the woman over and over, and Rhonda waited for the Gloria *she* knew to show through.

Paula was needy, whether toward her sister or Kim or other former Rockville residents with whom she'd reconnected. In most of her relationships, Paula, like someone much younger, seemed to require on-demand availability, reaching out through slews of text messages and voice mails, not waiting for a reply before trying again. Rhonda could feel how afraid she was of being alone. She drove around with a collection of teddy bears buckled into the back seat of her car and called them her "babies." She would not move them aside, not for grocery bags or passengers. She came over to Rhonda's one time with a stuffed bear so large it was human-size. "What the hell?" Rhonda said. "What *is* that?"

In other ways, though, Paula wanted space. She began pushing back against the requirements at Spain's—substance-abuse training, curfews. (Kim thought of Paula's occasional outbursts as "temper tantrums.") She wanted to live on her own terms; she wanted her own apartment. After about five months on the outside, she managed to move into a one-bedroom apartment that Catholic Charities helped her find, one of about a half dozen units in an older brick building at 38th Street and Meridian. After work she sometimes liked to just sit in the living room and look out the window at the view of the parking lot and the traffic beyond. But Rhonda was a little concerned. Paula kept her kitchen cabinets packed to bursting with canned food and snacks, multiple boxes of Ho-Ho's, some foods she wasn't even sure she liked—as if she might never have a chance to stock up again. "You don't have to buy everything all at once like this," her sister said. And she learned that every day at lunchtime, Paula would walk across the street from Five Guys to the bank, stand in line, and withdraw a small amount from the teller: lunch money. Every single day—as if she were taking out just enough to buy something from the commissary. Rhonda worried that part of Paula was still in prison.

She was working at getting her driver's license. But at forty-four, the last time Paula had driven a car (and not well) was nearly three decades earlier—and that had been the "joy ride" in Ruth Pelke's Plymouth. She failed her first test, a few months after her release, for going 60 miles an hour in a school zone; she finally passed the next spring. But she remained, unquestionably, a terrible driver. She often lost her way, and she had a terrifying habit of braking just after pulling into traffic, cursing out other drivers along the way.

By June, Paula had finished her year of parole. There would be no more required check-ins with Miss Jackson, no more monitoring of her everyday decisions, no more need to ask permission. She was now free to become the sum of her own choices.

Near the end of that summer, Paula celebrated her second birthday outside of prison—her first night out, free from parole. She and Rhonda and Mike dressed up and went to the Majestic Star Casino in Gary, where all three of them ran high on Paula's energy. The lights and the machines and the bells and the oversize buffet—she could not get over any of it. Rhonda, meanwhile, was trying to stay seated; she was in pain, still recovering from back surgery, and she whispered to Mike that she would probably need to head home soon. But Mike said, "Do you see her face?

Rhonda, you have to suck it up." Paula was playing the slots, and she looked as if she'd never had such a good time in her life. That's when she burst out with, "Oh my God, I *won!*" Rhonda rushed over. Her sister had won a dollar.

Another day, Paula visited and showed off a lottery ticket she'd just bought. "I *won!*" she announced. Mike was skeptical. She insisted— and reminded her brother-in-law that she had a college degree. Mike

Paula at Rhonda's house, Christmas 2014

gently pointed out that he had one too. "Take it back to the store and see if you won," he said. "Maybe you did, I don't know." Rhonda got roped into driving her sister back, and she watched as Paula strode inside on her own, ticket ready. The result was as expected.

Later that night, Mike told his wife, "She had to find out for herself." But Paula had a kind of optimism, in spite of everything. Maybe it was a survival instinct, a belief in her chances that defied logic.

That fall, at a Kentucky Fried Chicken, a man stopped Paula in the parking lot, his clothes covered in dirt from a landscaping job, and convinced her to take his business card. His name was LeShon. She called him that night and they spoke for a little while. She had dated someone since prison, a man named Michael who'd sent letters to her at Rockville, but that had not worked out.

The next day, LeShon sent her a Bible verse that a childhood friend had once shared with him—a boy who'd been left by his parents, who'd spent years alone with his brother, homeless. *This was on my heart to send to you*, he texted. *Read this and tell me what you think.* It was from Psalm

27:10: *Though my father and mother forsake me, the Lord will receive me.* LeShon was unaware that, as a child, Paula had leaned hard on this particular line from Scripture. Actually, he didn't know anything about her.

She took it as a sign and asked to meet up with him. At his apartment, she told him about her many years of incarceration. He wasn't shocked; he'd done time for handgun possession—not serious time, but he could relate. She stayed over that night, and he became more and more curious about her. He looked up her case online, but he didn't push. He let her take her time sharing her past. Her story opened him up to her.

They moved in together quickly. No more silent nights at her apartment. He took her with him on jobs, taught her to plant flower beds. He took her fishing on Eagle Creek, at the city's northwestern edge. She liked to sit outside together and listen to the birds calling back and forth.

LeShon, who she called "Daddy," was twice divorced with six kids and ten grandchildren, and he introduced them all to "Miss Paula." Like Ruth Pelke, Paula was poised to inherit a bevy of adult stepkids through this midlife relationship; as with Ruth, the family embraced her. LeShon had inherited some farmland in Glasgow, Kentucky, and they went to visit. About three months after meeting, on a Thanksgiving visit with Gloria, he got down on his knee and proposed. Still, LeShon wanted them to take their time getting married. Paula sometimes had bursts of intense anger, lashing out at him for what he thought was nothing much. At those moments, he did his best to remain steady for her.

During those same months, Paula started a new job, one she'd never anticipated: she began working in the office of the Indiana Federal Community Defenders, now run by Monica Foster.

Monica had handled perhaps twenty capital cases since her time with Paula, and she'd had countless clients who'd been raised in desperate situations. Despite the years of living with anxiety and insomnia, she'd been able to continue on with the work because she had eventually developed a strategy: *You put cases behind you, and they're behind you, and that's it. Put it in a box and put the box on a shelf.* She dealt only with what was directly in front of her. It was a primitive way of thinking, she thought, but she considered it a means of survival. And it made her more useful.

But then, after some twenty years of silence between them, Paula left Monica a message: "Hey, girl, this is a blast from the past." She knew right away who it was. And the feelings from that time, of her younger self, came rushing back.

The two women went out to dinner on Broad Ripple Avenue and sat outside on the deck, eating fried chicken and drinking wine, gossiping, laughing and doing impressions of people they used to know in common. They had *both* changed, middle-aged now, and there was an easiness between them. Monica had no expectations of their meet-up, but sitting with Paula after so many years had her consumed with joy—*Paula's* joy, which she found contagious. Above all, Paula loved indulging in boy talk: how a guy walking past their table had a nice ass, how their waiter was cute, how a good-looking man shouldn't be wearing those shorts. They began speaking regularly, meeting up every other week, and Monica and Bob would sometimes have Paula over for dinner.

Monica had major changes in mind when she took over the Federal Public Defender's Office. What had once been, in the words of one longtime attorney, "the home for semiretired white males," was on its way to steadily becoming the best federal law firm in the state. Monica wanted to focus on sentencing and mitigation, to hire social workers, to have a staff that was diverse. And now Monica had another idea: maybe her former client could take some shifts as their receptionist. Some of her colleagues hesitated, questioning whether or not the first person visitors to a legal office should see was someone convicted of murder. But Paula was given the chance. She'd been known as Renae at Spain's House, and Monica asked if she wanted to use her middle name at work too, for privacy. She declined. She would show up at the office, visited by the very crowd most likely to remember her, and she would do it as herself.

Paula had been a lay advocate while at Rockville, and her new job built on that. She answered phones and helped lawyers correspond with clients in jail; she worked on her typing and her legal terminology and took some tech courses. Paula loved the chance to dress like a professional and go into an office in a towering steel and glass building on Monument Circle. Even though she'd been incarcerated herself, she was pleasant when contacting prison officials—but she would not relent until they called back. She would leave voice mail after voice mail: "Hi, this is Paula Cooper. I called you yesterday, now I'm calling you again today, and I'm going to call you tomorrow."

She had a way of relating to their clients that the attorneys did not. Paula might slip in a note of encouragement with their correspondence—*Keep your head up*, something like that. If an attorney requested a photo of an incarcerated person's child for some purpose, Paula would always return the picture with a message saying that the kid was *the cutest we've seen*. She also had a gift for talking to mothers who might be concerned about the conditions in segregation, or how best to get their incarcerated son's or daughter's medical needs tended to. She spoke with the authority of experience. Monica thought Paula had grown into a person with an excess of empathy and a mysterious confidence for someone who'd lived her life. She thought she must have pulled that up from deep inside her.

Within months, the team brought her on full-time.

Paula left her friend Meshia's house quietly that morning, well before sunup, dressed in all new clothes and a new pair of sandals. She got into her black Toyota Corolla, her stuffed-animal babies strapped into the back seat. She drove for who knows how long—only Paula knows what route she took, how straight-ahead or how winding and hesitant—before pulling into a parking lot and cutting the engine.

It was dark out still, and the lot was illuminated here and there with the glow of the light poles. Now and then, cars sped by on I-465. She was at ITT Technical Institute; to almost anyone, this place, with its anonymous corporate architecture, would be indistinguishable from so many others. A strange choice for a person's final moment. But Paula was not far from LeShon's apartment, and he'd taken her for rides in this lot on the back of his motorcycle, a bike he kept in an equipment shed on the grounds.

Paula picked up a digital recorder and began speaking to the small number of people she held closest.

That Sunday, she had visited her friend Meshia at work—they knew each other from Rockville—and had broken down sobbing. Paula had argued with LeShon, but to Meshia it seemed bigger than that; she seemed like a child who'd run herself down, totally drained. Paula said, "Friend, friend, I can't take it anymore. It's the pain inside," pointing at her chest. "I just want it to be over." Meshia insisted she stay at her house.

The next day, yesterday, they'd had a Memorial Day barbeque and invited Rhonda. Paula held her sister tight, and Rhonda asked if anything was wrong. "Everything's fine," she said. "Everything's beautiful." That night, at Paula's insistence, she and Meshia drove to Walmart, the only store nearby open late on the holiday, and Paula bought a new outfit. In the middle of the night, when everyone was asleep, she did what she had for so many years: she wrote letters—to Meshia, Michael, LeShon, Rhonda—and placed them on the kitchen stove. And then, long before sunrise, she slipped out quietly and got in her car.

In the recording she left behind, Paula said goodbye, again, to the people she loved. In few words, she expressed the kinds of things you would expect: love and gratitude to Meshia, to Rhonda ("my queen, my everything"), and to LeShon. She apologized to LeShon for hurting him, and to Monica for leaving this way.

But with Gloria, this time, she was plainspoken. Her fantasy about a relationship with her mother had cracked; it was irreparably broken. "You didn't care about me," she said. "You cut me off. You judged me."

Nevertheless, Paula said, she still loved her.

To all of these people, she tried to give the *why* behind her actions that morning, falling back on abstract language:

This pain that I feel every day I walk around—I'm so miserable inside. . . . This is a reality that's too much for me to handle. . . . I must have peace—peace of mind, peace in my heart. . . . Forgive me, I must go now.

She placed the recorder on the seat of the car and stepped outside. Once before, as a child, she'd done this: stepped out into the early morning, prepared to end her life.

When the campus manager arrives, about two hours later, he notices a woman asleep underneath one of the ash trees. As he approaches, he senses she is too still. And then he sees it, the handgun.

Meshia's husband had discovered the letters in the kitchen not long after six a.m. and gone to wake his wife. Without waiting a beat, without a plan, Meshia had run from the house. She and LeShon are each now driving across the city, searching for the spot Paula might have chosen— a house she and LeShon considered buying, places they'd gone by Eagle Creek. Nothing. Finally, Meshia receives a call from a number she does not recognize: an officer is on the line. They have found the body of Paula Cooper.

In the letter to her fiancé, Paula had written, *I have taken a life and never felt worthy.*

Monica is on her way to the annual Federal Defender Conference in Omaha, Nebraska. She landed in Minneapolis, milled around the airport, and had just boarded her connecting flight. While waiting for takeoff, her phone lights up with a message: *Call the office 911.*

She makes the call, and is told by a staff member that Paula has killed herself.

"No, she didn't," Monica says. "No, she *didn't.* Who said that she did that? She didn't do that."

But then Monica has to turn off the phone: The flight is leaving, and she has no choice but to remain seated on the plane. One of her team members is with her, but he's ten rows back. Boxed into her middle seat, she cries hard, the entire way to Omaha.

The plane lands, and the two colleagues step into the airport. It's about ten a.m. in Nebraska, and they head to a bar near the gate and order vodka shots. "I can't stay here," she says. "I have to go home."

Her office arranges the flight back, but it will take all day—from Omaha to Wichita to Atlanta to Colorado Springs and then, finally, to Indianapolis. Along the way, the press begins to call. Monica finds herself telling a reporter, "You absolutely fucking *cannot* meet me at the airport."

It is nighttime when she arrives at her house, sobbing uncontrollably. Bob is beside himself; he does not know what to do. He calls her close friend, a federal judge. "You have to come over here." The judge finds Monica sitting on a bench in the backyard, wailing.

Monica often spoke to her clients about how their families had disappointed them, and how it was something they were learning to live with. She had not realized how deeply troubled Paula had been by her relationship with Gloria. Monica's approach had been "Okay, *fuck* your mother! Come on, we got all this good stuff going! I care about you, I love you. You don't need to be with your mom. Come to *my* house for Christmas."

That had seemed to be enough; Paula had seemed to be doing fine. If there had been signs, they were not obvious. The Friday before Memorial Day—three and half days before Paula took her own life—Monica turned up the music in the office, and the two of them started dancing and singing and cracking up about it. And in the early afternoon, others on the staff sent Paula in to ask Monica if they could go home early for the holiday. "Did the other ones send you in here because they know I won't say no to you?" Monica had stepped out into the hall and seen everyone milling about, smiling, waiting to hear word. She thought it was hilarious. She sent everyone home.

And then: Tuesday morning.

And now it is Tuesday night. And Monica is outside in the garden, letting out the sounds of an animal in pain. Her neighbor, just behind the yard, is Randall Shepard, who retired three years ago after twenty-five years as chief justice of the Indiana Supreme Court; he had led the court when they commuted Paula's sentence. He'd learned the news, so he calls the house. He asks Bob, "How is she?" In the midst of her grief, Monica never returns the call—but she will not forget that he rang. She disagreed with the man in so many ways, on so many issues, over so many years. And yet he reached out.

The next day, Paula's death is on the front page of the *Chicago Tribune:* WOMAN ONCE YOUNGEST ON DEATH ROW FOUND DEAD. *The Times* of Munster runs the banner headline COPS: KILLER COMMITS SUICIDE.

Monica goes into work. Everyone seems to be in a state of shock. She thinks, *I'm supposed to be the leader of this fucking office, and everybody is so badly hurting. What am I going to do?* As seems natural, she brings everyone together in a circle, and they take a moment to embrace one another. They talk about Paula, and they cry.

In Anchorage, Bill Pelke sits down at his desk. He logs online to check his email and finds a message from one of his daughters: *Dad, I'm so sorry.* There is a news link. He clicks on the item and bursts into tears.

Over the course of Paula's long prison sentence, Bill eventually visited her a total of fourteen times. They exchanged some two hundred letters and, as technology changed, perhaps a thousand emails. But Bill had not seen Paula since her release, and they had not been in touch for nearly a year.

A month before Paula left Rockville, a Chicago TV station had interviewed Bill. The reporter then contacted the prison in search of Paula's mug shot for broadcast, and she heard about it. She wrote to Bill that Gloria was *extremely upset,* anxious about this fresh wave of coverage, and questioned Bill's motivations. *I wonder if you have fully forgiven me*, she wrote. With only a few weeks left to her sentence, she cut him from her visitors list.

Over her years in prison, Paula had gone back and forth in her thinking about how to share her story once she was free again. She knew that Bill had a deep desire for her to join in his activism, to become his counterpart in the story he'd been telling on the road for so long. She was opposed to the death penalty, but she was more interested in, maybe, the possibility of speaking to kids who were on the cusp of hurting themselves or others—in a way, she was looking for a chance to speak to her fifteen-year-old self. But once her release was at hand, silence and anonymity became very appealing.

Around that same time, Carlo Santoro had written Paula from Rome and arranged to visit her at Rockville with Bill. But two days before the planned visit, she emailed Carlo to cancel; only when he promised to come on his own did she agree. And so, with her release a week away, Carlo had sat across from Paula in the visiting center while Bill waited outside in the car. Through Sant'Egidio, Carlo had recently offered to fly her to Rome to speak to young people there, possibly kids in the juvenile detention system, and Paula said she was grateful for the opportunity. But in person, she told him she was no longer interested. "I don't want to be known anymore," she said. "Nobody has to see my face."

Carlo thought he understood. But then she added, "And I don't want to see Bill anymore."

A devout man, and very earnest, Carlo was shocked by the statement. "But Bill *loves* you," he said, in his slow and steady English. "You also have a debt of love and compassion toward this man. He is a very good man."

Paula granted that. "But I have one mother." She had made up her mind as to where her loyalty must lie. Bill had been looking forward to Paula's release for many years, had woven her freedom into the larger narrative that had given shape to his life, and now their entire relationship was in question. Carlo felt for him.

Paula did eventually contact Bill, in the summer of 2014, shortly after her year of parole was up. He answered his cell phone while riding in a van with David Kaczynski, en route to a Journey event in Connecticut. It took him a moment to recognize her voice—and when he did, he was thrilled to hear from her. She asked about the Journey; she told him she'd been doing fine. Except something about needing to pay the IRS to keep them from seizing her car—which didn't really make sense to Bill, so he suggested she discuss it with Monica. Shortly afterward, they got off the phone. He'd felt awkward talking about money after the long silence. It was as if Paula did not understand how many cumulative hours he'd spent over the years telling others, often crowds of strangers, about his love for her. He decided to give her some space for a little while. Their phone call had lasted no more than a few minutes. He could not have known it would be their last communication.

At Rockville, a guard reads the news as it scrolls across the TV screen in one of the rec rooms and immediately calls the warden. Ms. Stout cannot believe what she is hearing. Paula had called her numerous times, her voice fast and excited, to talk about everything she was up to—when she got the job at Five Guys, got her driver's license, moved into her own apartment, just to say she was spending a weekend with family. Ms. Stout had hoped to have Paula visit someday to talk to the other women, tell them how well she'd handled her transition back into the world. There was a time when prison officials presumed the death of Paula Cooper to be an inevitability, sanctioned by the state; but today, the idea of her passing makes the warden feel ill. For years, she will turn the question over in her mind: *Why didn't you call me* then? *You called me multiple times. Why didn't you call me* then? This is the question she tries to avoid asking in life, *Why*. She thinks of it as "a suffering question. If you want to suffer, just ask yourself, *Why did this happen?*" A person can work with *How*, she thinks—*How am I supposed to deal with this?*—but not *Why*.

For Monica, the suffering question is *What if?* In the weeks and months that follow: *What if Paula hadn't killed herself? What if she didn't have the mother that she had? What if she'd had a better upbringing?* She plays *What if?* a lot—not only with Paula's story, but with her own. She thinks about the color of her own skin and what that's allowed her, the breathing room it's granted her. What if she'd had different parents? What if she'd been born a Black girl in Gary? What if some of the pieces of her own life had been handed, instead, to Paula Cooper?

For those first years in prison, as a teenager, there were two Paulas, and which one you believed in depended upon whom you consulted. She was a girl who'd been abused for years, a child in need of help; she was calculating, a great manipulator, as competent as any sociopath; she was both, someone split down the middle. Decades later, years into her time at Rockville, another Paula arrived, older, humbler, more capable of imagining a future for herself. The problem for this Paula was the realizations adulthood brought. She'd become weighted down with the enormity of twenty-eight years of missed opportunity, weighted down with guilt. Growing older meant carrying the full burden of what she'd done at fifteen years old.

Paula had told LeShon, in their many, many talks, that she could not shake the feelings of guilt for her actions thirty years ago. She thought of Bill Pelke, how he had forgiven her; she thought of her many years inside, how she'd trained herself over that time to believe she deserved another start. But there is a gulf between forgiveness in theory and forgiveness in practice. Paula was unable to fight her way to the other side of it. She had been the one to commit violence, and who was she to absolve herself?

Nor had her mother seemed willing to forgive Paula. That spring, her younger daughter called Gloria to ask if she and LeShon could come to her church in Hammond, make the two-and-a-half-hour trip up from Indy to spend some time together. Paula was clearly in a vulnerable position, trying to build a life, extending herself to the woman who had not been much of a parent to her. But Gloria rejected the offer. She made an excuse about Paula and her fiancé living together unmarried; she said,

"Let me talk to my pastor first." Paula did not believe her. "What it is, is that my mother doesn't want me to come down there to her church because of my past," she told LeShon. "I'm not that person anymore, but my own mother won't let the past go." At work, she went into Monica's office to talk about it, how her mother was ashamed of her. She began crying and shaking. And Monica said, "Look, she doesn't know you. She doesn't understand. It'll be okay. She has her own demons that she wrestles with."

Paula gave it two more weeks and then, with Mother's Day coming up, she called Gloria and again suggested a visit. Her mother was rude; in spite of her church talk, she cursed at her daughter. When Paula called LeShon, he offered to take off work to comfort her. "I'm going to be all right," she told him. Echoing Rhonda's refrain over the years, she said, "I'm not going to mess with my mom. I'm done." She phoned Gloria on Mother's Day, but it was no substitute for the gathering she'd imagined—a reminder that her mother had chosen not to be with her on the Sunday reserved for women to bask in their children.

Four days later: the Thursday that marked thirty years since Ruth Pelke's death. Two days after that: the anniversary of the start of Paula's decades of incarceration. Since she was a teenage girl, these were dates she had never failed to register in her mind, to dwell on. A part of how she marked time.

In the recording Paula made in her car that morning, and in the letter she left behind for LeShon, she gave detailed instructions for her funeral.

She wanted potted red begonias, the flowers LeShon had introduced her to on a landscaping job shortly after they met. She wanted Patti LaBelle and Chris Brown on the stereo, and she wanted the service "to be happy, quiet, and only for those who I care about." Guests should eat well: fried chicken, greens, mac and cheese, Hawaiian rolls. "I don't want people crying and having a lot of regrets, feeling they could have did more," she'd said as she sat in the front seat of her Toyota. "There was nothing anybody could do."

Paula asked to be laid out in a black outfit Rhonda recently bought for her, without any makeup, her hair rolled. But once the memorial was over with, she should be cremated. After so much time in prison, Monica thought, she did not want to be placed in a box and buried in the earth.

Monica organizes Paula's memorial: a private gathering to take place in Monica's backyard, where Paula had talked about getting married. She follows Paula's requests. She even offers to prepare the fried chicken and greens herself, but Rhonda cannot imagine an Italian American woman from Buffalo cooking soul food; she politely insists on doing that herself. Mike and Parish are there, and Rhonda's stepkids. Monica's entire office attends. Bill flies in from Alaska, and Victor Streib comes in from Cleveland. Archbishop Tobin says a prayer, a simple one, wary of giving some easy explanation for what has happened.

Gloria is not in attendance.

Rhonda had been the one to call their mother when Paula died. At that point, they had not spoken in nearly two months. She had struggled with her mother's drinking her entire life, helping to maintain her façade as a functioning alcoholic, and now she found herself propping up Gloria yet again, not far from where it all began. In response, Gloria continued to be rude to her, to say spiteful things to her face. Finally—this was shortly before their mother refused Paula's visit—Rhonda said, "Look, I can't do you and take care of me and my husband." Gloria stopped talking to her; even after Rhonda shared the news of Paula's death, that silent treatment continued. Rhonda does not let it bother her. Never in her life has she felt a motherly connection, that bond, not that she can remember. And she cannot cry over the loss of something she never had.

The day after Paula's death, Gloria and Monica met a detective at the downtown Indianapolis police station to make arrangements for Paula's body and possessions. Gloria had told Rhonda and Mike not to come that day, and Rhonda suspected her mother was in a rush to collect an apartment's worth of furniture, not realizing that Paula had sold her things before moving in with LeShon. Paula's car was not fully paid off, and so that wasn't available either, only the odd items inside the Toyota.

Rhonda had made a statement to the press, and she warned each journalist who called that those were her first and final words on the subject. Despite the warning, reporters rang with more questions, hoping for some new comment. Rhonda would not speak. Occasionally a journalist would show up at her door and refuse to leave, or show up multiple days in a row. Rhonda threatened to call the police. It all reminded her of that long period when she and Mike received *other* kinds of calls. Death messages. "Your sister should have died when his *mother* died," the voices had said, or "You should die, too, *bitch*." Messages about *your black* this and *your black* that. She became afraid of speaking to people she did not know well, afraid to make new friends, afraid of going to the store. She grew very, very tired, desperate to "shut down the noise." And so Rhonda avoided leaving home.

She had combed this girl's hair, been hit in the face for her, baked biscuits for her. They had danced together, alone in their house; they had run away together. Sometimes she thinks that her sister was the love of her life.

Gloria will have her daughter's body placed in a coffin and buried underground. And she will not mark her grave.

In Rome, where it was evening, Carlo had received the news standing in St. Peter's Square. He was handing out food to the homeless, as he does on Tuesdays, when Archbishop Tobin called. He could not believe what he heard.

The news weighs on him. As a pious man, he sits with it, turning over and over in his mind and in prayer what this could possibly mean. It must mean *something*.

He thinks of some of Paula's last words. *This pain that I feel every day*

I walk around—he hears in this the voice of someone describing the return of evil after a long respite (he sees the world in this way, divided between Good and Evil). An act of evil, he thinks, can haunt a person's soul until they believe they can never be forgiven; so many of the men he's met in Rome's prisons have seemed this way to him, haunted. For Paula, the weight of her crime had not been lifted by Bill's compassion.

Paula's death, Carlo thinks, is the victory of Evil. It makes him feel the way he feels whenever one of the homeless men he works with is found dead. Many are recovering alcoholics, and one day they start to drink again, and their body is discovered on a city sidewalk. Carlo thinks: Someone living in the street could die this very night—when he is robbed, or from the freezing cold, or because it's easy to get sick and hard to find help. But every day he lives out is a triumph. It is something.

For nearly thirty years, Paula had wrestled with Evil and held it back, with the help of so many others. They were family; they were family to her victim; they were attorneys and activists, fellow residents of Rockville or the Women's Prison, the Holy Father himself; they were a long list of strangers in other countries. Carlo thinks: Paula Cooper might have been executed, but she was not. She could have died in prison, but she did not. She could have been killed upon her release, but she stayed safe. She might have died in any other number of ways, but she lived to the age of forty-four.

This is the story, he thinks. This is the story he hopes will be repeated.

Twenty-Two

JUDGMENT

Now in his seventies, Jack Crawford has returned to Catholicism. Somewhat. He laughs at himself when talking about it, but, at this point, he pays attention to Pope Francis; he wonders what might happen when his life comes to an end; he is fearful of his day of judgment. He thinks it best to side with the believers.

So much has changed for Jack since his time as Lake County prosecutor.

After remaining unchallenged since his election in 1978, Jack resigned in the summer of 1989 to move his family "downstate" to the capital: the new Democratic governor, Evan Bayh, had appointed him director of Indiana's first lottery. In this way, Jack gained a highly visible statewide position, became the highest-paid head of a state department (with a salary higher than Bayh's), and found a new launching pad for a political life beyond Lake County—a path to power that had eluded him since his congressional campaign fiasco just before the Pelke case.

The goal was to launch an instant lottery by the end of the year— about six months to jumpstart a $600 million business—and million-dollar numbers games after that. At forty-one, Jack was determined to defy expectations again, this time by selling a not-so-Christian pastime in a conservative state. He would make the lottery an undeniable financial success.

After ten and a half years as a prosecutor, of being known (as he would later put it) as "the death penalty guy," Jack thoroughly enjoyed the *lightness* of being the lottery director. Who doesn't want to win a lot of money? And he was a natural at promotion. He would hype the lottery down on the court at Hoosiers games to big cheers. Hockey games, football games. He appeared in a local TV ad for *The Cosby Show*, dancing like the Huxtables. And then there was the *Hoosier Millionaire* TV game show each Saturday night on Channel 4. He became a celebrity in Indiana. Well-placed Democrats began talking about him for statewide office. When the lottery launched that fall, ticket sales exceeded expectations. By early December, Jack announced that sales had broken $100 million.

Jack considered Evan Bayh one of his best friends: They were close in age, and the Crawfords had worked hard campaigning for Bayh throughout Lake County—a county that had made a real difference in the election. But the governor, famously straitlaced, took issue with Jack's promotional style. He was uncomfortable with gambling to begin with, and Jack did little to downplay the lottery's carnivalesque nature. A reporter for *The Indianapolis Star* would later write of how Hoosiers could not help but be curious about "the lottery's brash, young director who was promoting the fledgling enterprise the way P. T. Barnum hawked a side show." It was possible that he was becoming *too* visible.

Still, he did not see it coming.

On a Sunday night that December, he was called in for a meeting at the Statehouse. When he arrived, Bayh was not there, but two of his senior aides were, accompanied by a state trooper. Two days earlier, the lottery's head of human resources had presented the governor's team with evidence that she had long been sexually involved with Jack. She claimed that it was harassment, a gross abuse of power; that for years he had linked her employment to sex; that, as prosecutor, there had been no one to report him to. Jack claimed their relationship had been consensual—but even if that were true, the governor's aides reminded him, he had violated state regulations against sex with a subordinate.

It was Mary Cartwright. He had hired Mary years earlier as a way to get closer to her father, Reverend Burns, the prominent Lake County minister, so that he could better access the Black churches and the Black vote during his run for prosecutor. Jack had made her his receptionist in Hammond City Court when he was city judge, then his executive secretary in the Lake County Prosecutor's Office; shortly after his appointment as lottery director, he'd brought her on board as head of human resources. And now Jack was being presented, in the governor's office, with notes he'd written her, including a revised will (on hotel stationery) leaving half of all he owned *to Mary L. Cartwright, my loyal and trusted office manager, in return for her many years of service and devotion.* This was dated about two weeks before Ruth Pelke's murder landed on Jack's desk, at the apex of his time as prosecutor.

If he resigned immediately, the affair would be kept quiet. And so he did.

But it was not kept quiet. The next morning, a radio station announced that Jack had stepped down after just six months on the job, something to do with a woman in his employ. And with nearly every day that passed, more details were revealed on the front pages of the major Indiana papers—coverage that would not stop for weeks and months to come. On Thursday, the governor felt compelled to hold a press conference and reveal that Jack's firing had been due to a sexual harassment allegation. And he confirmed reports that the woman involved was Mary Cartwright.

That same evening, Jack held a press conference of his own, in a barely furnished apartment (he and his family had yet to move into the new house he'd bought them). He invited in reporters and a cluster of television crews, offered everyone beers, and then—dressed in jeans, tennis shoes, and his Indiana University sweatshirt—sat down on a pair of pillows on the living-room floor. Klieg lights had been set up, and a wall of cameras all turned on him; the crush of reporters was silent.

For the next forty-five minutes, Jack worked to change the story. "This is simply a case of a love affair that went very bad. . . . I believe that Mrs. Cartwright was the victim not of sexual harassment, but of me leading her along during the course of a long relationship." Her aim in making her accusations had been retribution, Jack said, and perhaps he deserved it.

In a first, he made himself emotionally naked in public. He spoke without prepared remarks—a talent he'd learned early on, from the Black ministers he'd watched up in the pulpit. Sometimes he cried; one journalist would write that his "lower lip often quivered." As Jack had required of the many, many defendants he had charged over the years, he expressed remorse, aware that he had to sell it. He accepted blame for what had happened to his life and career. "The pain and suffering I have caused my family, the hurt I have caused a lot of people, is my burden to bear and no one else's," he said, "and I will bear it for many years to come." At the same time, looking up at the cameras, he asked the public to accept that he, too, was a victim. "I don't understand the treatment that I've been given." Those cameras captured an incredible image: that of Jack Crawford, Lake County prosecutor for a decade, once a viable candidate for Congress, seated cross-legged on the floor, with his face in his hands.

The next day, the story seemed to be everywhere. *The Indianapolis Star* ran a total of seven articles and an astounding photo that stretched from the top of the front page to below the fold: an enormous close-up of Jack in tears. WRTV (Channel 6), who'd chosen to interrupt their primetime programming to broadcast live from Jack's apartment, had doubled their ratings for the slot.

This public weeping—on television, seated on the floor in sweatshirt and sneakers—had been a spectacle of contrition. He wanted to be

forgiven, to be accepted as a complex person who still had a lot to offer. In the days after the living-room conference, he told a reporter that he'd never been dealt with in this way. "I was treated like I was nobody, like nobody even knew me, like I was some stranger who was going to become a homicidal maniac." He was, in other words, someone with a clean record who was being treated like a criminal; the nuances of his situation were not being considered. The governor's chief of staff had said of their office's hard-line response: "This was the pursuit of a principle."

A few weeks into the scandal, Jack, overestimating the political capital he had in reserve, began exploring a possible run for Marion County prosecutor. Shortly afterward, the governor's office released the remaining details they'd withheld about Mary Cartwright's allegations. Many details. Graphic details. Jack's career in politics had come to an end.

Jack's departure from Lake County had been a small relief to Earline Rogers. She had never fully trusted the man when he talked of protecting Gary. And she would never forget how he'd pushed so hard for the deaths of those teenage girls. Sometimes, to her mind, there is an absolute right and an absolute wrong.

Earline never left her city. She has lived on the same corner in the

Tolleston neighborhood of Gary, in the same house, for a half century. She only retired from political life in 2016, after eight years in the Indiana House of Representatives and twenty-five years in the State Senate. Her husband is recently deceased, but each time their son—a teacher like his mother, a college professor—suggests she join him where he's moved with her five grandsons, out West, she dismisses the idea. She tells her son at those moments, just as Ruth Pelke had told her stepson, "This is my corner, my piece of the Earth. And this is where I will remain until I'm not on this Earth anymore."

When Earline had taken all those trips downstate to participate in the General Assembly session, she had been one of few women, and certainly one of few Black women, among state legislators. She worked hard to convince many of her colleagues that they had any common ground on which to meet. By the time of her retirement, she had risen to Senate majority whip, and then Gary mayor Karen Freeman-Wilson honored her "ability to get things done in a General Assembly that often considers Gary a foreign land."

Since the end, in 1987, of Hatcher's five-term era, Gary has elected six Black mayors. But neither Hatcher, who died in 2019, nor any of his successors has been able to turn the city around. There had remained no substitute for the many thousands of jobs that were lost at the steel mill, and he had leaned heavily on federal funds to develop the city. He had invested millions in Gary's depressed downtown, building a convention center, a transportation hub, a sports arena. But the hotel chains did not follow; big businesses did not follow; the convention center did not attract marquee events or large conferences. The predominantly white-run shopping centers of Merrillville were so nearby and, at this point, so convenient, that many of Gary's own residents spent their money in the suburb at stores that were hard to compete with. And when President Reagan made dramatic cuts to federal aid in the early eighties, the city became truly strapped. The population is now less than half of what it was then, and the small collection of businesses left are hardly enough to serve the remaining sixty-nine thousand residents: some fast-food restaurants and dollar stores, hair salons and barbershops, a record store, cash-checking services, a few auto shops, the office of *The Gary Crusader*. The Palace Theater has long been out of use, and the offices of the *Post-Tribune* long ago moved to Merrillville.

Earline's family has been in the community for five generations now. They are known here, and she does not take that lightly. Through her many years in public service, she tried to create a lifeline for her home-town, any opportunities she could grab. She'd seen an opening in the bill that legalized gambling in Indiana back in 1988—the same bill that cleared the way for the state's first lottery. To Earline's mind, that bill meant jobs for her city, for her neighbors, and when it passed, it was not long before she'd helped broker the opening of a pair of riverboat casinos in Gary; only a few years ago, she helped ease the deal for a Hard Rock Casino outpost. She was aware of the criticisms of gambling culture, but she asked in response, "When's the last time somebody wanted to invest three hundred million dollars into Gary, Indiana?" They had agreed to hire from within the community, and that was what she cared about.

She had also fought, for nearly forty years, to improve the Gary public school system—as a teacher herself and as a representative, authoring or pushing through reforms to better conditions for educators and students. Looking back, at eighty-seven years old, that is what she's proudest of. But several of the schools in which she and her colleagues taught have since been shuttered; many have become abandoned shells, vandalized. In 2001, a law was passed that allowed students to attend school in a district that was not their own, and the decline of Gary's public schools was all but guaranteed. Children who could be bused or driven by their parents to neighboring towns, like Hammond, went ahead and attended charter schools, razing the number of pupils enrolled in Gary. Meanwhile, as enrollment numbers dropped, so did funding for resources to help the remaining students succeed. So test scores for Gary's schools *also* fell. And soon the state and local governments saw no point in the upkeep of the schoolhouses.

Roosevelt, the first high school built for Gary's Black students, just a few years before Earline was born, remained in use until recently, and Earline still finds the building beautiful. She belongs to a committee that is trying to raise funds for repairs, to save the place from being torn down. Not long ago, she told a reporter, "I'd lay in front of a steamroller before they let it go."

Lew Wallace High School, where the girls in the Pelke case had gathered back in 1985, was recently demolished, reduced to a fenced-off, city-block long stretch of rubble.

Of those four girls, only one still lives: Denise Thomas, who, at fourteen, had required a booster seat on the witness stand. Of her thirty-five-year sentence, she spent eighteen in prison, and returned home to Gary in 2003; unlike Paula, she had been portrayed as a minor player in the killing of Ruth Pelke, and so her release happened quietly. Today Denise lives in Indianapolis and has no desire to share her experience with the press. She has not spoken publicly since her appearance in court nearly forty years ago.

April Beverly had known Mrs. Pelke and sent the girls to the house on Adams Street. She was the only one whose family hired an attorney, and in a plea deal, she was sentenced to twenty-five years in prison (the shortest sentence of them all). She served fourteen years and moved back to Gary upon her release in 1999. April had trained to use the AutoCAD computer program while in prison and had a talent for it, and so she had a job waiting for her, drafting plans for a small architectural firm. A few years into her life outside, she was killed by an abusive boyfriend. The event—a Black woman in Gary killed in an act of domestic violence—went unnoticed by the media.

Karen Corder, who had taken part in the stabbing of Ruth Pelke, was spared the death penalty in 1986 but sentenced to sixty years. After the crime, no one, including her public defenders, had spent much time exploring the events that had left the twelve-year-old girl pregnant by a seventeen-year-old. Once she was sentenced to prison, Karen's young son was placed, like the Cooper sisters, in the Thelma Marshall Children's Home, around the corner from the Jackson family house. She saw little of him after that.

In 2000, at thirty-one years old, Karen began filing a series of petitions for early release, without the help of counsel. Each time, she outlined the whole array of prison programs in which she'd enrolled, from thousands of hours of vocational training to multiple kinds of therapy. She mentioned the certificates of distinction she'd received in piano lessons and drama class, and how she had helped with the Christmas murals at Ronald McDonald House and sung gospel solos in the chapel choir. She requested a reduction of sentence to forty years and a move to a treatment center to ease her reentry into society. Her requests were denied.

All four girls, as women, had eventually ended up at Rockville together, and Karen and Paula had spoken every day. Karen had a thick heart—hypertrophic obstructive cardiomyopathy—and around Thanksgiving of 2008, she had a defibrillator implanted in her chest. A month later, she told an officer in her dorm that she didn't feel well, and she was advised to lie down in her bunk. Paula's room was across from Karen's, and Paula looked on as she struggled and passed away. She had served more than twenty-two years of her sentence, and had five years left until her likely release. Some of the long-termers who'd gotten out— women who'd been in prison with Karen, and knew she didn't have any family support—picked up her body and made arrangements for a funeral service a couple of hours from the institution that had brought them together. Among Paula Cooper's few possessions at the end of her life were the photos she was sent of Karen's memorial.

———————✦———————

After the lottery scandal, Jack Crawford struggled to find a place for himself. No one was prepared to hire him, not even as a poorly compensated public defender. And so he opened up his own modest practice on Indianapolis's less-polished northeast section. He pitched himself to prospective clients as a defense attorney who understands what it's like to feel shut out and desperate for help.

It worked. And after four years passed, he was once again on the front page of *The Indianapolis Star*: "JACK FIGHTS BACK: With stubborn determination and hard lessons learned, Jack Crawford is rebuilding his life . . ." The head-in-hands 1989 portrait had been resurrected, but it was now juxtaposed with that of a suited-up, smiling, reinvented man. In little time, he'd climbed back up to annual earnings close to his lottery salary, and he'd bought himself a red Mustang convertible. Jack was forty-five at the time of his reemergence, around the same age at which Paula Cooper would later attempt her "second chance."

Today Jack's law office occupies part of the bottom floor of a large historic redbrick building, around the corner from two Black churches. When he and his second wife Kim bought the building in 1995, to convert into a shared practice, it was abandoned, a shell; now the place is in the historic registry, another piece of the northeast's revitalization.

After several visits with Jack and numerous hours of conversation, it is not difficult for me to imagine the career he might have had. Now in his early seventies, Jack is less camera-ready than he was thirty-odd years ago; he has a growth about the size of a cashew nestled between his right eye and the bridge of his nose, and he has recently undergone heart surgery. But the charisma remains: that particular politician's brand of easy confidence, the projection of that confidence onto you, the sense that you are sharing a moment that's of greater historic import than anticipated.

The dominant impression, however, is of a man mourning his legacy.

On one visit, at my request, he had laid out across a tabletop in a small conference room photos from another era: images from the Pelke case file; images of him and his first wife as a smiling young political couple; of him and their sons and the family dog; of him and Evan Bayh, then recently elected governor; of a local rally he'd helped to organize for Ted Kennedy's presidential run; of political appearances in a Gary nightclub, in a Knights of Columbus meeting hall, alongside future Chicago mayor Richard M. Daley. He said that gathering up the photos had depressed him. "Because, I mean, is this a life? A few photographs?"

Multiple times over the course of our talks, he will mention his ex-girlfriend Cathy, the woman who had called to confront him about pursuing the death sentence for Paula and Karen. He wonders aloud how his career and his life might have been different "if I'd gone *her* way"—further to the left. Maybe he would be more in sync with the present, his time in office remembered more fondly. When I point out how far that is from the work he actually pursued, as a hard-line prosecutor who leaned heavily on the death penalty, he agrees. "Well, I've changed," he says. "I've evolved. That's *okay*, isn't it—for people to evolve?"

Jack is now against the death penalty—mainly, he says, because of the racial bias in how it is meted out. He says he is against the death penalty for juveniles because of what we've learned about the development of the brain. But when I ask Jack, after so much time has passed, if he would have handled the Pelke case differently in any way, he answers with a statement that has become a refrain in our conversations: "I don't know."

"If you're in politics," he says, "you want to win, and you have to be sensitive to what you think people want. And people wanted a hard line on crime—they wanted a very hard line." He reminds me that, during his time as prosecutor, support for the death penalty was high, and three-strikes laws were common across the country. "Is my job to represent what people think, or is my job to lead them to what they *should* think? I don't know."

On occasion, at this point in his life, Jack thinks of his own death, imagines his own moment of judgment. "What if I get up there and, first of all, God's a *woman?*" he says. "So I get up there, and I've got some woman—and she's a *Black* woman? And she's gonna ask me, 'How did you treat your fellow human beings during the course of your life, Mr. Crawford?' So yeah, I'm going to hedge my bets." He will tell this Black, female God that he does not have an answer.

As prosecutor, he *did* have an answer, had been certain that he was doing the right thing, that justice was whatever the largest number of voters defined it as being. Now, he says, "I'm not so sure." And he does not go much further than that.

Twenty-Three

STORYTELLING

In the spring of 2020, the Covid-19 pandemic arrives. Across the country, people avoid touching each other or standing closer than six feet apart or gathering indoors. They wear surgical or double-ply fabric masks when outside their homes. People divide themselves into those they live with and those who live in other houses. Those taking precautions live in fear of those who refuse to. And the number of deaths continues mounting, reaching a hundred thousand within a few months.

As requested by the Centers for Disease Control, Bill Pelke, in Anchorage, hardly leaves his house. He is growing out a beard that's gray and biblical. Since the first caravan through Indiana, there have been two dozen Journeys, mostly throughout the South and the Midwest, some states four times, five times. Members of the group have told their stories in Southeast Asia, East Africa, and Western Europe. Bill alone has traveled to Italy twenty-six times. At the age of seventy-two, this is the longest stretch he's spent at home for thirty years.

An unofficial moratorium has halted executions in most states, mainly out of safety concerns for the correction officers, execution team, attorneys, and witnesses who would be brought together for such an event. But in the summer, the Trump administration, through Attorney General

William Barr, proceeds to revive federal executions for the first time in seventeen years—nearly as far back as the execution of Timothy McVeigh. Only three have been carried out since the death penalty was reinstated in 1976, but beginning in July 2020, through the following January—up until the inauguration of Joseph Biden as the next president—a string of thirteen people will be sent to their deaths by lethal injection. When this sequence begins, nearly 150,000 Americans have died from the virus as President Donald Trump continues to claim that "99 percent" of cases are "totally harmless"—and that number will grow exponentially. The presidential election campaign is accelerating, and these state killings are perhaps an attempt to convey that this administration is still in control.

With federal execution dates being announced, Bill begins to feel useless. He thinks about using his frequent-flyer miles to travel from Alaska to Indiana, to stand across from federal death row in Terre Haute. As many times as possible, as many times as necessary. The prospect scares him, but he believes he cannot stay at home.

Bill talks it over with Kathy. She's not happy with the idea of him boarding a series of flights a few months into a global pandemic—especially considering his age, his diabetes, his diet of steak and calorie-free soda, the arthritis that occasionally causes him to lose feeling in his fingers. But he tells her he needs to do it. "I'll wear my mask," Bill says. "I'll wash my hands." One night, as these conversations continue, he references Second Timothy in the Bible, telling his partner, "Ours is not a spirit of fear." Kathy knows Bill well enough to understand that nothing will stop him. For a long time now, this work has been his calling, and, in the end, that makes decisions simple.

And so Bill shaves his beard, packs a bag, and flies and drives a total of nine hours to stand across from the federal penitentiary. He does this again and again. He travels to stand among a cross-section of the supporters who often come to these events: local organizers and national organizers, members of faith groups and civil rights groups, death-row family members. Some in attendance—a nun, an imam, a Unitarian minister—serve or have served as spiritual counselors to the condemned. And though their numbers are unpredictable—sometimes strong, more often modest—they show up. They stand in clusters across from the prison entrance, on a grassy spot in front of a Dollar General.

On a small stand they have erected a large bell, and each time an execution is carried out, those gathered take turns striking it. One by one, in the daylight or in the dark, they hit the steel with a mallet, and it rings out. This is a tradition that began when a nun reached out to convents around the country to suggest they toll their bells on the eve of McVeigh's execution and of any more to come. Bells were rung in thirty-one states; Terre Haute's Sisters of Providence ring their bells now. After the deaths of Daniel Lee, Wesley Purkey, Dustin Honken, Lezmond Mitchell, Keith Nelson, William LeCroy, and Christopher Vialva, Bill Pelke steps up to swing the mallet.

Paula Cooper remains one of the youngest people ever to be sentenced to death in this country. No one under the age of eighteen may now be executed. And in the years since *Roper*, a string of Supreme Court cases have also made it harder for a teenager to be sentenced to die in prison, a punishment only the United States hands down.

But the Court will continue its move further to the right. There will soon be four justices on the bench who take the very conservative, originalist view of the Constitution once represented by Scalia, including Trump appointees Neil Gorsuch, Brett Kavanaugh, and Amy Coney Barrett. And in the spring of 2021, the Court will use this approach to reverse course regarding the punishment of juveniles. In the case of *Jones v. Mississippi*, the 6-to-3 conservative majority will reinterpret their recent decisions as leaving room for life without parole in cases of homicide, *without* the need to rule on whether that young person has a hope of rehabilitation. In her dissent, Justice Sonia Sotomayor will call this *a shock* and *an abrupt break from precedent*. She will write, *The Court is fooling no one.*

In this way, the Court will give license, once again, to judges who would sentence teenagers to die in prison, regardless of their potential for transformation. Regardless of how they may evolve in five, ten, twenty-eight years. If so little value is placed on the rehabilitation of a class of people whose character science has found still to be developing, then the system is questioning whether *anyone* who has committed an act of violence has the capacity to change.

On a morning at home in the late fall of 2020, after a fresh snow, Bill Pelke steps outside to shovel the driveway. Kathy is at work, at a local utility company, and he wants to get his car out to run some errands.

He collapses right there. A neighbor sees Bill lying on the ground in front of the house and dials 911.

When Kathy arrives at the hospital, the doctor says that he tried to restart Bill's heart but did not succeed. Kathy finds it ironic: she had worried so much about him dying from the virus.

She calls the rest of her family in Alaska; she calls his family in Indiana. And then she sets into motion a phone chain of activists, organizers, attorneys, whoever else—people in several countries who should be told of Bill's passing before they read about it online.

A wake is held at a funeral home in Anchorage at which, in compliance with pandemic regulations, no more than fifteen people are in attendance. Others watch on their laptops: a live stream of William Pelke, laid out in a dark blue suit. In honor of his military service, the American flag is draped over his coffin. And after "Taps" is played, a pair of soldiers fold the flag into the shape of the tricorn and present it to his partner.

————— ⚘ —————

Bill and Rhonda had known each other for thirty-five years—most of her life, half of his. They began as adversaries, and Rhonda's suspicion of Bill, of this older white man, persisted for a long time.

When she thinks of Bill in that courtroom in 1986, Rhonda thinks of a tall guy with hair all over his face: a big wolf. He wanted the death penalty for her sister, and he made that clear. Rhonda, at nineteen, had thought to herself, *This man, he acts like he wants to tear my head off*—and she would have liked to tear *his* off. She wanted nothing to do with any of the Pelkes. And so when the Pelke grandson reached out to her family, showed up at her grandfather's house with a basket of fruit, saying that he felt called to help her sister, Rhonda was beside herself. The man must have some ulterior motive.

Over the years of Paula's appeal, and then the course of her long prison sentence, Bill reached out to Rhonda. Now and then, he mailed her modest checks to send to her sister, along with small notes: *Hey, Rhonda, how are you doing?* She never replied. Dozens of voice-mail messages and emails over time—she did not answer. "Hey, Rhonda, got your number and just wanted to call and see how you were doing." She thought, *Really?* For years and years, she resisted Bill's overtures of friendship. She realizes now that she was still afraid of him.

They saw each other at Paula's memorial and became friendly, though it was more of an uneasy truce in honor of Paula's memory. At one point, Rhonda fell silent on Bill for about two years' time, and it disturbed him. Because if Paula Cooper's sister disapproved of him, then how might that alter the story he was telling? And hadn't he done the good, right, peaceable thing, made an enormous gesture, forgiving the girl who had killed his grandmother?

They had been at odds, the Cooper sisters and Ruth Pelke's grandson, in this one undeniable way: the story that Bill felt compelled to tell again and again, year after year, to as many people as would listen, was the same story that had brought both Paula and Rhonda shame. Later, Rhonda would describe it as *"Hey, Rhonda, how are you doing? I've forgiven. Come on over to this side, I'm forgiving you and Paula.* Well, you don't have anything to forgive *me* for, Bill." What was left unsaid is this: Bill Pelke had never considered the life of Paula Cooper before that day in the spring of 1985—that is to say, he had never considered the life of a Black teenage girl in Gary; he had never considered the life of a kid who had run from home so many times, passed from one emergency shelter or foster home to another. He was not the only one. Hurt and ugliness that belonged to *all* of Lake County, that could have been a shared responsibility, had instead been kept out of view through a collective effort. Some problems are called Black, some are called poor, some are called drunk or strung-out or unchristian. As if the fates and conditions of so many families are in no way connected. It is a choice to think this way. It is a perspective that requires effort and indoctrination, by family and faith and community.

Rhonda did not feel an obligation to Bill—but she paid close attention to him. From a distance, she followed the man, reading what was written about him, watching videos of talks he'd given that were posted online. The same terrible story, yet again. She never wanted to go listen in person, but she wanted to know what he was saying (was he getting out of line?) and the kinds of comments others might make. Because she'd lived through many ugly words, the racist threats, the people who wished her whole family dead. Each time Bill gave his talk, she worried all of that might start up again.

But then one morning, about two years ago, Rhonda got a call from Mike at his job. "Guess who's going to be at Indiana University today?" The Gary campus, blocks from their house. She would go and finally see for herself.

She took a seat in the front row of the auditorium, the last seat on the end.

Rhonda had listened to Bill talk so often; it was so familiar. But on this particular day, as he spoke about Ruth, Rhonda found herself listening closely. Maybe enough years had finally passed; maybe she had let enough of the anger and pain run out of her that she could hear the experience of this man on the other side and imagine herself into his grief and his happiness. She thought, *He's just telling his story his way.* Rhonda felt her resistance fall away, and she was moved. After more than thirty years.

And now he stopped speaking. He was staring at her. Rhonda was skinnier now, had lost the weight from her hiding-from-the-world days, and she was wearing a dark red wig. Bill asked from the stage, "Rhonda— are you Rhonda?"

That was the day she decided he was "a true God's friend," a person she was meant to know. After that, they were in touch every week, maybe twice a week. He was still the one reaching out—but now when he called, she answered. And soon she began calling *him*. And whenever he traveled back to Indiana he'd let her know, and she'd make the effort to say, "Did you want to meet up, Bill? Where would you like to meet up?" There were times when he'd ask, "Is this really real?" and she had to admit that it was. She had few people in her life that she could trust—she does not trust easily—but Rhonda began to think of Bill as a best friend. His attention made her feel good. She thought, *I can let my hair down around him, and he can let his hair down around me.* They could share with each other and not feel bad or bitter at whatever was said. They could simply know one another.

Rhonda traded messages with Bill that morning, in what would be his last few hours. She was suffering. There was the isolation, the pandemic forcing her back into her house, and now her back pain had returned and it was serious. The situation had her very low.

She sent Bill a text, and they began a back-and-forth. She desperately needed to talk, and she knew that, long ago, Bill had studied to become a pastor: that was the voice she wanted to hear. Not because she believed in any particular church—she'd tried so many congregations over the

years, from Jehovah's Witness and Pentecostal to Catholic and Sancti-
fied, and none of it had spoken to her much. After all, her childhood
congregation, the one that abandoned her, had been Christian; so many
of the people who had wished for her sister's death, who'd said murder-
ous things to her too, had been Christian. But she had faith *of some kind.*
And that day Rhonda wrote to Bill and asked him to speak to her like a
spiritual person, a pastor, a preacher. *Why so much pain?* she asked. *Why
does God make me suffer so? Why me?*

At first, Bill did as she asked. He wrote to her about God and faith
and personal strength. He took his time.

But soon, he let go of the quotes and the uplifting phrases, and he
changed his tone. He had known pain in his life too, and he did not know
the purpose of it. *But one day,* he wrote, *we'll know the answer why.* This
was the best he could do to help Rhonda. His message was imperfect,
but she hung on his words.

R honda avoids taking herself back to the yellow house in her mind.
She couldn't go back to look at it, even if she wanted to: the place
burned down years ago.

She thinks of her life thus far as having been lived "in the background
of this evilness that has taken place in my family, and me trying to re-
write things." Now she has accepted that what happened can never be
revised. It has its place, and it will not give way.

It is a little easier, with Bill no longer reminding her of what passed
between their families. But the loss of him is a great sadness to Rhonda,
that friendship that was impossible for more than thirty years and then
suddenly so easy.

Bill had clung to Paula, as a way to give shape and purpose to his
loss. But she belongs to her sister. And when Rhonda thinks of Paula, she
thinks of a child. Someone always young, and without a father, without
a mother. Rhonda thinks of her partner, her girl. She used her every

chance to smooth the way for her sister. That is a fact that can never be rubbed out, not even by her most unsettling memories.

Her own childhood was so short, and now a piece of Rhonda is trying to reimagine herself in that state of possibility. Some days, she dresses up. She has new friends; she helps care for her grandkids. She feels, suddenly, that she can breathe, as if her center is wide open, able to take in more. Sometimes she can talk to a person she's just met—about herself, about Paula—and not regret it.

During the first months of their correspondence, Paula had written to Bill about the rhythms of her life, her habits, the never-ending noise of the prison, her parents, her anger, her body pains, her pen pals, her surprise at the breadth of her language as she answered her many letters. But at one point—she was sixteen and he had just turned thirty-nine— she told him there was a limit to what he could know about her, a limit to what this list of details could convey. She was getting used to that idea, she said, that each of us lives with this kind of missing out, these gaps, the things we realize later, late, or never.

you may never see inside of me to see & under stand the person I really am, she wrote. *but one day we will come to grips.*

Acknowledgments

My first thanks go to Bill Pelke, who became a real friend. I miss him. I will always remember how generous he was, and how damn funny. He made fun of how long it seemed to be taking me to write this thing—"Are you writing the *Encyclopedia Britannica?*"—and I wish I could now share it with him. My deepest condolences to Bill's partner Kathy Harris, and to all his family.

I would like to thank all the members of MVFR and the Journey who freely volunteered the stories of their most difficult life experiences. I was especially grateful for the time and generosity of SueZann Bosler, Marietta Jaeger, George White, Reverend Jack Sullivan Jr., Terri Steinberg, and David Kaczynski. It was an honor to get to know each of them through one-on-one conversations, through long rides in the Journey vans, and as a member of the audience for some of their many talks. Their stories are far richer and more complex than the parameters of this book allowed me to capture.

Many thanks to Bob and Rachel Gross, for the times they welcomed me into their home and for their insight into the earlier days of the Journey (Bob is now their executive director). Many thanks to the brilliant and unflappable Abe Bonowitz for his insight into the death penalty abolition movement, in which he's been engaged for decades. His Death

ACKNOWLEDGMENTS

Penalty Action Network is doing robust and effective work organizing and educating the public about capital punishment. Thanks also to Gary Wright, who was generous in sharing the story of his life after his attack by Ted Kaczynski—and the subsequent deep friendship that sprung up between him and Ted's brother David. My conversations with him and with David helped me to better understand life in the wake of violence, and to imagine the possibilities that can arise when families on either side are able to connect.

Thanks to Monica Foster for many long talks. Her openness, and her deep connection to Paula, made me feel I should and could write this book. The tenacity and the truly awesome commitment she brings to her work are a thing to witness.

Thanks to Rhonda LaBroi, whose generosity in sharing her perspective, her intimate memories, and her insights was a tremendous gift. I am very close to my own sibling, and Rhonda's love for her sister was, for me, one of the most moving aspects of this story. She hopes someday soon to complete a memoir of her experiences, and I look forward to reading it.

Thanks to the archivist Regina Longo, whose determined efforts early on tracked down some of the European media about Paula's case; to my Italian translator (a writer in her own right) Janna Brancolini; and to my brilliant "law guru" Annie Hudson-Price. Thanks to MacDowell, where I was a Calderwood journalism fellow, for the support of a residency during the book's first stages. As with my first book, my time there was both incredibly freeing and focusing—there are few places that support artists the way in which MacDowell does. Thanks also to Aspen Words, where I was a writer in residence. Running away to the Colorado mountains at just that moment truly helped to move the work forward.

To my agent, Sarah Burnes: Thank you for your very smart guidance, and for believing in this book—even through the upheaval of the pandemic. Thanks to the team at Penguin Press, including the very patient and always helpful Victoria Lopez.

And to my editor, Emily Cunningham: I have never met an editor so dedicated, clear-headed, and thoughtful—and who gives such irritatingly flawless notes. I am so happy we were able to work (relentlessly) on this book together.

Thanks to my friends who supported the writing of this book, in all sorts of ways, during these past five years—Idra Novey, Nicole Cota, Reyhan Harmanci, Jonathan Ames, Allistair Banks Griffin, David Siegel, Jodie and Guillermo Maciel. The pandemic has been a time of confusion and heartache for nearly everyone I care about. Here's to better times.

Abrazos to Sylvie, whose big spirit I love and admire, and to my beautiful adopted sister Genevieve. And thanks to my beautiful and spirited Greco-Cuban family, who have given me so much and whom I love dearly.

And finally, a very deep thank you to my partner, Todd—my champion, my protector, my greatest stroke of luck. The five years I put into this book would not have been possible without your own sacrifices, your many-layered support, and your unshakeable belief in the project.

A Note on Sources

Seventy Times Seven is a work of nonfiction based upon hundreds of hours of interviews with some eighty individuals; thousands of pages of documents, unpublished letters and emails, newspaper features, and photographs; and dozens of hours of archival footage. For the purpose of this research, over the course of the past five years I made eight trips to Indiana, a trip to follow Bill Pelke and the Journey through Texas, a trip to Italy, and four shorter trips to D.C. and to Ohio for other Journey-related events. Biographical information, scenes, events, and dialogue are all based on interview subjects' personal recollections, archival documents, and/or media reports at the time; whenever possible, I confirmed accounts with other surviving sources. To re-create the experiences and perspectives of subjects who are now deceased, I relied upon interviews they gave to the press at the time, as well as my own conversations with surviving family members and colleagues, and personal correspondence when available. In the rare instances where there was disagreement or lack of clarity about a particular event, I acknowledge that in the chapter notes below.

For their coverage of decades of events specific to Lake County, Indiana, the following newspapers were significant sources for me: *The*

Times (now the *Northwest Indiana Times*), the Gary *Post-Tribune*, *The Indianapolis Star*, and the *Chicago Tribune*. The more lifestyle-focused coverage of the Black-owned and Black-run *Gary Crusader* and *INFO* were also invaluable for their insight into Gary's Black community. I was able to view the archives of these papers at the Lake County Public Library in Merrillville, the Indiana State Library, and New York City's Schomburg Center for Research in Black Culture. Over the past few years, the National Death Penalty Archive (NDPA) at the State University of New York at Albany was a dream resource, in that it holds the collections of multiple scholars and activists important to this story (more details below). Special thanks to head archivist Brian Keough and digital curator Mark Wolfe; extra-special thanks to supervisory archivist Jodi Boyle, who was an extraordinary and patient guide during my many, many visits.

Authorities of particular help in researching the history of capital punishment in the United States and Supreme Court death-penalty jurisprudence included: the Death Penalty Information Center, the American Civil Liberties Union, Cornell Law School's Legal Information Institute, the Pew Research Center for its surveys on shifting public views on the death penalty (including polls broken down by religious affiliation), and the Bureau of Justice Statistics for its annual reports on capital punishment in the U.S. Oyez.org was very useful for its audio recordings of Supreme Court oral arguments and opinion announcements. Other significant sources included: David Garland's *Peculiar Institution: America's Death Penalty in an Age of Abolition* for its general history but especially for its contrasting of American ideas of punishment versus those of Western Europe; Maurice Chammah's *Let the Lord Sort Them* on the history of the death penalty, with a focus on Texas; Todd C. Peppers's *A Courageous Fool* (with Margaret A. Anderson) on Marie Deans's work to end capital punishment (with a focus on Virginia and South Carolina), for its intimate view of advocacy on death row; *The New York Times*'s coverage of the Supreme Court's death-penalty decisions over the years; the Marshall Project's present-day reporting on the death penalty and mass incarceration; Liliana Segura's coverage of the federal executions of 2020–21 for the Intercept; Jill Lepore's *New Yorker* feature "The Rise of the Victims'-Rights Movement." Coverage of mass incarceration by The Marshall Project and The Sentencing Project, Michelle Alexander's classic on the topic *The New Jim Crow*, and the work of the Vera Institute of Justice were all helpful resources.

When quoting from the Bible at various points in the book, I chose to use the New International Version (NIV), in spite of the fact that a Baptist such as Bill Pelke was raised with the more formal King James Version. I did so because of the NIV's closer resemblance to contemporary speech; I wanted readers to be able to absorb that language from less of a remove. Worth noting: The phrase "seventy times seven" is part of an alternate translation of Matthew 18:22 in the NIV, found in a footnote to that line (in the body of the text, the NIV translates the phrase as "seventy-seven times"). I chose to use that alternate translation because it matches that of the King James Version and was the phrase Bill himself used—a point of overlap between the two translations, and a more emphatic expression of that passage's underlying meaning. The Revised Standard Version Catholic Edition, used by many English-speaking Catholics, also translates the phrase in this way.

The present tense of the book refers, throughout, to the present tense of the storyline. In keeping with this stylistic choice, any descriptions of legal standards, the working of the courts, and financial sums are accurate for that moment in time but not necessarily today.

I have chosen to capitalize "Black" and not "white" in keeping with a journalistic standard currently favored by the Associated Press, *The New York Times*, and others—though there is an ongoing debate in favor of "White," which is a style used by the National Association of Black Journalists and *The Washington Post*.

Chapter 1

My description of the moment when Gloria Cooper attempts to take her own life and those of her two young daughters is based on Rhonda LaBroi's recollections; her father Ron Williams's testimony at Paula's trial; the July 1986 *Indianapolis Star* story "From Runaway to Death Row Inmate"; and *The Times*'s July 1986 story "Cooper's Life Led to Sorrow." (Gloria Cooper—now Gloria Reese—has yet to speak publicly and did not respond to repeated requests.) Where reporting was in conflict with Rhonda's memories, I gave greater weight to Rhonda's account.

I learned a significant amount of information about Paula and Rhonda's childhood from her case file, interviews with Rhonda, Ron Williams's testimony, and local coverage in the months after the Pelke murder and at the time of her sentencing. In March 1986, *60 Minutes* reported that Herman Cooper "has consistently denied beating his children." Both parents left the state months before Paula's sentencing. Neither has since spoken publicly on the topic; Herman, as I note in chapter 21, died in 2010.

p. 13 "crazy" is taken from Ronald Williams's testimony about what the caseworker in question told him, and is not a direct quote from her (she is deceased).

Chapter 2

For information on Ruth Pelke's family background and earlier life on the outskirts of Peru, Indiana, in Miami County, I turned to: her grandson Bill Pelke, her granddaughter (Bill's cousin) Judi Weyhe, the research department of Peru's Miami County Museum, and members of the current Center Chapel congregation—including Roger and Darlene Holiday, Doris Owings, and Rosanna Bloxson, who was one of Ruth's Sunday school students at Center Chapel and who recently died at the age of 102.

I was surprised by how relatively few books have been written on the history of Gary and of Lake County overall, but the following titles were of particular help in my research: James B. Lane's *City of the Century: A History of Gary, Indiana*; *Racial Politics and Urban Planning: Gary, Indiana 1980–1989*, written by Mayor Hatcher's planning adviser from 1982 to 1987 and the former chairman of Indiana University Northwest's Department of Minority Studies, Robert A. Catlin; and Raymond A. Mohl and Neil Betten's *Steel City*. Beloved local historian (and first *Gary Crusader* editor) Darathula "Dolly" Millender's *Yesterday in Gary: A Brief History of the Negro in Gary* and *Gary's Central Business Community* were also helpful, as well as Kenneth Schoon's *Calumet Beginnings* and Powell A. Moore's *The Calumet Region: Indiana's Last Frontier*.

I based my description of the May 14, 1985, murder of Ruth Pelke on extensive legal documents and transcripts from the cases of all four of the girls, particularly those of Paula Cooper and Karen Corder, as well as the details of the coroner's report and crime scene photos. I chose to take Paula's initial confession (on May 17, 1985) and her guilty plea testimony (on April 21, 1986) at face value, and they form the foundation of my understanding of that event and its immediate aftermath. In these transcripts, Paula implicates herself completely, and she never contradicted those statements, even though she would later imply (if never explicitly claim) that the other girls were more deeply involved in the violence than they admitted. Worth noting: reports at the time said that Ruth recited the Lord's Prayer during the attack, but Paula herself never claimed this; she later wrote to Bill that she did *not* hear his grandmother pray, but rather she heard her say the line I have quoted in chapter 2, "If you do this, you'll be sorry."

Chapter 3

To better understand the many facets of the criminal justice system in Lake County from the late 1970s through the late 1980s, I interviewed the following individuals: then prosecutor Jack Crawford, then deputy prosecutor (and eventual Indiana Supreme Court justice) Robert Rucker, then deputy prosecutor (and current federal judge) Andrew Rodovich, then deputy prosecutor (and current chief public defender) Tom Vanes, a former deputy prosecutor who did not wish to be named, Judge Richard Maroc, then public defenders Kevin Relphorde and Rich Wolter, then chief appellate defender Bill Touchette, former Kimbrough executive assistant and investigator Patti Wolter, then Lake County Juvenile Court Magistrate (and soon judge) Mary Beth Bonaventura, and current juvenile court judge Tom Stefaniak.

Former Indiana supreme court chief justice Randall Shepard's Princeton undergraduate thesis on the mayoral campaign of Richard Hatcher, based in part on interviews with the mayor's staff and former campaign workers, was hugely useful; it can be found in the Princeton University Library. Conversations with people who were residents in Gary during the 1970s and '80s—including Rhonda and Mike LaBroi, Earline Rogers, and Judge Robert Rucker—helped me to get a deeper sense of the city during that era, as well as archival issues of *The Gary Crusader* and *INFO*.

None of my sources could confirm Jack Crawford's account of either his lunch meeting with Mayor Hatcher or his consultation with some of the county's Black ministers in the immediate wake of the Pelke murder—and both Hatcher and Reverend Burns are now deceased. But I was told by Mary Cartwright, as well as a former deputy prosecutor, that both of these events sounded very plausible.

Chapters 4–6

In these interrogation and courtroom scenes, and wherever relevant throughout the book, any obvious typographical errors in official transcripts were corrected to make the text more readable. These instances were rare, unambiguous, and did not change the substance of the text being quoted.

For Judge Kimbrough's biographical information, I spoke with several of his former colleagues, including Jack Crawford, Richard Maroc, Rich and Patti Wolter, and Bill Touchette. His wife Faye and his former law partner Fred Work are now both deceased.

I spoke with Jack Crawford's ex-girlfriend Cathy over the phone; she did not wish for her last name to be used.

p. 74 "Three weeks later, a group of Black kids went into a house a block from his grandmother's place and killed a Black couple: the coverage amounted to a short newspaper item and nothing on TV."—This is based on Mike and Rhonda LaBroi's memories. I was not able to find corresponding coverage of such a crime.

p. 67 "As she enters, Paula is smiling, laughing actually, as if in response to something the officer has said."—This is based on Bill Pelke's memory of his first time seeing Paula Cooper.

When Kimbrough sentences Paula, he at one point uses the phrase "It is a viable alternative." This phrase, in the court transcript, read "an inviable alternative"; I changed it for sense, within the context of the judge's statement.

II

Chapter 7

I interviewed Bill Pelke many times from late 2016 until shortly before his death in 2021, and those conversations formed the basis of my account of Bill's life and worldview. Interviews with his ex-wife and friend Judy Pelke (now Judy Knapp); his partner and widow Kathy Harris; his friend Leanna Mula; and his cousin Judi Weyhe were also of great value. (Bill's first wife, Mary Jane, did not wish to speak with me for the book.) For more on Bill's long career at Bethlehem Steel, and basic facts about the mill as it was run during that period, I spoke with his former coworker and friend Dennis Eaton and was given a tour of the mill by Bill's former foreman Joe Wolodzko.

Chapter 8

This chapter is based on extensive interviews with Monica Foster, and conversations with Patti Wolter and Bill Touchette.

Chapter 9

Bill Pelke shared his many letters from Paula with me, as did Father Vito Bracone, at the monastery where he now lives, in the seaside town of Monopoli in southern Italy. With regard to quotations from Paula's letters in this chapter and throughout the book: from the age of sixteen, Paula was a compelling writer—to the surprise of everyone, including herself. But as can be expected from a young person who was rarely in class in the few years before her incarceration, her spelling, capitalization, and punctuation were sometimes dodgy. I tried to preserve the feel of her correspondence, but in those instances when such errors were a distraction, I corrected them in favor of clarity. No slang or personal peculiarities of language use were altered.

As for the letters Bill wrote to Paula, those were lost—but I was able to reconstruct some of them through a few copies that were in Father Vito's personal collection, as well as drafts that Bill preserved in his personal papers (at the NDPA since his death).

Chapters 10–13

I interviewed journalists Anna Guaita and Giampaolo Piolo, and my freelance translator, Janna Brancolini, helped to translate their newspaper articles into English from Italian. Janna was also kind enough to hunt down some of Guaita's missing articles on Paula for *Il Messaggero* in the

National Central Library of Rome. One challenge of translating the interviews Paula gave Guaita and Pioli was that Paula's words had already been translated (in 1986) from English to Italian, and so we were left to speculate (to some degree) as to what her precise words had originally been. The one instance in which I chose to veer from the most obvious translation from the Italian was on p. 142, where she was originally quoted as saying "flesh and bone" (an idiomatic expression in Italian) rather than the more common English-language expression "flesh and blood." In that case, I changed the wording to what seemed to be the more likely phrase, based on context.

I was able to spend two days visiting Father Vito Bracone at the Monopoli monastery, where he shared with me his many personal scrapbooks of photos and newspaper clippings related to Paula's case, as well as many letters from her and from Bill. At the Monastery of St. Francis in Indianapolis, I spoke with Father Justin Belitz, who accompanied Father Vito on his visits to see Paula on death row. In addition, my translator helped me review several Italian-language interviews Father Vito gave to the Italian Radical Party's radio station, Radio Radicale, about Paula and Bill. For background on the Franciscan order and the life of St. Francis (San Francesco), I turned primarily to *Francis of Assisi: The Founder: Early Documents*, vol. II, as well as the contemporary scholarly work *Francis of Assisi: Performing the Gospel Life* by Lawrence S. Cunningham.

On the Radical Party's involvement in Paula's case, I met in Rome with Ivan Novelli, who organized Non Uccidere (Thou Shalt Not Kill) alongside Father Greganti and Father Vito. Novelli was also a source on Greganti (now deceased), with whom he had become close friends through their work. For international petitions and letters to Governor Orr asking for Paula's sentence to be commuted—primarily from Italian citizens, but also from people throughout Western Europe and Scandinavia—I turned to the collection of the Indiana Historical Society.

I interviewed Victor Streib over the phone multiple times and read several of his published works from the 1980s, including: *Juvenile Justice in America*, *Death Penalty for Juveniles*, "Death Penalty for Children," "The Eighth Amendment and Capital Punishment of Juveniles," and "Executing Juvenile Females." I also read through his papers in the NDPA. I based my representation of the communication between Streib and Kevin Relphorde in 1985 on a letter to Relphorde from Streib from July 15 of that year that references their recent phone conversation (in Streib's NDPA collection). I was also able to read through the NDPA's Watt Espy papers for a better sense of Espy's process.

Chapter 11's sections on Earline Rogers are based on interviews with Rogers at her home and over the phone, as well as extensive local newspaper coverage of her bill.

For my passages on the lead-up to and oral argument for *Thompson v. Oklahoma*, I relied on interviews with Streib and Rick Tepker. Tepker also contributed a detailed essay—"*Thompson v. Oklahoma* and the Judicial Search for Constitutional Tradition in Celebration of Victor Streib," about his experience with Streib on the case—to *Ohio Northern University Law Review* 38, no. II,, from which I drew some of my details. Jeffrey Toobin's *The Nine: Inside the Secret World of the Supreme Court* offered insight into the evolving makeup of the Court over the second half of the twentieth century.

Chapter 14

I interviewed former Chief Justice Randall Shepard at length on the Indiana Supreme Court's decision in the Paula Cooper case. I also interviewed State Deputy Attorney General Gary Secrest, Bill Touchette, and Victor Streib on the lead-up to and the day of the oral argument. To better understand Shepard as a legal thinker, I also read his articles "Second Wind for the Indiana Bill of Rights," "Indiana Law and the Idea of Progress," and "Indiana's Place in American Court Reform." The tensions between some of the Indiana Supreme Court justices during that era—particularly between Richard Givan, Alfred J. Pivarnik, and Chief Justice Shepard—were rigorously reported in 1989 through an eight-part *Indianapolis Star* series entitled "A Court Divided."

III

Chapters 15–16

For the background on Center Chapel, I visited with members of the current-day congregation and was able to see their salvaged church ledgers from 1900–1920, their archive of Sunday school books, and a photo of the congregation from 1910. With the help of an archivist at Peru's Miami County Museum, Ann Sullivan, I was also able to trace Ruth's family tree and locate the deed to her family farm; I visited the original site of the farm (mostly open fields now), and visited the burial plots of her parents and siblings at nearby Paw-Paw Cemetery. For background on the area, one useful source was *History of Miami County, Indiana, from the Earliest Time to the Present*, published in 1887 by Brant & Fuller.

For the story of Bill Pelke's participation in the Pilgrimage from Florida to Georgia (the event was formally called "The Pilgrimage of Light"), the Texans Against the Death Penalty March, and the Albany meeting that led to the expansion of Murder Victims' Families for Reconciliation, I interviewed Bill Pelke and reviewed the NDPA collections of Pelke, MVFR, Marie Deans (MVFR's founder), and Bob Gross. Gross helped to organize the Pilgrimage, took part in the TASK March, and played a key role in making the 1993 Journey through Indiana happen; he is currently the Journey's executive director. It is worth noting that the full legal name of the group is Journey of Hope . . . from Violence to Healing.

My description of the 1993 Journey is based on about thirty hours of home-video footage that was shot by Judy Knapp, thousands of photographs taken by Journey participants, thousands of pages of internal documents, correspondence, and publicity materials preserved by the steering committee, as well as press coverage of the event. To re-create that first Journey and to better appreciate the many Journeys that followed, I interviewed Bill and Judy; Bob Gross and his wife, activist and Death Row Support Project founder Rachel Gross; activist and Death Penalty Action Network cofounder Abe Bonowitz; MVFR members and current Journey board members and cofounders SueZann Bosler, Marietta Jaeger, and George White; activist and Texas University professor Rick Halperin; and 1993 Journey coorganizer Laura Van Voorhis. (The steering committee for the 1993 Journey included Bill Pelke, Bob Gross, Toni Moore, and Maureen Kelly of Amnesty International, and Laura Van Voorhis.) Also helpful to me in fleshing out the stories of those involved in the Journey—beyond my extensive archival research—were Micki Dickoff's independent documentary about the 2000 Journey through Texas, *Step by Step*; *From Fury to Forgiveness*, a 1994 Discovery Channel documentary featuring Pelke, Jaeger, and Bosler; Jaeger's 1983 memoir *The Lost Child*; Pelke's 2013 self-published memoir *Journey of Hope . . . From Violence to Healing*; and the chapter on Bosler in Jill Monroe's 2012 book *Don't Kill in Our Name*.

Over the past five years, I've traveled with the Journey through Texas (2017), and attended Journey events in D.C. (2017–2019) and the first leg of the Ohio Journey (2019). Through these events, I absorbed a sense of the rhythm, pace, and emotional life of the Journey experience for those attending and for those taking part.

Chapter 17

For background on daily life at the Indiana Women's Prison, from the Department of Correction standpoint, I spoke with former IWP superintendent Dana Blank Rowe (the previous superintendent during Paula's time there, Clarence Trigg, is now deceased). To better understand the life of women incarcerated at IWP, I spoke extensively with Shirley Cooper, who was incarcerated alongside Paula (she has since been released and has become an advocate for prison reform with the group Faith in Indiana); corresponded briefly with Donna Stites before her death in 2018; and spoke with retired prison chaplain Priscilla Hutton, as well as a few regular visitors to the two facilities (including Rhonda, Monica, and a close friend of Donna's). Paula's letters to Bill also included extensive descriptions of her experiences while incarcerated. My account of the episode that led to Paula's three years in segregation at IWP is based in part on documents from her disciplinary review hearing, which include testimony by other incarcerated women and corrections staff.

Chapter 18

This chapter was based on extensive interviews with Monica Foster and an interview with Bob Hammerle. Descriptions of Bill and Judy's relationship were based on interviews with each of them, as well as letters from Paula to Bill in response to his confiding in her about his romantic life and marriage. The description of the death of Carolyn (Judy's sister) and its aftermath was based on conversations with Judy and local coverage. Letters from Perry Steven Miller to Bill can be found among Bill's papers at the NDAP.

Worth noting: I compressed the timeline of some events in chapters 17 and 18 for fluidity and thematic cohesion, but without impacting the factual clarity of events. Paula's attack on an officer at IWP took place in the summer of 1995; the execution of Gregory Resnover and its aftermath took place in the end of 1994 through mid-1995; Tommy Schiro's sentence was commuted in 1996; and Bill and Judy's anniversary, and the death of her sister, took place in the fall of 1996.

Chapters 19–20

For the lead-up to *Roper v. Simmons* and the oral argument, I spoke with Seth Waxman, Waxman's cocounsel Danielle Spinelli, James Layton, Lawrence Steinberg, Stephen Harper, Steve Drizin, and Juvenile Law Center cofounder Marsha Levick. For additional background on the movement to abolish the death penalty during that period, I spoke with attorney George Kendall, who was deeply involved in the NAACP LDF's Supreme Court strategy in the era preceding *Roper*. (Patricia "Patti" Puritz did not wish to be interviewed.) For background on the cognitive neuroscience regarding adolescent brain development, I spoke with Beatriz Luna. Regarding the MVFR amicus brief, I interviewed coauthors Emily Sack and Kate Lowenstein (longtime national organizer for MVFR), and MVFR member Linda White. Of great help in shaping my initial grasp of the lead-up to *Roper v. Simmons* was the Juvenile Law Center's oral history of those efforts, *"Roper v. Simmons*, Ten Years Later," published online in 2015; this history includes interviews with Puritz, as well as with Bernardine Dohrn and Elizabeth "Buffie" Scott, neither of whom responded to requests for interviews. Steinberg was another source, for me, on Scott's involvement.

Worth noting: Shortly after the *Roper* decision, internal disagreements led MVFR to split into two organizations, MVFR and MVFHR (Murder Victims' Families for Human Rights). Also, shortly before their trip through Texas (described in chapter 19), the Journey became its own nonprofit, distinct from—though sharing members with—MVFR.

In my summary of the *Atkins v. Virginia* Supreme Court decision, I use the phrase "intellectually disabled," but the terminology used then was "mentally retarded"—now considered to be language that is dated and offensive.

My descriptions of Paula's life at Rockville were based on an interview with Rockville warden Julie Stout, who also gave me a tour of the facility; letters from Paula to Bill; conversations with Shirley Cooper, who was incarcerated alongside Paula at both IWP and Rockville; interviews with Rhonda; limited correspondence with Donna Stites, who was also at both facilities with Paula; Anna Guaita's 2000 *Il Messaggero* feature on Paula's life inside, "Paula Cooper, Fifteen Years Later"; and journalist Robert King's 2016 *Indianapolis Star* feature "The Executioner Within."

IV

Chapter 21

I interviewed Rockville warden Julie Stout about the period leading up to Paula's release; Monica Foster about Paula's life and work after prison, as well as their friendship; Shirley Cooper about her visit with Paula after her own release from Rockville; Cardinal Joseph Tobin, Archbishop of Newark (then Archbishop of Indianapolis), about his interventions on Paula's behalf; and Rhonda, about their relationship in Paula's final years and her struggles with adjusting to life outside. Rhonda was also generous enough to share with me the letter her sister left behind for her. For some details about Paula's life after prison, I am indebted to King's "The Executioner Within" (in particular, information he gleaned through interviews with LeShon Davidson, Denise Jackson, and Kim Kidd), as well as the Intercept reporter Liliana Segura's 2015 story, "The Life and Death of Paula Cooper" (in particular, her interview with Meisha Linton), and Sharon Cohen's 2015 AP feature, which ran in *The Chicago Tribune* as "No Escaping Brutal Past."

My depiction of the aftermath of Paula's death was based on interviews with Rhonda, Monica, Bill Pelke, Julie Stout, Cardinal Tobin, and Carlo Santoro of the Sant'Egidio community in Rome. Descriptions of Paula's mother's response were based on interviews with Rhonda and Monica.

Chapter 22

For the story of the lottery scandal, I spoke with Jack Crawford, his ex-wife Ann, and Mary Cartwright. As I mention in that chapter, there was extensive media coverage of these events; all details I cover can be found in *The Indianapolis Star* and *The Times*.

My description of the death of April Beverly was based on information from Shirley Cooper and Donna Stites. My depiction of the later years and death of Karen Corder is based on documents from her case file, information from Shirley and Rhonda, and photographs of her funeral service (in Paula's personal collection) that Rhonda shared with me. Denise Thomas did not wish to speak with me for this book.

Chapter 23

Bill's partner and widow Kathy Harris had the tremendous grace and generosity to share her memories of his final days with me, as well as her perspective on his pandemic life and frustrations. Activist, frequent Journey volunteer and coorganizer, and Death Penalty Action Network cofounder Abe Bonowitz shared his detailed memories of the protests in Terre Haute of the 2020–21 federal executions.

I mentioned a "string" of Supreme Court decisions that addressed life without parole (LWOP) for juveniles: 2010's *Graham v. Florida* made a life sentence without parole unconstitutional for juveniles convicted of non-homicide crimes; 2012's *Miller v. Alabama* made mandatory LWOP for juveniles convicted of homicides unconstitutional; and in 2016's *Montgomery v. Louisiana*, the Court made the *Miller* decision retroactive, vacating all such sentences. The brilliant attorney and activist Bryan Stevenson (himself a murder victim's family member) argued *Miller*, and Bill Pelke took part in an amicus brief to support the argument.

After Bill's death, Rhonda spoke to me at length about the evolution of her relationship with him. She also shared with me Bill's final text messages.

Image Credits

Index

NOTE: *italic page numbers* indicate photographs